BEHIND EVERY GREAT MAN

*The Forgotten Women
Behind the World's Famous
and Infamous*

MARLENE
WAGMAN-GELLER

Published by Sourcebooks, Inc.
P.O. Box 4410, Naperville, Illinois 60567-4410
(630) 961-3900
Fax: (630) 961-2168
www.sourcebooks.com

Library of Congress Cataloging-in-Publication data is on file with the publisher.

Printed and bound in the United States of America.

VP 10 9 8 7 6 5 4 3 2 1

PREVIOUS BOOKS

And the Rest Is History: The Famous (and Infamous) First Meetings of the World's Most Passionate Couples

Eureka!: The Surprising Stories Behind the Ideas That Shaped the World

Once Again to Zelda: The Stories Behind Literature's Most Intriguing Dedications

To my great women: Gilda Wagman and Jordanna Geller.
And to all great women everywhere.

"For most of history, Anonymous was a woman."

—*Virginia Woolf*

CONTENTS

REMEMBER THE LADIES

Over the centuries, the saying, "Behind every great man is a great woman" has proven to be more than a girl-power chant. As it turns out, the long shadows cast by alpha males throughout history have obscured many stories of truly intriguing women who acted as their right hands and muses, the magicians behind the screen. For these intrepid females, supporting their famous husbands and partners by helping them achieve their destinies was frequently a Herculean task, accomplished in spite of sagas of alcoholism, infidelity, breakdowns, divorce, and despair (usually on the men's part).

How did these women do it? Were they members of some more evolved species than the rest of us—equipped to handle the good, the bad, and the ugly sides of power? By casting light on the wife (or girlfriend) behind the famous man, we can begin to understand these "better halves" who left indelible lines on the visage of history through their husbands and their own works. The fairer sex has consistently been relegated to the footnotes of time under the label of "so-and-so's lover," "wife," or "widow." As Dorothy Parker observed in "The Little Hours," "Oh, well, it's a man's world." It is time for them to emerge from the shadows, both because their stories shed new insight on the famous men featured in history and because their own lives are equally as fascinating. In the feminist essay, "A Room of One's Own," Virginia Woolf stated, "A woman must have money and a room of her own if she is to write fiction." *Behind Every Great Man* explores the biographies of those who never received a room of their own to shine or whose rooms and stories have never been properly explored.

Wives have generally been the untold half of history, so this book offers a different perspective on history than what we expect: it tells the story of these famous men (and one woman) from the wives' point of view. Public lives and private lives are indivisible, and the detail of the marital relationships of some of the most well-known men gives a rounded picture that helps history come alive. Each chapter explores the real-life Lady Macbeths and Carmela Sopranos whose love humanized their men while often dehumanizing themselves.

But the women profiled here are not those who commandeered time in the spotlight themselves, as their biographies and stories are already part of our cultural psyche. Hence there are no chapters devoted to Eleanor Roosevelt or Hillary Rodham Clinton. The criteria for inclusion entail marriage to a famous spouse who outshone them in the pages of time. While Oscar Wilde is known as the literary great imprisoned for "the love that dare not speak its name," few know of Constance (an apt name for Oscar's *semper fidelis* spouse), who found herself wed to Europe's most (in)famous homosexual. Mohandas Gandhi is a world icon, depicted with his ever-present spinning wheel, but what about Mrs. Mohandas? She bore him four sons, fasted when he was imprisoned, and died in Aga Khan Prison for complicity in fighting to wrest her country from the yoke of the British Raj. While everyone is familiar with Germany's notorious Nazi dictator and his trademark mustache, few know much about his mystery woman, Eva Braun—Hitler's consort for fourteen years and wife for forty hours. Their relationship leaves lingering questions: was she the First Lady of Nazism or just an apolitical blond who lived in his Bavarian mountain retreat, oblivious to the genocide of which her lover was architect? Can one love a monster and yet not be evil oneself? Find out the answers to these questions and countless others about the remarkable yet little-known women behind history's famous (and infamous) men.

After the joy that ensued from my first three books, I desperately desired a fourth, but inspiration, like love, does not come when summoned. In this case, I found it in the most unlikely of places: former First Lady Laura Bush sparked the idea for *Behind Every Great Man*. In a White House roast, she likened herself to a character from television's *Desperate Housewives*. She told the audience, "I am married to the president of the United States and here is our typical evening: nine o'clock, Mr. Excitement here is sound asleep, and I am watching *Desperate Housewives*. Ladies and gentlemen, I *am* a desperate housewife!"

After reading this, I rolled my eyes—she was married to the president, her daughters look like they posed for a Norman Rockwell painting, and her wealth was as vast as her native Texas. She, I felt, couldn't possibly know what it was like to be a real desperate housewife. Many American wives congregate every day at work, at home, online, anywhere, bemoaning their lives plagued by drug-addicted family members, threats of foreclosure, and credit card bills with as many digits as phone numbers. But then I wondered if there was more to Mrs. Bush's quote, and it led me to think of the real desperate housewives of history, those who lived and died with their lives forgotten, swallowed by the long shadows cast by the alpha males who garnered the spotlight. Creation is a conjugal act; it is a miscarriage of justice for the great men of history to skimp on spousal credit due to their wives and partners who helped them become who they were (or are). *Behind Every Great Man* helps settle the score.

The women profiled were chosen by the following process: First I thought of a colorful famous man, and if his wife dwelled in the shadows, I investigated. If her life was an intriguing one and shone light on a hitherto unknown aspect of her husband, she merited a chapter. To illustrate the forgotten wives and partners are not bound by geography, I included ladies from various locales: Emilie Schindler (Germany), Betty X (the United States), Gala Dalí (Spain), and many more. During this process, I discovered fascinating, strange, and sometimes inspiring new information. For example, when Warren Buffett's wife, Susan, departed for San Francisco to become a "geriatric gypsy," she asked Astrid Menks, a middle-aged, never-married, Latvian immigrant to look after her husband. Soon, Christmas cards were signed "Warren, Susie, and Astrid." After Susan passed away, Buffett married his mistress, making her the spouse of the world's second-richest man. This certainly offers hope to all middle-aged Latvian cocktail hostesses.

As with all relationships, upon the conclusion of *Behind Every Great Man*, I dwelt on the ones that got away—chapters not included. Katharina von Bora, disenchanted with life as a nun, escaped her convent hidden in a wagon that delivered herring. From this odorous start, she became the wife of the great reformer, Martin Luther. The bell tolled for the poet-priest John Donne when he secretly wed the seventeen-year-old daughter of Sir George More. His none-too-pleased father-in-law had him thrown in Fleet Prison where he wrote his wife: "John Donne, Anne Donne, Undone." They don't make 'em like Renée-Pélagie de Montreuil anymore, wife of the world's most prolific pornographer, the Marquis de Sade (who gave us the word "sadism"), her tale lost in the shadow of the Bastille. She stood by her sadomasochist spouse through his sex scandals and jail terms and lived in a convent to provide him with the luxuries he felt his due. There was also the tale of Charles Dickens and the woman—his wife—who bore him ten children before she was supplanted in his affections by actress Ellen Ternan, his muse for *Great Expectations*. Bugsy Siegel named his Vegas hotel after his lover Virginia Hill, whom he nicknamed "the flamingo" due to her long, slender legs. Both casino and mistress led to his Mafia murder.

The desperate housewives of Greek mythology had nothing on their nonfictional counterparts. There is a nod to these archetypes: the Harpie (Mrs. Salvador Dalí), Galatea (Mrs. Richard Wagner), and the vast spectrum of wives and partners in between. And no self-respecting bird's-eye view of marriage would be complete without the eternal love triangle. While the trio of Paris, Helen, and Menelaus caused the Trojan War, the one between Catherine of Aragon, Henry VIII, and Anne Boleyn caused England to divorce Catholicism.

It is time to honor the historic helpmeets, the real-life Suzy Homemakers and muses whose loyalty to their famous men—for better or worse—proved far more extraordinary than what they ever imagined. For these women, the exchange of vows of love (whether formal or not) often equaled trauma-ever-after. Fanny Vandegrift Osbourne, who journeyed to Samoa with her husband, Robert Louis Stevenson, expressed this anti-metronome existence, "My life resembles a wild ride on the crest of a wave that rolls and never breaks."

Abigail Adams, the Founding Mother, admonished in a letter to John, "remember the ladies." It was her plea that the new American Congress not overlook women as they proclaimed freedom from tyranny. Alas, in the end, women were relegated to the shadows, though it did not stop them from leading from the sidelines. In the same way, the wives in *Behind Every Great Man* became marginalized by history, but never by their impact, though this may not be an insight to which even they were privy. However, sometimes self-effacement was voluntary. As an anonymous Russian literary spouse stated, "The more you leave me out, the closer to truth you will be." But as with the other wives profiled, their remarkable lives do not bear this out.

I hope in this volume you glean some interesting biographical tidbits and, in doing so, let great female figures emerge from the dustbin of time. Perhaps beleaguered spouses today can also take solace that no matter what insensitive or egregious acts their husbands or partners may have committed ("I can't believe you didn't take out the trash again!" or admittedly far worse for some of us), their experiences are likely nothing compared to those of these historic women. It is interesting to ponder, if in retrospect, these intrepid wives, when standing at the altar, had they been privy to what lay ahead (in the vein of "If I Knew Then What I Know Now") would have said "We don't" in lieu of "We do."

In a variation of the title of James Agee's classic novel, let us now praise these unfamous women and let them step out of the cloak of anonymity in which they have long been shrouded. *Behind Every Great Man* parts the curtain, allowing the wives of the famous or infamous to finally take their place on center stage. I hope Abigail Adams would be pleased in this remembrance of the world's great ladies.

CHAPTER ONE

THE ENCHANTED PRINCESS

Mrs. Karl Marx

The Argentinean-Cuban revolutionary Ernesto "Che" Guevara remarked, "Let me say, at the risk of seeming ridiculous, that the true revolutionary is guided by great feelings of love." Fellow zealot Karl Marx was likewise the possessor of passion; however, the woman he loved was obscured by the red shadow he cast over the world.

The founder of communism exhorted the workers of the world to throw off their chains, but there was one who continued to carry these heavy links after marriage—Marx's long-laboring wife. Johanna Bertha Julie Jenny von Westphalen was born high on the royal hierarchy of Trier in the Kingdom of Prussia; her father was Baron Ludwig von Westphalen, a descendant of Prussian nobles and the Scottish House of Argyll. The indulged heiress, renowned for beauty and brilliance, was always ensconced in silk, from clothes to pillows to sheets. The family's parlor knew no shortage of eligible suitors, yet she rejected them when the "boy next door" (or rather the ruffian from the less affluent side of the tracks of Trier) proffered his heart.

This was, in fact, Karl Heinrich Marx's first revolutionary act. It was nothing short of audacious for the young man to court Trier's princess, as his blood had no semblance of blue that her family sought in a son-in-law. Marx was descended from a long line of rabbis, though his father, Hirschel, became Heinrich when he converted to Lutheranism (a baptism undertaken for expediency rather than religious conviction). Marx garnered his *chutzpah* because of his deep-seated belief that class should not be an impediment to love—and life without Jenny would be unbearable. It may seem surprising that a twenty-two-year-old manor-born beauty should have fallen for a bourgeois boy four years her junior instead of a dashing officer in braided uniform and of private income. However, the Prussian Jenny subscribed her feelings to the French quote, "The heart has its reasons that reason knows nothing of." The couple was secretly engaged in 1836 before Marx left for the University of Berlin to study law, followed by a stay in Cologne to edit a leftist newspaper. He returned seven years later, where Jenny, like the biblical Ruth, faithfully waited. By this time, the baron had passed away and Jenny's mother, realizing her twenty-nine-year-old daughter's devotion, bestowed blessing and a dowry—both of which Jenny would desperately need in years to come.

The marriage banns were published announcing the imminent wedding of "Herr Karl Marx, doctor of philosophy, residing in Cologne, and of Fraulein Johanna Bertha Julie Jenny von Westphalen." Marx was overjoyed his hometown beauty had chosen him—a fellow student had described him as "nearly the most unattractive man on whom the sun ever shone." The bride well understood she was marrying not only a man but a cause and willingly pledged herself to both.

The long-delayed nuptials took place in the Protestant church at Kreuznacher Pauluskirche (the Kreuznach Church of St. Paul) on June 19, 1843. It was a small affair, boycotted by the bride's disapproving family except for her mother and brother Edgar. Marx's radicalism did not extend to his honeymoon, which was a conventional trip to the Rhein-Pfalz, the German version of Niagara Falls. The baroness had given Jenny sufficient cash to cover expenses, carefully secured in a double-handed strongbox. The honeymooners left the strongbox open for needy hotel workers to partake.

Unfortunately, their first brief romantic interlude was to be their last. Jenny had hoped her brilliant husband would secure a niche as a philosophy professor; however, his voluble social advocacy made this impossible. He raged against a world where royals lived in splendor and the masses were duped into accepting their lot through the anesthetic of religion. He espoused his theories as a journalist for a Parisian newspaper, and they became friends of Heinrich Heine, the famed poet who waxed eloquent on Jenny's considerable charms.

Unfortunately, Marx never honored a deadline and was dismissed from his post. The Marxes were confronted with abject poverty until they made the acquaintance of their "angel," aptly named Engels, who used his extensive family wealth to aid the economist whose vision mirrored his own. Marx and a pregnant Jenny fled Paris when the king of Prussia, who did not appreciate the philosopher advocating the demise of his empire, ordered his arrest, and they were forced into a desperate odyssey across Europe: from Paris to Cologne to Brussels. The births of three children increased the pressure of their nomadic existence until they found refuge in England. Other women would have decried their lot—exile in a country where they had no relatives and did not speak the language. However, Jenny stated, "In these hard times, you must be plucky and keep your head unbowed. The world belongs to the brave."

The Marxes' milieu was Dickensian; they lived in a three-room slum with their ever-growing brood. The adjective that most aptly described their home would be "squalid," based on one visitor's description: "There is not one solid piece of furniture. The table is covered with an oil cloth, and on it lies manuscripts, books, and newspapers as well as the children's toys, his wife's sewing basket, several cups with broken rims, pipes, tobacco ash. To sit down becomes a thoroughly dangerous business. There is a chair with only three legs."

Ironically, despite being the world's foremost economist, Marx was ignorant of capital when it came to household finances. Jenny's home away from home became the pawnshop where she parted with the remnants of her dowry—including a silver dinner service bearing the crest of the Scottish House of Argyll—while Marx's retreat when the family bedlam became overwhelming was the reading room at the British Library. Still, despite working on his great tomes, which he believed held the antidote to the sufferings of the proletariat, he took time to humor his children. When Marx was writing *The Eighteenth Brumaire of Louis Bonaparte*, he was harnessed to a chair (supposedly one with four legs) so his children could play horse and carriage while he served as horsey.

Despite the ever-present specter of poverty, Jenny also found contentment, later writing, "The years I spent in his little study copying his scrawled articles are among the happiest of my life." She had an unfailing belief in her husband's brilliance and believed the world would ultimately embrace this truth. The family lore was Marx was the modern Prometheus, engaged in an epic struggle against bourgeoisie gods.

Jenny accepted her Job-like torments with little complaint— flight across Europe, pregnant with toddlers in tow, abject poverty, alienation from family—and that in and of itself is remarkable. She was a fierce adherent of the vow, "For better or worse." In 1850, Jenny, despite carrying her fourth baby, undertook a tour to raise money for the communist cause. (Marx could not do so as he was immersed in his manifesto, advocating revolution to the masses.) Jenny entrusted the care of her family to Helene Demuth, nicknamed Lenchen, who had accompanied the family from Prague as housekeeper and received room and board in lieu of wages. During his wife's absence, Marx committed an Arnold Schwarzenegger—he impregnated the maid. Apparently Lenchen had interpreted too literally Jenny's words to take over household duties while she was gone.

Marx was chagrined at Lenchen's condition, not on moral scruples, but rather because he felt it might be construed as his having taken advantage of a proletarian. However, he could also have viewed his simultaneously pregnant wife and housekeeper with a variation of his adage: "from each according to his ability, to each according to *his* needs." Thankfully for Marx, Comrade Friedrich Engels obligingly claimed paternity and the boy, christened Freddy Demuth, was adopted by a working-class family. Engels did this both to save the Marxes' marriage and because the news would have provided lethal ammunition to Marx's enemies. When Jenny returned, she commiserated with Lenchen and admonished Engels. Freddy's true paternity was buried for decades in the Marx mystique as Stalin desired to whitewash the unsavory tidbit and stuff it deep in the Soviet archives. Ironically, Freddy was the only one of Marx's children to live to see the advent of the Russian Revolution of which his father had been architect.

The Marxes had further reason to berate the capitalist system: they blamed it for the deaths of four of their children as a result of illness born from malnutrition, lack of medical care, and unsanitary living conditions. After losing two children in infancy, their third born, Charles Louis Henri Edgar (Musch), died of intestinal tuberculosis at age eight. Marx poured out his grief in a letter to Engels, who stood by him, helped with his writing, and provided financial support. His son's demise plunged him into a two-year depression compounded by the stillborn passing of his final, unnamed baby. Of the latter Marx had first bemoaned he could not afford a cradle, and then he could not afford a coffin.

The tragedies drew husband and wife yet closer, united by shared grief and commitment to their daughters Jenny Caroline, Jenny Laura, and Jenny Eleanor. In fact, despite all its pitfalls, the marriage of the father and mother of communism remained rich with love (though devoid of capital). On a trip to their Prussian hometown to discover the contents of his mother's will, Marx wrote to his wife, "Dear sweet darling Jenny, every day and on every side I am asked about the 'most beautiful girl in Trier' and the 'queen of the ball.' It's damned pleasant for a man, when his wife lives on like this as an 'enchanted princess' in the imagination of a whole town."

But even such intense love could not buoy Jenny forever. She had been experiencing intense internal pain, and in 1881, she was diagnosed with liver cancer and passed away at age sixty-seven on December 2 of that year. Marx was inconsolable—life without Jenny was unbearable. While fate had not spared Jenny much, her death did spare her bearing witness to the tragedies that befell her girls. Two years after her death, bladder cancer claimed her firstborn, Jenny Caroline, which proved a second and lethal punch to the man who had recently become a widower. Weakened by despair and his health compromised by years of drinking and smoking, in 1883, Karl Marx joined his spouse and child in Highgate Cemetery.

The next two daughters shared their mother's questionable taste in men. Jenny Laura died in a cyanide-induced suicide pact with

her husband Paul Lafargue. His suicide note proclaimed, "Long live communism!" The youngest, Jenny Eleanor, also ended her life with
cyanide when she discovered her common-
law spouse, Edward Aveling, had embezzled
her funds and legally married a young actress.

However, Jenny also never lived to see her
husband's vision turn into a tidal wave of a political movement that changed the history of the world
and made his name immortal, though quickly snubbing her part
in the process. But she would not have raged against his place in
history even though her own legacy was lost. It would have been
enough for her that she was the mother of what she had always
prayed would be an egalitarian brotherhood. Although the baron's
daughter had more than her fair share from the quiver of the arrows
of misfortune, she at least lived her life with the husband who, to the
last, always saw her as Trier's—and his—enchanted princess.

CHAPTER TWO

◇◇◇◇◇◇◇◇◇

SENTA

Mrs. Richard Wagner

Behind a great man—Franz Liszt—was his daughter Cosima, who was also behind another great man, Richard Wagner, as his wife. This triumvirate was united by music and by lives so melodramatic they could have sprung from a Wagnerian opera.

Franz Liszt, arguably the world's greatest pianist and the nineteenth century's nearest approach to a contemporary superstar, embarked on an affair with a married mother of two, Countess Marie d'Agoult, and in the wake of the scandal, they fled Paris. In a hotel in Lake Como, Italy, on December 24, 1837, Marie gave birth to Francesca Gaetana Cosima, the middle of their three children. The couple split on an acrimonious note, and the Countess returned to France. She was persona non grata to her aristocratic family as long as she kept her illegitimate offspring, and for the sake of preserving social standing, her daughters Blandine and Cosima and her son Daniel moved in with Liszt's mother in Paris.

Although Marie attempted to visit her estranged children, the vindictive Liszt exercised veto power and forbid her from doing so. In reproach, Marie accused him of "stealing the fruits of a mother's womb." When mother and daughters finally reunited after five years, Liszt retaliated by removing the girls from the nurturing environment of their grandmother's house to the draconian lair of Madame Patersi, whose iron-rod rules were a form of child abuse. Whenever her charges were reduced to tears—which was frequently—the Nurse Ratched of governesses responded, "Tears are just water." The result was that early on in her life, Cosima's milk of human kindness dried up, and except for Richard Wagner down the road, her heart was impregnable.

After nine years of touring, Liszt returned to Paris, and despite having been an absentee father, Cosima had endless admiration for his musical genius. He was accompanied by the world's most politically incorrect composer, who was destined to be the fifteen-year-old Cosima's soul mate. They would eventually be bound by their mutual love of music and hatred of the Jews. At that time, Richard Wagner took little notice of Liszt's younger daughter, whose only bid to beauty was luxuriant blond hair. A few years later, when Madame Patersi succumbed to the infirmities of age, Liszt took Blandine and Cosima to Berlin to live with the family of his pupil, Hans von Bülow, ardent apostle of Wagner. This time, the piano bench served as a matchmaker for the teenaged Cosima, who married von Bülow in St. Hedwig's Church in 1857. Although not in love, she sensed he would become a musical colossus; when he disappointed, it shattered her dream to wed a man as brilliant as her father. Despite despair at a marriage that left her emotionally adrift, she gave birth to Daniela and Blandina, named after her deceased siblings; her brother had succumbed at age twenty to an undiagnosed disease, her sister had passed away at age twenty-six from complications during childbirth.

Cosima's life had begun as the result of a love triangle, and another love triangle sidelined her destiny. On a trip to Zurich with von Bülow some years after they married, she became reacquainted with Richard Wagner and experienced what she referred to as her *coup de foudre*, a bolt of lightning, in which twin souls found one another. Unable to quench the symphony of their passion, the twenty-five-year-old Cosima fell hopelessly for the fifty-year-old composer, despite their respective spouses and his current mistress. Wagner later recounted, "She fell at my feet and covered my hands with tears and kisses… I pondered the mystery, without being able to solve it." It was not that much of a mystery—von Bülow had seduced the teenaged Cosima to the strains of a Wagner composition. But the ardor at that point was one-sided. Ten days after Cosima's impassioned gesture, Wagner wrote a lecherous note to a very different lady, the daughter of a Viennese pork butcher, "I hope your pink drawers are ready."

But Cosima was not deterred by this apparent lack of interest. Since her husband was an impassioned Wagnerite, a social relationship was easily arranged. In 1892, Wagner and von Bülow shared conducting duties—as well as Cosima. A year later, Wagner and Cosima took a lengthy carriage ride together. Cosima recounted in her copious diaries, "We gazed mutely into each other's eyes. A fierce desire to acknowledge the truth seized us…with tears and sobs we sealed the pledge that we belonged to each other alone. It came as a relief to both of us."

To the music-mad Cosima, Wagner was the incarnation of the romantic figure in his opera *Der fliegende Holländer* (*The Flying Dutchman*). Its tale centered on a sea captain doomed to sail on his ghostly vessel until the end of time, the only redemption a woman faithful unto death. His salvation came from Senta, the woman who freed him from Satan's curse. Cosima was convinced she was her musical lover's Senta.

By 1866, Richard was ensconced in Munich in a villa provided by his new patron, the teenaged Ludwig II, "the mad king of

Bavaria." Sitting amid the splendor of Neuschwanstein Castle (later used to house Nazi plunder and the inspiration for Disneyland's Sleeping Beauty's Castle), the king was an obsessive fan of Wagner, in the true sense of fanatic. With the passing of Wagner's wife, Minna, with whom he had an on-and-off relationship, he desired a new spouse and his thoughts harkened to Cosima, who shared his musical persuasion and fed his voracious narcissism. He was also desperate for a muse and felt she was his intended, though he probably loved her more for her slavish devotion than for her charms: she was of angular build and had inherited Franz Liszt's nose, which suited her father more than it did her.

The first step in Wagner's plan was to arrange for the von Bülows to relocate to Munich, with Hans as his conductor and Cosima as his lover. All of Europe seemed to know what was going on—except for von Bülow. (Sometimes the husband is the last to know.) Nine months later, Cosima gave birth to a third daughter, Isolde; although her surname was von Bülow, she was Wagner's daughter. If von Bülow remained oblivious to the fact that his wife spent more time in her lover's bedroom than his own, the baby's name should have provided a hint: it was from the heroine of a Wagner opera.

When babies Eva and Siegfried followed, there remained no doubt of paternity—and no dearth of scandal. Nevertheless, von Bülow kept on working with his rival, either in adulation of Wagner or fear of the controlling Cosima. He stated, "If it had been anybody but Wagner, I would have shot him." In 1870, despite her Catholicism and her father's disapproval, Cosima petitioned for a divorce. Von Bülow reluctantly threw in the towel, which finally severed his bond with Wagner—he became a devotee of Johannes Brahms.

Cosima said of her beloved, "My single prayer: one day to die with Richard in the selfsame hour. My greatest pride: to have rejected everything in order to live with him." The couple was married on August 25, 1870 (King Ludwig's birthday), in the Protestant Church in Lucerne. Cosima wrote in her diary, "At 8 o'clock we were married. May I be worthy of bearing R's name! My prayers were concentrated on two points: R's well-being—that I may always promote it; and Hans's forgiveness." She explained to her children that because of his work, their father would be permanently on tour and that was why she was marrying "Uncle Richard." Another thing they were made to understand, as were their two stepsisters—their lives were to be subordinated to their brother, nicknamed Fidi. In later years, when Isolde threatened to expose Siegfried as a homosexual (and to the Wagners, homosexuality was just below the hierarchy of horrible under Jews), Cosima retaliated by pronouncing the name "Isolde" verboten. She stated, "Just think, it is as if my feelings in this regard have died." She hardened herself against her child's anguish: tears were, after all, just water.

Cosima moved into the Munich mansion (which always contained a dog) along with her five children. Wagner, whom she called Herr Meister, set himself up in the role of Cosima's mentor. One of his pronouncements: Jewish blood is more corrosive than Latin blood. Another: the highest creation is the dog.

Cosima was born to be the spouse of a megalomaniac. The new Mrs. Wagner set about becoming the handmaiden to greatness, going so far as to preserve her husband's eyebrow clippings and who knows what else. She harnessed her force-of-nature personality as a conduit for Wagner as well. In a desire to please, she even converted to the Protestant faith for him, though he remained the core of her idolatry.

Barring the gift of the Taj Mahal that Shah Jahan erected at the dying request of his wife Mumtaz Mahal, who passed away

delivering his fourteenth baby, few women received as wondrous a present as Cosima did on her thirty-third birthday. When she awoke, it was to the strains of fifteen musicians at the foot of her grand stairway, playing the ethereally beautiful "Symphonic Birthday Greeting," which became renowned as the *Siegfried Idyll*. She confided to her diary the rapture of the immortal moment—far more magical than the birth of her own babies.

Although Wagner was engaged in composing the most controversial, sexually explicit, and lengthy of operas and Cosima was presiding over a mansion that included a megalomaniac husband, five children, and dogs, they still found time to create the Bayreuth Festival, dedicated to the music of Wagner and German purity. The composer designed the world-famous *Festspielhaus* on a wooded Bavarian hillside outside the city of Bayreuth. The foundation stone was laid in driving rain on May 22, 1872 Wagner's fifty-ninth birthday. At that moment, Wagner said to Cosima, "Each stone is red with my blood and yours." The moment was the apex of Cosima's life, though it would have been significantly clouded had she known Wagner still had more arrows in Cupid's quiver. During the opening of the festival, he embarked on an affair with Judith Gautier, daughter of a French poet.

The Wagners loved dogs, but when they fought, they did so like cats. In 1883, while in Venice, to the accompaniment of a violent storm on the Grand Canal, a row broke out between husband and wife over twenty-three-year-old soprano Carrie Pringle; despite his age, Wagner was unable to keep his *bâton* in his pants. Indeed, this row may have precipitated his fatal heart attack. Cheated from her dream of expiring at her Richard's side, Cosima made her husband a parting gift, cutting off her abundant hair and placing it in a velvet coffin cushion on which his head rested. When his body was interred (his beloved dog Russ was later buried at the feet of his master), Cosima plunged into the open grave where she lay upon the glass-topped coffin till Fidi led his anguished mother to Wahnfried, the Wagner villa.

After his death, Cosima never wrote another word in her million-word diary—without her Herr Meister, she ceased to exist. Weeks after the funeral, the widow was still willing herself to die when she had her epiphany: She could serve her beloved by keeping the flame of Bayreuth burning bright. She dedicated the rest of her years to her mission, ensuring that everything remained as it had been under "dear Richard." It was because of Cosima and Bayreuth that a half a century after his death, Wagner became the court composer of the Third Reich. The strains of Wagner were played during the Nazis book-burning ceremonies and when concentration camp prisoners walked to their deaths. Hitler briefly took time off from marching his six-thousand-strong army of Brownshirts up the Bayreuth Hill to nip into Wahnfried. He shared a close relationship with Siegfried's wife, Winifred, and their children called him Uncle Wolf.

Cosima passed away in 1930 at age ninety-two. Her urn was buried at the head of her husband's grave in the garden at Wahnfried. After forty-seven years of separation, the Flying Dutchman was finally reunited with his Senta.

⋄⋄⋄⋄⋄⋄⋄⋄⋄

CHAPTER THREE

THE IMPORTANCE OF BEING CONSTANCE

Mrs. Oscar Wilde

The seventeenth-century fictional Hester Prynne was forced to wear a scarlet letter for running afoul of Puritan Boston; her life closely paralleled the nineteenth-century nonfictional Irish writer, Oscar Wilde, who thumbed his nose at the rigid rules of British society before Queen Victoria's unamused eyes. In both cases, they were more sinned against than sinners. But there is one who was more sinned against than all: Oscar Wilde's little-known wife.

No one was ever more suitably christened than Constance Lloyd, whose constancy would be tested through a seemingly masochistic fidelity to an irresponsible, brilliant literary husband. She was born in 1858 in Dublin in an upper-middle-class family. Their house was elegantly appointed, but her father, Horace, a Queen's Counsel, was an absentee parent who had been arrested for exposing himself to nursemaids. Family life further deteriorated when he passed away when Constance was sixteen, leaving her in the clutches of her mother, Ada. Like the queen in *Snow White*, Ada Lloyd bitterly resented her daughter's beauty which had eclipsed her own. The girl's life-preserver was her brother Otho, who arranged for her to live with their paternal grandparents before he departed for Oxford.

Constance had the usual ladylike accomplishments—playing piano, painting, needlework—but she aspired higher, reading

Dante in Italian and taking a university class on Shelley in an era when women were not allowed to earn degrees. Soon the bohemian-dressed beauty was attracting admirers of all sorts. But she preferred artistic bad-boy types and fell passionately in love with the king of them all: Oscar Fingal O'Flahertie Wills Wilde. They shared the commonalities of Dubliners, children of professional fathers who were arrested on sexual charges, and Freudian dream mothers—ones who bequeathed to their offspring a host of psychological issues.

Constance felt an instant connection when she discovered Wilde, a flamboyant man-about-town, had a deep admiration for Keats, and she listened intently about his pilgrimage to the Protestant Cemetery in Rome where he had laid flowers on his idol's grave. He ended the evening by whispering she was poetry incarnate; hearts have surrendered for far less. On the drive home, he told his mother, Lady Wilde, "By the by, Mama, I think of marrying that girl."

Unaware of his words, Constance worried he was either being flirtatious—as he was known as a ladies' man, keeping company with beauties such as Sarah Bernhardt and Lillie Langtry—or still on the rebound from Florence Balcombe, who had ended their relationship when she married Bram Stoker, master of the undead, author of *Dracula*. After Wilde's visit to the Lloyd home for tea, she wrote Otho, "O. W. came yesterday at about 5:50 (by which time I was shaking with fright) and begged me to come and see his mother again soon. I can't help liking him, because when he's talking to me alone he's never a bit affected, and speaks naturally, excepting that he uses better language than most people."

Their courtship was curtailed when Wilde left to the United States on a lecture tour that made him famous on both sides of the Atlantic and allowed him to deliver his *bons mots* at the New York

City Customs Office, "I have nothing to declare but my genius." It also allowed him to indulge in his favorite pastimes of talking to captive audiences and meeting celebrities: Henry Wadsworth Longfellow, Oliver Wendell Holmes, and Walt Whitman (the latter of whom declared Wilde "a great, big splendid boy"). Two years later, after Wilde's return, Constance wrote Otho, "Prepare yourself for an astonishing piece of news. I'm engaged to Oscar Wilde and perfectly and insanely happy." Otho sent his Irish version of *mazel tov* by the next post, "If Constance makes as good a wife as she has been a good sister to me, your happiness is certain. She is staunch and true." On May 29, 1884, at 2:30 p.m., Constance and Oscar, wearing matching bands designed by the groom, exchanged vows at St. James's Church, Sussex Gardens.

Their cloud nine continued with a Parisian honeymoon in a flower-filled hotel suite overlooking the Tuileries Garden. Upon their return, they leased a property at 16 Tite Street in the artistic neighborhood of Chelsea; residents included Carlyle, Rossetti, Whistler, and Stoker. The Wildes lavished attention on each avant-garde detail till Oscar deemed their temple to aestheticism "The House Beautiful." Invitations to their dinner parties (dubbed "at homes") were coveted, and the famous gathered in their salon to revel in the company of history's most brilliant conversationalist. At gallery openings, Mr. and Mrs. Oscar (the name bestowed on the couple by the press) proved stiff competition to Lillie Langtry as the main magnet for celebrity watchers.

During this golden era, Wilde wrote *The Picture of Dorian Gray*, the fairy tale *The Happy Prince*, dedicated to his spouse whom he addressed as "the great lamp of a cathedral shrine," and *The Selfish Giant*, a story of Christian

DEDICATED TO THE GREAT LAMP OF A CATHEDRAL SHRINE

redemption. Constance, not wanting to be just her husband's ornament like his omnipresent green carnation, tried her hand at writing as well. Although her talent did not match Wilde's (whose did?), she published a book of children's tales titled *There Was Once*. An ardent feminist, she was a member of the Rational Dress Society, which likened corsets to binding women's feet and advocated that the fairer sex should not be expected to don undergarments weighing upward of seven pounds (although they stopped short of burning bras). She was also a patron of Dorothy's restaurant, where women could dine and, more shockingly, smoke alone. Most evenings found the couple together, and when Wilde left on business to Scotland, he wrote, "I feel your fingers in my hair and your cheeks brushing mine. The air is full of the music of your voice, my soul and body seem no longer mine, but mingled in some exquisite ecstasy with yours."

Wilde, who adored all experiences novel, added another to his life's résumé, fatherhood, with the arrival of sons Cyril and Vyvyan. The proud new papa could not stop urging his male friends to wed and told Constance, "I feel incomplete without you." The Wildes dwelled in their Tite Street Eden until a snake, Lord Alfred Douglas, nicknamed Bosie, entered their garden. He was a beautiful aristocrat (he coined the phrase "the love that dare not speak its name") who could twist Wilde around his bejeweled finger—and quickly did. Douglas was also a practicing homosexual, and he chose to practice with Wilde, who proved to

be quite open to the opportunity. Post Bosie, Wilde's two hit plays, *The Importance of Being Earnest* and *An Ideal Husband*, took on ironic overtones.

Wilde felt he was a rope in a tug-of-war-between his wife and lover, and it was the narcissistic Lord Douglas who proved victor. On one occasion, after spending nights in a hotel room (claiming he needed solitude to work) he returned home to spend time with his children and found an opportunity to pull the wool over Constance's eyes. After reading them a story, he admonished his sons about naughty boys who make their mothers cry; Vyvyan asked what happens to absent fathers who make their mothers cry. For once, Wilde was bereft of words.

Libido triumphed guilt and Wilde continued his affair. His quip, "In married life, three is company and two is none," had chillingly transformed into truth. Bosie brought out all of Wilde's worst qualities, especially his selfishness and narcissism, which his wife had tempered. Besotted, he spent wildly on his young lover, buying costly cigarette cases, taking him to dine at the Café Royale, and staying in suites at the Savoy Hotel. As with everything else, he indulged in a lavish midlife crisis. Constance, eventually forced from denial, confided to a friend, "I know that the one I am jealous of fills a place I cannot fill," and determined to continue her marriage; although it was devoid of sex, it still possessed love.

The turning point in the love triangle occurred when the Marquess of Queensberry, Bosie's father, left a calling card—replete with misspelling—at Wilde's club: "For Oscar Wilde, posing as a somdomite." Bosie convinced Wilde to press a charge of libel against his despised father. The problem? Wilde was guilty of the accusation, and in London's high society, it was an open secret. The trial was sensational, involving the peerage, the celebrity playwright, and rent boys (male prostitutes). However, lost in the shadows was Constance, who faithfully appeared each day at court. What added to her mortification of being the spouse of Europe's most infamous homosexual was extreme physical anguish: she had tripped on a loose carpet on her stairs at the House Beautiful and had tumbled to the bottom, seriously injuring her spine.

It was hubris that caused Wilde to stay and face trial, believing his wit and charm would sway the jury. When asked by the prosecution if he had kissed a certain boy, Wilde answered with his celebratory wit, "Oh, dear, no. He was unfortunately extremely ugly." While Constance's former rival Florence's husband was lauded as the author of *Dracula*, Constance's own husband was now viewed as the Count's nonfictional counterpart. The marriage of the Wildes proved the veracity of an Oscar quote, "The book of life begins with a man and a woman in a garden; it ends with revelations."

The result was that Wilde not only lost his suit against Queensberry but was in turn tried and convicted for "acts of gross indecency" (homosexuality). He was sentenced to two years of hard labor at Reading Prison. Constance voiced her compassion, "He is such a poor, poor fellow. What a tragedy for him who is so gifted."

After the trial, the once enviable life of Constance became akin to the Walls of Jericho: the egg thrown on her husband landed on her. The court costs had drained their financial resources, her two sons were targets of bullying, and she could only walk with great difficulty. Constance was equally victimized by the hypocrisy of Victorian society.

Her brother Otho, once again a lifesaver, arranged for her to leave England and relocate to the Continent where she changed her surname to Holland, a family name that was also Otho's middle one. Nevertheless, she did not seek a divorce; although she had married the wrong man, she loved him just the same. Constance epitomized Oscar's observation, "There is nothing in the world like the devotion of a married woman; it's a thing that no married man knows anything about." In addition, though she dreaded returning to England, she did so to deliver the heartbreaking news to her husband that his beloved mother had passed away. She could not wrap her arms around Wilde as she was separated from him by bars that forced them to remain three feet apart. During the brief time permitted, he poured out his grief to his wife for the pain of losing his mother and his hatred of his Dorian Gray (Bosie), whom he swore he would kill if he saw again. He related how someone had spat in his face and how, each day at the same hour, he wept, remembering the indignity. He bitterly stated, "If this is the way Queen Victoria treats her prisoners, she doesn't deserve to have any." After the visit, Constance poured out her own grief in a letter to her friend: "He is very repentant and minds most of all what he has brought on myself and the boys. It seems to me that by sticking to him now, I may save him from even worse."

When Wilde, broken in body and spirit from his incarceration, was released, Constance informed him she would provide an annual stipend from her trust fund and invited her prodigal husband to rejoin his family in Genoa. He was making plans to do so when he instead decided to meet up with Bosie (whom Constance referred to as "that appalling individual") in Naples. Preferring his Judas to his wife led even Constance to her breaking point; she declared Wilde was "weak as water," and at long last, the marriage of the Wildes ended sadly, madly, badly. Wilde lost his parental rights; he was never to see wife or sons again. But again, even though their marriage ended, their love never did. In her last letter, Constance wrote to Otho of Wilde's final literary work, "The Ballad of Reading Gaol": "I was frightfully upset by this wonderful poem… it is tragic and makes one cry." The line that carried the most personal resonance: "Each man kills the thing he loves." Tragically, Wilde, unlike his Selfish Giant, never achieved redemption.

Constance underwent an operation and passed away on April 7, 1898, with only a nurse in attendance. She was interred in the Campo Santo Cemetery in Genoa. The following year, Wilde visited her gravesite and broke down in tears. He wrote to his friend Ross, "It was very tragic seeing her name carved on a tomb—her surname, my name, not mentioned. I had a sense of the uselessness of all regrets. Life is a very terrible thing." In 1963, her family added an addendum to her tombstone: wife of Oscar Wilde.

After life with her flamboyant and tortured genius, Constance deserves to recline and remember the time before Wilde wore his variation of Hester's scarlet letter.

CHAPTER FOUR

BA

Mrs. Mohandas Gandhi

In the 1990s, a photograph appeared in a newspaper; in the top corner was a rainbow-striped apple with the slogan "Think Different." The lone image was of a follicle-challenged, emaciated man wearing a loincloth and oversized spectacles. But his small frame belied his huge achievement. A half century beforehand, Mohandas Gandhi, known as Bapu (father), had freed his nation from the yoke of the Raj. However, obscured by the giant shadow of the diminutive leader was Ba, mother of India.

The woman who was to prove the mettle behind the Mahatma, Kasturba Kapadia, was born in 1869 in Porbandar, the daughter of an affluent merchant. In order to cement a friendship with a local family, she was betrothed at age seven and married six years later to a groom of the same age, Mohandas Karamchand Gandhi. Later he recounted, "As we didn't know much about marriage, for us it only meant wearing new clothes, eating sweets, and playing with relatives. The carnal desire came later." Even as a teen, he harbored misgivings about having no voice in his life's companion; Kasturba, however, accepted the event as the natural cycle of life, much like the annual monsoons. This was a natural response for a girl raised on tales of ancient India's faithful modest wives.

Gandhi, however, refused to accept old traditions. Instead, he taught his partner to read, and they perused the newspapers, never imagining one day his image, albeit greatly altered, would peer back.

Later Gandhi stated that had they not enjoyed such a libidinous life, there would have been more time for his wife's education: "I am sure that had my love for her been absolutely untainted by lust, she would have been a learned lady by now."

As they grew into adulthood, his desire to push the boundaries of tradition subsided. In the patriarchal society, Gandhi soon assumed the role of a traditional MCP—male chauvinist pig—and demanded his wife seek permission before leaving home. As a girl from a traditional background, Kasturba could not openly defy her husband; however, she discovered a loophole. When her mother-in-law asked her to accompany her to temple, she could not ask Gandhi, who was at school. When he raised an objection, she responded, "Are you suggesting I obey you and disrespect your mother?" At age fifteen, two tragic events occurred: the death of their first son who lived for a few days, and the passing of Gandhi's father.

Three years later, on the advice of a Hindu priest, Gandhi decided to study law in London; the enterprise was financed by selling his wife's jewels, wedding gifts from her parents. What helped assuage Kasturba's loneliness during this time was the birth of their son Harilal, and Gandhi's acquiescence when his mother requested that he not touch wine, women, or meat while abroad. Upon his return, a second son, Manilal, arrived. When Gandhi's Bombay practice failed because he was too shy to speak in court, he accepted a position in South Africa, a part of the British Empire where its sun never set. In 1893 white officials forced him from a train when he refused to vacate its first-class section, arguing he had paid for its ticket. The incident served as a catalyst and made Gandhi a David fighting against the Goliath of social injustice. He founded the Natal Indian Congress, which united his countrymen and drew widespread attention to South Africa's racial regime. Lonely, he returned to India to bring his family to the continent where he was to embody the slogan "Think Different."

Kasturba was apprehensive about moving to a country dominated by apartheid, where the Indian minority was derogatorily referred to as "coolies." However, she felt comforted she would be with her husband, who had scarcely had any contact with his two sons. Her first taste of what was to lie ahead came before the Gandhis even set foot in Durban. Their ship, the *Nadir*, was forced to remain in harbor for twenty-three days, ostensibly because the authorities were afraid its passengers had been exposed to the plague rampant in Bombay. In fact, the ship had been placed in quarantine not for fear of disease, but for fear of Gandhi, an unwelcome thorn in apartheid's side. The welcoming committee ashore consisted of a mob of white South Africans who did not want the agitator, Gandhi, whom his people had taken to calling "Bapu," to return. When they finally disembarked, the pregnant Kasturba and the two boys were spirited to safety, but Gandhi was assaulted with bricks, rotten eggs, and fists. The police interceded but he refused to press charges, saying, "The weak can never forgive. Forgiveness is the attribute of the strong."

Kasturba, badly shaken at this violent welcome, derived comfort from her beautiful new house, the Beach Grove Villa, modeled after European architecture. Their family grew with the births of their next two sons, Ramdas and Devadas.

To Kasturba's dismay, life in the villa came with an expiration date. Gandhi, who donned philosophies for a midlife crisis as other men did cars, adopted a belief in *aparigraha* (nonpossessiveness) and determined his wife and sons engage in communal living. He established the Phoenix settlement, situated in the midst of miles of sugar cane. When they traveled, it was only in third class, and when questioned why he did so, he quipped, "Because there is no fourth." To promote his view of simplicity, Gandhi bought shears to cut hair and studied a childbirth manual so he would be able to deliver any subsequent babies. However, the latter never occurred because of his next philosophy, *brahmacharya*, sexual abstinence. Gandhi was burdened with lifelong guilt that he had been in the throes of lust with his teenage wife when his father breathed his last, without his son at his side. This may have been the subliminal reason behind his decision to channel his sexual urges into working for the communal good. He stated, "One who conserves his vital fluid acquires unfailing power." Gandhi claimed Kasturba was compliant with his decision; this is understandable as her plate was more than full with raising four sons and a husband who, well, thought differently. Another quirk was that he always slept with a light burning by the bedside. Entirely unafraid of the British, he was afraid of the dark.

The philosophy for which he had most need of saving his bodily fluids was *satyagraha*, the Indian equivalent of Christ's "turn the other cheek." Ironically, although this method of nonviolent civil disobedience is the one with which he is most associated, it originated with Kasturba, whom he had tried to control as a young wife. She had simply turned the other cheek at his outbursts. Interestingly, these were in some ways the birth of his tenet of passive resistance, one later adopted by Dr. Martin Luther King Jr.

Kasturba also often joined him in his protests toward the outside world. In his role in fighting for his people, Gandhi was arrested on innumerable occasions; with each incarceration, in solidarity,

Kasturba subsided on the same meals as her husband and ate nothing but cornmeal porridge. Her true religion was her husband.

On one occasion, she became seriously ill and the prison officials informed Gandhi that if he admitted guilt, he could walk through the prison gate. The price of freedom was too high and he wrote home, "I am not in a position to come and nurse you. If it is destined that you should die, I think it is preferable that you should go before me. Even if you die, for me you will be eternally alive." He went on to reassure her that he had no intention of remarrying after her demise and told her that her death would serve as "another great sacrifice for *satyagraha*." Kasturba survived and for her part in civil disobedience was sentenced to three months of hard labor. Denied a vegetarian diet in the labor camp, she resorted to a fast; General Smuts, avid adherent of white minority rule, not wanting her to die as a martyr, ultimately conceded.

In 1914, after two decades in South Africa, Gandhi decided it was time to return to India, the land Queen Victoria had dubbed "the jewel in her crown." His reputation had preceded him, and he was referred to as the Mahatma, the "enlightened." It was a title he disliked, saying, "The woes of Mahatmas are known to Mahatmas alone." The same sentiment was felt by Mrs. Mahatma. After establishing a spiritual retreat, his famous ashram (where he slept naked beside similarly undressed young girls to prove his power over preserving his vital fluids), he set about trying to right the wrongs imposed by the British Raj, which used his country to line England's coffers. It was there he adopted the garb of the Indian peasants and wore only a loincloth and a shawl when cold.

Once more, he began his acts of civil disobedience, which landed him in jail where he fasted in protest. Winston Churchill was incensed by the agitator who he referred to as that "half-naked fakir" and determined that he be crushed. When that proved problematic, a meeting was arranged between the Mahatma and the king of England. In 1931, he arrived with his entourage: a goat to provide milk and a collapsible spinning wheel. When someone asked how he could have dressed in a loincloth to meet royalty, he replied, "The king had on enough for both of us." The conference bore no fruit, and shortly after his return to India, he was arrested on order of the country that had erstwhile served as his host.

In retaliation, Gandhi embarked on a lengthy fast. His people now viewed him not just as Bapu, but as a *dhoti*-clad demigod. He was the Indian Moses; his life's mission was for the British to let his people go. From his prison, he urged his followers to eschew violence, a plea that often went unheeded. He stated, "There are many causes I am prepared to die for, but none I am prepared to kill for."

Kasturba was direly afraid for her husband and was simultaneously dealing with her prodigal son, Harilal, who had been estranged from his parents for many years. His entire life had been spent in the shadow of his father, and he lived it rebelling against everything Gandhi represented. He was angered his parent had spent all his time being the Bapu to his people and never one to his sons. At one point, when Gandhi and Kasturba were in a train station, a feeble voice was heard to say, "*Kasturba ki jai*," instead of the customary "*Gandhi ki jai*." Harilal, in rags and toothless, approached and offered an orange to his mother. When Gandhi asked what he had brought him, his son replied, "Nothing. If you are so great, it is because of Ba." Privy to what went on behind the homespun curtains, he knew it had been his mother who had been her husband's metaphorical walking stick.

Gandhi and Kasturba were incarcerated in the Aga Khan Prison where they fasted, a situation detrimental to a woman who at this point had suffered two heart attacks and had chronic bronchitis. Despite this, she tried her best to nurse her husband and work at her spinning wheel. She eventually came down with pneumonia and Harilal, greatly intoxicated, visited her sickbed. He insisted she take penicillin while Mohandas demanded she undergo traditional Indian medicine. Understandably tired, she only agreed to sip water from the Ganges. Afterward, she lay down and alternately called out, "*Ram Hai Ram*" or for her husband. Saddened there was no reconciliation between father and son—or perhaps unable to bear it—Kasturba placed her head on her husband's lap and breathed her last.

A photograph shows Gandhi huddled in a corner, a shadow of himself. Kasturba was clad in a white sari woven by her husband, and after her body had been consumed in the funeral pyre, Gandhi moaned, "I cannot imagine life without Ba." His only solace was that she had passed away in *satyagraha*, a woman who had spent her life turning the other cheek. After Gandhi was assassinated, his ashes were interred next to Kasturba's in the prison courtyard.

When Sir Richard Attenborough was producing his epic film *Gandhi*, Jawaharlal Nehru told him, "Do not deify him. He was too great a man to be turned into a god." It was a sentiment to which Kasturba would have wholeheartedly agreed. If someone had inquired if she had known her arranged marriage was to be deranged, would she still have desired it, she would have nodded acquiescence. For a life of unimaginable turmoil, she deserves a tranquil spot by the Ganges, free from the monsoons of the life she spent with her "think different" Gandhi.

None of this is meant to diminish Bapu's legacy; the Mahatama, despite his flaws, was a man of iron integrity. Many of the world's greatest freedom-fighters were inspired by Mohandas Gandhi: Russia's Leo Tolstoy, South Africa's Nelson Mandela, the United States' Dr. Martin Luther King. However, as Harilal realized, if his father was so great, it was because of Ba.

CHAPTER FIVE

DOXERL AND JOHONZEL

Mrs. Albert Einstein

An iconic image of the twentieth century depicts Albert Einstein sticking his tongue out in his variation of "Say cheese." As a man so famous he stopped Fifth Avenue traffic in the same fashion as The Beatles and Marilyn Monroe (who called him the sexiest man on earth), he could afford such irreverence. However, the woman at whom he figuratively stuck out his tongue was a little-known girl of his youth, the one who labored and loved by his side.

Milos and Marija Maric viewed their daughter Mileva as possessing two disabilities: a severely displaced hip that made one leg three inches shorter than the other and a genius intellect. Although she had a dark Slavic beauty, they despaired of her marrying because of her "problems." These were daunting issues in nineteenth-century Novi Sad (modern-day Serbia). Still, Milos admired his daughter's smarts and obtained special permission to enroll her in an all-male high school. His labors paid off—her grade in physics was the highest ever awarded. A prefeminist fighter, her dream was to be a physicist. By the time Mileva graduated from secondary school in 1894, the Austro-Hungarian Empire stood firm in its conviction to bar female students from university. Hence, when her scientific thirst remained unquenched, her parents financed her educational aspirations and she left for Switzerland's exclusive Zurich Polytechnic, the MIT of Europe.

Mileva was only the fifth female to pass through the school's venerated doors, and it was here the twenty-two-year-old met the seventeen-year-old Albert Einstein, possessor of thick, curly hair and brown bedroom eyes. It was not love at first sight, but it was a meeting of minds—akin to E meeting mc². Albert was intrigued a girl could converse on his life's passion: the realm of physics. Mileva was enthralled that Einstein, unlike her hometown macho males, was not threatened she passed the Matura (entrance exam) on her first try, even though it took him two.

For the first semester, the two blossoming geniuses maintained a platonic friendship. Mileva, who did not have a nonserious bone in her body, kept her eye on the prize of a diploma, while Einstein was carrying the flame for Marie Winteler, from his native Ulm, who adoringly did his laundry. A year later, platonic gave way to passionate, and they embarked on a union fueled by shared interests in music and math. Einstein's friends were puzzled by his interest in the melancholy girl with the limp; her small circle of eastern European friends questioned her feelings for the boy with disheveled hair and mismatched socks. Einstein brushed off such criticism: "Once you accept the universe as matter expanding into nothing that is something, wearing stripes with plaid comes easy."

When separated, they wrote letters in which he would address her as Doxerl (little doll) and she would lovingly respond to her Johonzel (Johnnie). For pillow talk, they had electrodynamics and atomic kinetics. During a family vacation in Milan, Einstein first showed his mother, Pauline, a photo of the woman he loved; she fell on her bed in tears when rather than seeing the lovely Marie Winteler as she expected, she was confronted with a dark-haired, brooding woman. Her mood did not improve when her son supplied details: Mileva was older, from the backwaters of the Balkans, and, horror of horrors, a *shiksa*. In between sobs, she admonished him, "If she gets a child, you'll be in a pretty mess." The twenty-two-year-old Einstein, as fixed in his own romantic beliefs as he would be in his professional, brushed off his mother's agitated warning. He dashed off a poem in a letter, "Oh my! That Johnnie boy! So crazy with desire/While thinking of his Dollie/His pillow catches fire." His next letter was of a more prosaic bent when he sent his lady an outline of his foot, requesting she knit him a pair of socks because his big toe always made holes in those from a store.

When Einstein graduated, he accepted a position in the Swiss Patent Office in Bern, which provided economic autonomy from his parents. In celebration, he and Mileva enjoyed a rendezvous in Italy's Lake Como district, shaped like a horseshoe and nestled in the lap of the Alps. Perhaps there is something in the water, as Franz Liszt conceived his daughter Cosima in Lake Como, as did Einstein. When Mileva informed him of her pregnancy, it was Einstein's Big Bang moment: should he listen to his mother or Mileva? Eventually, unwilling to commit, Einstein ignored the pleading look in his girlfriend's dark eyes and she returned to Novi Sad. On January 27, 1902, she gave birth to a daughter, Lieserl, and the absentee father wrote, "Is she healthy, and does she cry properly? Which one of us does she resemble? I love her so much and don't even know her yet!" After this initial letter, the baby vanished into the Balkan night, either given up for adoption or a victim of scarlet fever. Neither Mileva nor Albert mentioned her again, at least in any recorded source.

The next year, after his father, Hermann, gave a deathbed blessing for their union, Einstein asked for Mileva's hand, a proposal based on both love and guilt—the pregnancy had forced her to leave school and had branded her with a scarlet letter. The January 6 wedding was a simple ceremony in the town hall in Bern and a celebratory dinner at a local restaurant. What followed was the time that would one day be described as "the good old days." In 1904, a son, Hans Albert, was born, which helped mend the hole in Mileva's heart from the loss of Lieserl. On Sundays, the proud papa could be seen in the streets of Bern pushing a stroller, pipe in mouth, notebook ever at the ready.

However, when the baby was asleep, Albert and Mileva could return to the partnership of their student years at the prestigious Poly, and the nocturnal air was filled with talk of atoms, rather than any atomic love at that point. Einstein said if he could only discover the single law that governed the universe, he would be able to "read the mind of God." An avid partner, Mileva worked alongside in his quest, and in 1905, the merging of their minds bore fruit. It was to become known as Einstein's *Annus Mirabilis* (Year of Miracles), one that was to prove the lowly patent clerk was on an intellectual par with Newton, Galileo, and Aristotle. He published five scientific papers that ushered in the birth of modern physics and irrevocably altered the course of history. The twentieth century was born in those pages. He wrote of his collaboration with his brilliant wife, "How happy and proud I will be when the two of us together will have brought our work on the relative motion to a victorious conclusion!"

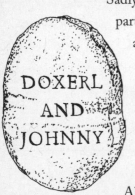

DOXERL AND JOHNNY

Sadly, history would never view them as an equal partnership. When Helene, Mileva's dearest friend, asked why she never affixed her name to the papers, she replied, "We are *ein Stein*" (one stone). But the nights no longer revolved solely around theories of relativity because a second son, Eduard ("Tete"), was born in 1910 in Zurich, where the family had relocated when Einstein became Herr Professor. Although the missus labored into the night with

her husband on his work, the responsibility of
the children was hers alone. As the resident
genius, he bore a "do not disturb" sign—
one can imagine Mileva with a finger
permanently affixed to her lip, silencing
their children: "Shhh...Daddy's working
on unlocking the secrets of the cosmos."
Although Mileva was content to dissolve into

Einstein's ever-lengthening shadow, she still experienced heartache when the Nobel Prize in chemistry was awarded to
the husband-and-wife team, Pierre and Marie Curie.

Mileva's *Annus Horribilis* coincided with the start of World
War I—and lasted as long—when Einstein accepted a position at
the University of Berlin. Mileva was opposed to relocating because
the Germans looked down on ethnic Serbians, and she suspected
her husband harbored romantic notions for his first cousin Elsa
Löwenthal (née Einstein), daughter of Pauline's sister. She proved
as astute in this observation as she had been in her scientific theories. The divorced mother of Ilse and Margot was the polar opposite of Mileva: blond, blue-eyed, Jewish. Moreover, unlike Mileva,
who only cared about cerebral affairs, Elsa was so vain she refused
to wear glasses. At a dinner party, she had started eating a flower
arrangement, mistaking it for salad. She was nevertheless clever
enough to understand the cliché "the way to a man's heart is through
his stomach," and she prepared Einstein's favorite: goose crackle.
When he returned home, he wrote his cousin/mistress, "Mileva is
an unfriendly humorless creature who has nothing from life herself
and smothers the joy in life of others through her mere presence
(*malocchio*)!" (evil eye).

When the young Einstein was two and a half, his sister Maja
was born. He had been expecting some kind of toy, and when he

saw the baby, he expressed his dissatisfaction she did not come with wheels. The adult Einstein was also now dissatisfied his wife no longer had the "wheels" he required. The flame of his earlier passion for Doxerl had been extinguished. Einstein felt conflicted between duty to his sons and his carnal cravings. His later quote indicated which side he would land on: "And the moral of the story/(Which one hardly ever discusses)/Is that the upper half plans and thinks/ While the lower half determines our fate."

He drew up an agreement that contained the stipulations for the couple remaining together for the sake of Hans Albert and Eduard. It was as cold as a mathematical equation. "A. You will see to it (1) that my clothes and linen are kept in order, (2) that I am served three regular meals a day in my room. B. You will renounce all personal relations with me, except when these are required to keep up social appearances. You will expect no affection from me... You must leave my bedroom or study at once without protesting when I ask you to." From the document, it is apparent that emotionally Albert was no Einstein. He had once famously remarked, "God does not play dice with the universe"; however, he did just that with his wife. Mileva's response to the misogynistic manifesto was a nervous breakdown that required hospitalization. When she recovered, she realized that although she desperately wanted an intact family, she still had enough vestige of pride from her years at the Poly not to submit to life as an unglorified maid. Einstein once again ignored the pleading look in his wife's dark eyes to rekindle his earlier love, and she returned to Zurich, sons in tow.

On Valentine's Day 1919, the Einsteins were divorced, and that

same year, Albert made his first cousin his second wife. Mileva, con-vinced the theories they had worked on would get the recognition they deserved, wisely demanded that her divorce settlement include earnings from any future Nobel Prize, which he garnered three years later. The wild-haired physicist, adorned with laurel, made no mention that his ex had helped discover relativity. Neither all of his learning nor liberalism prevented him from making his mate an appendage to his own identity.

The Jewish scientist became a target of the Nazis, and in 1933, he and Elsa and her two daughters immigrated to the United States, where he became the wild-haired, sock-shunning Princeton professor who wept that his mathematical equation had led to Hiroshima and Nagasaki. Despite serial infidelities, the Einsteins remained married until Elsa's death. He later quipped that he was doing well considering he had survived two World Wars and two wives. However, rather than castigate himself for his roving eye, he immersed in self-pity, saying, "I am a completely isolated man and though everybody knows me, there are very few people who really know me." He also commented to a friend that he admired his father because the man had stayed with the same woman his entire life, "a project in which I grossly failed twice." The great man could see past space and time but had limited insight into his own heart.

Seven years later, Hans Albert Einstein followed his estranged father's footsteps and served as a professor at Berkeley, but the two had minimal contact. This was not, as Einstein believed, because his ex-wife had poisoned the children against him. Rather, as Hans Albert bitterly explained, "The only scientific project my father ever gave up on was me."

While Albert was forever feted, Mileva retreated into obscu-rity, poverty, and despair. Her life in Zurich was a never-ending quest to care for Eduard, whose brilliant mind was blindsided by schizophrenia. She kept him at home, despite violent out-bursts; when she passed away in 1948, he was committed to the Burghölzli Psychiatric Institute, where he remained till his death. Albert, who had not seen Eduard for thirty years, lamented the wasted potential of his brilliant son, isolated from any loved one after his mother's death. He wrote it would have been preferable had Tete never been born.

We will never know how much input Mileva had in Einstein's magnum opus. But what we do know is it was fashioned from the days when Einstein was a young man in love—in the days of Doxerl and Johonzel.

CHAPTER SIX

A ROSE IS A ROSE IS A ROSE IS A ROSE

Mrs. Gertrude Stein

T he girl power chant, "Behind every great man" had a variation in 1920s Paris: "Behind every great woman is a woman." Indeed, this proved true for the high priestess of modern art and her consort, who provided a salon in 1920s Paris that served as a Mecca for the leading lights of the Lost Generation.

Gertrude Stein had remarked of her Oakland, California, childhood home, "There is no there there." Alice Babette Toklas, whose life was to be forever knitted with Stein's, felt the same about her native San Francisco. This was not an indictment of the city, rather a commentary on her mundane existence. As a teen, she had studied music at the University of Seattle and displayed such talent she considered a career as a concert pianist. Her dreams dissipated at age twenty when her mother passed away and she took over her role of running a household that consisted of an Orthodox Jewish grandfather, wealthy Polish immigrant father, and ten-year-old brother. They appreciated her outstanding cooking but, finding her odd (for one, she sported a mustache), treated her as if she were merely a housekeeper.

Alice's salvation was the devastating San Francisco earthquake of 1907. Through her neighbor (and possibly lover), Harriet Lane Levy, Alice made the acquaintance of Michael and Sarah Stein, who had relocated to France but were in San Francisco to assess damage to their properties. Alice proved a rapt audience; her favorite author

was Henry James, the American novelist who penned *The Portrait of a Lady*, and she was intrigued to hear of the places his characters roamed. Michael further piqued her interest when he showed her a portrait by Henri Matisse that showcased the French painter's wife with a green stripe running down her nose. Toklas, who possessed an avant-garde nature, related far more to the modernist portrait than to the Old Masters. When Sarah invited the girls to visit if they ever came to Paris, Harriet and Alice commenced packing. They were determined to get there—to escape to a world less conventional than their own. Little did Alice know when she departed she was to become not merely a permanent Parisian but one half of the most celebrated lesbian couple in history.

In her 1963 memoir, Alice wrote of meeting the one on whose axis her world was to revolve the very day she arrived in France: "She was a golden brown presence, burned by the Tuscan sun and with a golden glint in her warm brown hair." Alice was immediately smitten by Paris and Gertrude Stein (Michael's sister), and the two instantly were joined at far more than just the hip. She adopted the role of cook, muse, and confidante to her life companion and beloved. In Cecil Beaton's photographs of the pair, Alice is always behind Gertrude, content to dwell in her shadow. But it was a common consensus among their circle that without Alice, Gertrude would not have been Gertrude. One of the foremost feminists of the day, she nevertheless needed a soul mate, one who would be willing to worship at the skirt of her genius.

The couple, although both vertically challenged, were a study in contrasts. Stein, rotund, wore her hair in a Roman emperor cut and favored mannish outfits; Alice, rakishly thin, favored couture attire, though her appearance proved far from what their designers had envisioned. In a nod to "out of the mouths of babes," Michael Stein's

three-year-old son remarked he liked the man, but why did the woman have a mustache? Two years later, Toklas moved in to what was to become an iconic address—27 rue de Fleurus, her own niche in the pantheon of modern art—as a core member of Gertrude's charmed circle.

The new living arrangement did not sit well with Gertrude's eldest brother, Leo, whose avant-garde taste did not extend to his sister's lifestyle and selection of companion (whom he would never describe by the name of Henry James's novel *Portrait of a Lady*)— and he took his departure from the home they had shared since moving to Paris. Although Leo had been the first to champion the unknown Picasso, Gertrude kept his canvasses while Leo opted for the Cézannes. Delighted at having their own domicile, Alice and Gertrude scattered love notes around their home, signed DD and YD (Dear Dear and Your Dear). The women strolled the streets of their adopted city and browsed flea markets, walking their enormous white poodle, Basket, who, upon his passing, was replaced by Basket II. In 1908, in a country setting, Gertrude proposed and presented "wifey" with a ring. Ms. Stein wrote of the day, "It happened very simply that they were married. They were naturally married."

Alice would have been content to live in the fringes of French society, but Gertrude needed to be lionized. Hence, they opened their door to soirees that became a Mecca for the modern-minded. On a typical evening, one would have found Gertrude, swathed in brown corduroy, sitting in a high-backed Renaissance chair, feet dangling. Guests included Picasso with his latest mistress, Matisse and wife (sans green stripe running down her nose), and Hemingway, who remarked he and Gertrude were "just like brothers." While Gertrude dominated in the drawing room, Alice held court with the geniuses' wives where she engaged in her favorite pastime of gossip. She also reigned in the kitchen and was acknowledged as one of the finest chefs in Paris of her time. All ingredients were purchased from Fauchon, the city's elite greengrocer. Picasso was smitten with her bass, poached in wine and butter, and rewarded Alice's artistry by designing a needlepoint pattern that she used to make a tapestry for a footstool. In a more grandiose gesture, he created a canvas of Gertrude; when someone commented her portrait did not look like her, Picasso replied, "It will."

Despite Alice's diminutive stature, she was a fierce guardian of the gate and held veto power over entry. One of the exiled was Hemingway, who, though Alice and Gertrude were godmothers to his son John (whom they had nicknamed Goddy, as they were his godmothers), became persona non grata when Alice felt he was getting too chummy with Gertrude. In his memoir, *A Moveable Feast*, he recounted an argument between the two hostesses: "I heard Miss Toklas speaking to Miss Stein as I have never heard one person speak to another, never, anywhere, ever."

The true apotheosis of Gertrude, however, began in 1933 with *The Autobiography of Alice B. Toklas*, which was actually penned by Gertrude writing in her lover's voice—a paean to hubris. One vignette recounted Alice's first meeting with Gertrude: "I must say that only three times in my life have I met a genius, and each time a bell within me rang and I was not mistaken, and I may say in each case it was before there was any general recognition of the quality of genius in them. The three geniuses of whom I wish to speak are Gertrude Stein, Pablo Picasso, and Alfred Whitehead." Each page dripped anecdotes of their famous friends, and because it was not written in the odd cubist style of her earlier works (verses like "a rose is a rose is a rose is a rose"), it became a bestseller and was followed by an enormously successful American tour. The ladies made the front pages of major newspapers, and a revolving billboard in Times Square spelled out in lights: Gerty Gerty Stein Stein is back back back. Alice, described as the writer's "constant companion," appeared in outfits topped with a feathered chapeau while Gertrude wore a deerstalker cap. Other highlights in the country from which they had been self-exiled for thirty years was tea with Eleanor Roosevelt in the White House and cocktails with Charlie Chaplin in Beverley Hills. Gertrude had once stated, "I always wanted to be historical, from almost a baby on, I felt that way about it." The tour cemented her wish.

When World War II broke out, friends cautioned Alice and Gertrude to return to America; after all, as Jews and lesbians, they were prime targets of the Nazi bull's-eyes. Gertrude refused, saying, "America is my country, but Paris is my hometown." However, they did escape Paris and fled to their country retreat in Bilignin in the south of France. They managed to evade deportation through the aid of Bernard Fay, ironically a Nazi collaborator, who nevertheless used his influence and the Stein wealth to buy them immunity. Post liberation, Gertrude wrote to Alice, "I love you so much more/every war more and more and more." When they returned home, Alice was devastated that in a Gestapo raid their Picasso petit-point footstool and a pair of Louis XV candlesticks were stolen. The Nazis had not snatched the art, believing it degenerate. Gertrude comforted her, saying they still had their paintings and each other.

In 1946, Gertrude experienced abdominal pain and was diagnosed with stomach cancer. When the end was near, she was transported to the American hospital in Neuilly-sur-Seine. Alice sat up in tearful vigil, already grieving the remaining empty years. As Gertrude lay dying, Alice listened to her "deep, full, velvety, contralto's voice for the last time ask, 'What is the answer?' followed by 'What is the question?'" Alice mourned, "I am but a memory of her. I wish to God we had gone together as I always fatuously thought we would—a bomb—a shipwreck—just anything but this." There had been a Basket II to replace Basket the poodle, but there would be no replacement for Gertrude.

Gertrude always loved words but they fell short in her will. She bequeathed all her paintings to Alice, and after her lover's own passing to her nephew Allan. However, through a legal loophole, the Stein attorney, Edgar Allan Poe (the author's great-nephew), arranged for their removal to a Paris vault when Alice was in Italy taking a mud cure for arthritis. When she returned, all that remained on her walls was the haunting imprint of the masterpieces. If Gertrude had been privy to this horror, she would have bemoaned, "a thorn is a thorn is a thorn is a thorn." Alice was evicted from the apartment where she had lived and loved with Gertrude and relocated to an austere flat. Destitute, in 1954, she penned *The Alice B. Toklas Cookbook*, which mixed reminiscences and recipes, the most famous for hashish brownies: "In the menu, there should be a climax and a culmination. Come to it gently. One will suffice." Alice's surname gave rise to the vernacular "toke"—the inhaling of marijuana.

Gertrude had once noted, "Life is funny that way. The ones that should naturally offer do not, and those who have no reason to offer it do, you never know you never do know where your good fortune is to come from." In her last years, Alice languished in a nursing home, dribbling on a dirty house-robe, when she was befriended by Doda Conrad, a friend from the old days. He took over her upkeep and brought her groceries from the local market, deceptively wrapped in a bag from Fauchon. He took her out to dine despite the fact that when she ate oil coagulated on her whiskers. Ironically a stranger came to her aid when her lover's family, and her own, would not. Life is funny that way.

Gertrude never believed in an afterlife: "there was no there there." However, Alice, in a desperate hope to be reunited with her lost love, converted to Catholicism. She asked her priest, "Will this allow me to see Gertrude when I die?" When Alice passed away in 1967, she was interred next to Gertrude in Père Lachaise Cemetery. As Alice had instructed, "Toklas" was inscribed on the back of their shared tombstone. Even in death, she stood aside so her lover could shine.

◇◇◇◇◇◇◇◇◇◇

CHAPTER SEVEN

THE STEPPING STONE

Mrs. Bill Wilson

I n a country music classic, for a sip of whiskey, a gambler offers the advice, "You've got to know when to hold 'em/Know when to fold 'em/Know when to walk away." However, unlike the gambler, there was a wife who, though justified beyond belief, refused to walk away. By remaining steadfast, she saved her man and, by extension, brought salvation to millions.

The woman who became the cornerstone of a movement was born in Brooklyn Heights in 1891. Lois Burnham's formative influences were her father, Clark, a respected surgeon, and her mother, Matilda, staunch believers in the Swedenborgian faith, founded in the eighteenth century, which counted among its faithful Helen Keller and Robert Frost. The family's lavishly appointed home on Clinton Street was filled with the happy noise of six children, and summers were spent in Vermont where Dr. Burnham treated his wealthy vacationing New York patients. (One well-heeled Vermont neighbor was Abraham Lincoln's grandson.) The adjective Lois used to describe her childhood was idyllic.

Life irrevocably changed when a local teen knocked at the Burnham door and asked Lois to buy some kerosene lamps that were tied to a pole slung across his shoulder. She recognized Bill Wilson as her brother Roger's friend but was not interested in either boy or product. Wilson, who carried a chip on his shoulder along with the lamps in his hand, felt the wealthy city girl looked down on the poor country bumpkin. Later, noticing her sailing on Emerald Lake, he decided to give her a dunking. He refurbished his grandfather's old rowboat, drove a pole through its center, and fastened a bedsheet for a makeshift sail.

The race that morning was not conducted on an equal water playing field—Lois was a seasoned sailor with a state-of-the-art skiff, and Wilson was handicapped by inexperience and a sailboat meant to be rowed. When Lois looked back and saw a bizarre contraption heading toward her, piloted by the kerosene lamp boy, she was stunned. A moment later, a gust of wind hit the pole, and Wilson was flung into the lake wrapped in the white bedsheet, a drowning Vermont mummy. Lois rescued him, and once in her boat, perhaps nudged by the beauty of Emerald Lake, feelings stirred. In 1916, Wilson bought his fiancée a small, twenty-five-dollar amethyst ring from Tiffany's, and took her to a barbeque in Staten Island. They had placed their steaks on a grill when the breeze from the bay blew the burning embers and ignited a fire on the dry grass. Wilson used his jacket to quell the flames; though his clothes were destroyed, the Tiffany box remained intact.

The couple would have waited until Wilson was financially stable before marriage, but with the advent of World War I and Wilson facing imminent departure with the army, they were wed in the Swedenborgian Church on January 24, 1918, followed by a reception on Clinton Street. After Wilson shipped out, Lois was devastated when she miscarried. Soon after, she asked the YMCA to send her overseas as a nurse in the hope of being stationed near her husband, but was turned down because they did not consider the Swedenborgian faith Christian.

In Europe, while thousands of soldiers fought the horror of trench warfare, Bill Wilson struggled with another kind of battle. In England, when the first butler he had ever seen offered him a drink, a Bronx cocktail, the second lieutenant did not refuse. Liquor transformed him from an awkward quarryman's son to a sophisticated officer. He claimed he had found "the elixir of life."

Although Wilson never experienced combat, he returned home shell-shocked, and matters were not helped when the world's respect disappeared once he took off his uniform. Lois's friend helped Wilson land a job on Wall Street, but though lucrative, it was soul-sucking, and for solace, he began his ever-escalating inebriation. On the evening of Lois's second miscarriage, one that annihilated her dream of ever giving birth, Wilson arrived at the hospital falling-down drunk. Her hopes of adoption were also destroyed because of his chronic alcoholism.

With Wilson's depression over his job and Lois's misery over her infertility, they latched on to his get-rich-quick scheme. Lois believed in her husband; after all, Thomas Edison had been so impressed with the young man he had once offered him a position in his laboratory. Wilson's plan was to travel the country on a three-wheeled Harley-Davidson to conduct studies of successful companies. When the Wall Street executives approved his first analysis, he celebrated by leaving Lois on the side of a muddy country road with the motorcycle while he went to get hammered. So what would any self-respecting, college-educated daughter of an affluent doctor do: a) obtain a restraining order, b) get a Reno divorce, or c) run him over with the Harley? Lois stood by her man, believing unconditional love would lead to sobriety. With the failure of the far-fetched business venture, they returned to New York where she worked at Macy's. Nearly destitute, they moved back into Clinton Street. Desperate for drink, Wilson pilfered from his wife's purse, sold her family heirlooms, and panhandled. One rainy night after work, she stopped at Slavin's drugstore—which doubled as a bootleg establishment. Vulnerable, she almost succumbed to the owner's sexual advances. Filled with self-loathing and despair, that night she was awakened by the sound of a lamp crashing and her husband futilely attempting to stand. Infuriated, she pounded on his chest while screaming, "You don't even have the decency to die!"

After seventeen torturous years of marriage, on Kenny Rogers's "train bound for nowhere," Wilson had his lightning-bolt moment in a hospital. Aware he had reached rock bottom, he "turned over his life to a Higher Power." Five sober months later, he went to Akron, Ohio, on a business trip. When it fell through, he was lured by the siren song of bottles emanating from the Mayflower Hotel's bar. Fighting an overpowering urge, he underwent his epiphany: only a drunk can help another drunk. He connected with an alcoholic Akron physician, Dr. Bob Smith, and the two men not only saved one another—they launched Alcoholics Anonymous. The Clinton Street house that Lois had once envisioned filled with children instead became a haven for the local Bowery drunks where she fed the desperate men and Bill initiated meetings: "My name is Bill W. and I'm an alcoholic."

Ironically, just as Wilson found his life's calling, Lois began to flounder emotionally. Her mission had always been to save her husband, a pattern that had begun when she rescued his sail-entangled body in Emerald Lake. She felt resentful he was always involved in AA and that his fellow alcoholics had done for him what she had failed to accomplish. A turning point came when resentment boiled over and she threw her shoe at him with all her might. This led to her own epiphany: the families and friends of alcoholics were as sick as their loved ones. She

realized that for every man sitting in her smoke-filled house—nicotine substituting for booze—there was a woman waiting outside in a car for him. She invited these desperate by association in, and Al-Anon was born, which provided therapy for the families and loved ones of AA members, based on the Alcoholics Anonymous Twelve Steps Program.

The Wilsons were fueled with their respective fellowships until their momentum came to a grinding halt in 1939 when the bank foreclosed on the Clinton Street property. Thus began a two-year homeless odyssey, living as guests in borrowed rooms. Their nomadic existence, which entailed fifty-one moves, ended with the publication of *Alcoholics Anonymous*, also known as the Big Book, which explained in twelve steps how to free oneself from the purgatory of addiction. It became one of the best-selling books of all time—President Richard Nixon was presented with its millionth copy. A permanent address came when a fan of AA offered her sprawling home in Bedford Hills to the founders at far below the market price. It had taken twenty-three years, but Lois finally had a home of her own. Perched on a hill, the property could only be accessed from the driveway by a series of rugged stone steps, which led to its double entendre name: Stepping Stones. Lois hoped to spend her remaining years there developing her long-latent interior designer skills but instead became consumed in running Al-Anon as Lois W.

During the first half of their marriage, the couple had been known to their circle as the drunk and his wife; however, in the second half, they were hailed as "the royal couple of recovery." At the initial international convention of Al-Anon in Montreal, an audience of 45,000 gave the diminutive Lois a standing ovation. Eventually the world came to recognize Bill Wilson for the great man Lois always knew he was, and he was offered an honorary

degree from Yale University that he turned down, as he did *Life* magazine's offer to place him on its cover. When he refused, they suggested he just appear with his back turned, but he again declined in order to maintain the power of anonymity so crucial to his organization's ideals and success. Aldous Huxley pronounced Wilson "the greatest social architect of our time," and he was in the top twenty of *Time* magazine's one hundred heroes and icons of the twentieth century. Because of Lois's refusal to walk away from her husband, though he had taken her on endless tours of Dante's circles of hell, she too should have been listed as one of its she-roes.

The one thing Wilson did not become was a megalomaniac; whenever his head swelled, Lois would tease, "Sweetheart, your halo's on crooked." In tribute, on their 1954 wedding anniversary, he wrote on a card, "Come any peril, we know that we are safe in each other's arms because we are in God's." The Tiffany engagement ring could serve as a metaphor for the Wilson marriage—it had survived the flames and emerged intact.

Despite their newfound wealth, lovely home, and societal accolades, it was never easy to navigate the terrain as Mrs. Bill W. As it transpired, Wilson was a serial adulterer; at AA meetings, after he had finished delivering his Twelve Steps, he embarked on an unofficial thirteenth: hitting on recovering young women. These affairs stayed in the realm of physical adultery until he fell in love with Helen Wynn, a former actress with whom he had a fifteen-year relationship. It finally ended when he decided not to dissolve his marriage to his long-suffering wife. In addition to slipping under nonmarital bedsheets, Lois had to put up with his other pastimes, namely experimentation with LSD and the occult. Despite everything, Lois took the advice of the gambler: she knew what she wanted to keep and what she wanted to throw away. She remained committed to Wilson.

After retirement, he told his foundation, "Let go and let God," and retreated to his hilltop home. There his chronically addictive personality began its final addiction, this time to nicotine. He became a chain-smoker, and as he had once done with his bottles, he squirreled away cigarettes from his wife's eagle eyes. He developed emphysema but, undeterred, alternated inhaling from his oxygen tank and his cigarettes. When he died, he was interred in Vermont where he was joined by Lois, who passed away at age ninety-seven. Her *Los Angeles Times* obituary stated she "left no immediate survivors." In a sense, however, through Al-Anon, she had left thousands.

Today, the Big Book, *Alcoholics Anonymous*, is the "newest Testament" for millions of recovering alcoholics and their families. It was penned by Bill W., but it could not have been written without Lois, his ever-supportive stepping stone.

<><><><><><><>

CHAPTER EIGHT

LIFE'S LEADING LADY

Mrs. Alfred Hitchcock

Alfred Hitchcock's place in the pantheon of great film directors rests on a secure niche of psychological thrillers, thanks to classics like *Psycho* (or *Psyyyy-cow*, as he pronounced it) that led generations to shudder when showering at a motel. He is one of only two movie directors whose faces are as familiar as some of the actors who starred in his films (the other is fellow working-class Londoner Charlie Chaplin). Hitchcock's renowned silhouette in his movies depicts his enormous girth, but lost in his towering shadow was his partner, Alma Reville.

The woman destined to succeed in the male-dominated early movie industry (though in a largely unrecognized role) began life in the city of Robin Hood fame, Nottingham, on August 14, 1899. Her father worked in the costume department of the United Kingdom's largest motion picture studio, Twickenham, where she obtained a position as a rewind girl when she left school at age sixteen. Ever enterprising, she was promoted to cutter, where she would splice and glue together pieces of film. She also worked as a script girl, which gave her exposure to the embryonic movie industry, a niche few women of the time were granted access. When the studio closed, she was hired by an American company, Famous Players-Lasky, at its Islington location.

It was in this studio Alma met Hitchcock, who had just been hired to write title cards for the silent pictures. Their first encounter was not promising. Alma later recalled how he strolled across the set with a deadpan expression before disappearing, without a glance in her direction. For the next two years, he never met her eyes or exchanged a word. He later attributed his aloofness to shyness, the fact she was higher on the studio hierarchy, a repressive Catholic upbringing, and his belief she was a "trifle snooty."

The silence was broken when the branch closed and Alma was once more unemployed. In 1923 she received a phone call from Hitchcock, requesting her presence at a meeting; he had been made assistant director on the film *Woman to Woman* and was in need of an editor. The interview was cut short when Alma, as fiery as her red hair, rejected the proposed salary. After she left the room, the portly Hitchcock raced down the corridor and made a better offer. The two entered into a business partnership and eventually began dating, a relationship born of commonalities: Alma had been born on the same day, a few hours after Hitchcock, and both were monomaniacal about all things having to do with movies. At age twenty-seven, Alma was the first woman, other than his beloved mother, with whom Hitchcock let down his guard. Their relationship, however, was chaste. He made the admission he was still ignorant of "the mechanics of sex" and confessed that during this time, he "never so much as touched her little finger."

The couple worked together at Gainsborough studio where Hitchcock was beginning to garner a reputation as a virtuoso behind the camera. Some believed Alma could have become one as well, but she shrugged off any such suggestion with a reference to her 4'11" frame, saying, "I'm too small. I could never project the image of authority a director has to project." Nevertheless, her skills did not go unnoticed. In 1925, the *Picturegoer* ran a piece: "Alma in Wonderland: An interesting article, proving that a woman's place is not always at home." And though Hitch (as Alma called him) was the consummate narcissist—he made a cameo appearance in every film—he acknowledged how much he depended on her opinion. This was revealed in the Anglo-German production of *The Pleasure Garden* in which Alma served as assistant. In an interview with François Truffaut, Hitchcock described the chaos of working on a low-budget production and how he depended on Alma to find extra money and listen to his litany of woes. One of these troubles was he did not want to tell his Hollywood star that it was his first movie as director and money was in short supply. He told Truffaut, "I did a really mean thing. I managed to twist the facts and put the whole blame on my fiancée...I always make my fiancée do all the dirty work."

On Christmas Eve, on the return trip to England, Hitchcock asked for Alma's hand on a storm-tossed ferry. She was seasick when he produced the engagement ring, and in a decidedly unromantic proposal, he ventured, "I thought I'd catch you when you were too weak to say no." She weakly nodded assent before she resumed retching. In order to please Hitchcock, Alma relinquished her Protestant faith and they exchanged vows on December 2, 1926, in the Church of the Oratory in Knightsbridge. This was followed by a honeymoon in St. Moritz, Switzerland, where they vacationed at the Palace Hotel, which became their favorite destination.

Two years later, the event that Hitchcock always referred to as his "finest production" arrived—the birth of their only child, Patricia Alma. He was absent during the delivery, explaining he could not bear the suspense. The family stayed at their London flat during the week and on weekends in their idyllic country retreat, Shamley Cottage. Patricia recalled home was a happy place where her father would contentedly puff cigars while she and her mother attended to their menagerie of pony, Arabian stallion, and a number of dogs. Although Hitchcock's fame placed him on the A-list, he was happiest in his ancient cottage. He was never known for his bubbly people skills. To Pat's dismay, no other sibling arrived. This was because though Alma and Alfred were soul mates, sexual chemistry soon migrated from their domestic nest. In fact, unlike other macho directors, Hitchcock implied he suffered from chronic impotence and described himself as celibate.

Life changed dramatically in 1939 when the siren call of Hollywood summoned England's greatest director to Tinseltown. The Hitchcocks purchased a home on the fifteenth fairway of the Bel Air golf course that they filled with masterpieces by Rodin, Klee, and Utrillo. Alfred's string of successes allowed Alma to live a lifestyle she could never have imagined when a cutter at Twickenham Studios. Although living in America, they remained Brits at heart, and had the *The Times* and British food flown in weekly. Food was very important to the couple, and Alma, as accomplished in the kitchen as she was in the screening room, produced culinary masterpieces. Hitchcock even analogized his approach to moviemaking with dessert, saying, "Some films are slices of life; mine are slices of cake." Every Thursday they dined at their favorite restaurant, Chasen's, where they would order steak for their adored dogs salivating in the chauffeur-driven limousine. Waiters would routinely overhear Alma urging her portly husband to forgo the second pudding. In a reverse Jack-Sprat-and-his-wife fashion, Hitchcock grew in girth over the years while Alma remained slight. On their evenings out, Hitchcock would greet fans with his trademark "good e-ve-ning"; an obsessive creature of habit, he was never without dark suit and skinny tie. (His contemporary JFK dressed in a similar fashion, but the vibe was different.) Film and food remained the twin passions in the Hitchcock marriage, and Alfred was known to quip that he and his wife had only had sex once, when they conceived Patricia.

The director of psychological thrillers was the master manipulator of the macabre, and his apogee was *Psycho*, based on Wisconsin
body-snatcher Ed Gein. Paramount got cold feet over the project,
feeling moviegoers would not appreciate a picture involving voyeur-
ism, a mother who was the victim of taxidermy, and a cross-dressing
leading man. However, the Hitchcocks were committed and bank-
rolled its $800,000 budget. Although *Psycho* is forever intertwined
with its director, Alma left an indelible fingerprint. It was she who
suggested the heroine be killed off half an hour into the film (contrary to Hollywood convention) and who recommended Anthony
Perkins (with his rumored secret homosexual life) for the role of
Norman (a name whose final letter *n* could never be supplanted by
the letter *l*; thankfully "normal" was not an adjective to represent the
consummate mamma's boy).

Janet Leigh was cast as the doomed Marion Crane; her blond
beauty was in keeping with other Hitchcock starlets, such as Grace
Kelly, Ingrid Bergman, and Kim Novak. In a nod to Freud's eternal question Hitchcock opined, "I never understood what women
wanted. I only knew it wasn't me."

Alma also left her mark on the climactic
moments of the film. Alfred was adamant
that the shower scene have no accompanying music; his wife convinced him otherwise. The decision proved prescient as the
background score of the shrieking violins is
enshrined as one of the greatest scenes in
film. And though the Bates were effective at
eliminating guests, it was Alma who cinemati-
cally finished off Janet Leigh. She was the only one
who noticed the actress swallowed after lying dead on the bathroom
floor and brought attention to the oversight. Indeed, it was Alma's

MADAME WANTS ME HOME.

MR. HITCHCOCK

unsung role that led critic Charles Champlin to write, "The Hitchcock touch has four hands, and two of them are Alma's." In the studio, everyone deferred to the director, who only deferred to his spouse. If she phoned, no matter how busy, he would state, "Madam wants me at home," and would leave.

To outsiders looking in, Alma appeared to have a storied life: wife of the director acclaimed on both sides of the Atlantic, a daughter who had bypassed teenage angst, and a multimillion-dollar fortune. However, rumors circulated that Hitchcock was a Peeping Tom and his actresses his Lady Godivas. While Alma fondly called Hitchcock by the first syllable of his surname, his reluctant blonds often referred to him by its second. The grapevine warned that the Hitchcock casting couch entailed bench-pressing a 300-pound director as they fended off his advances. The greatest detractor was Tippi Hedren, whom Alma herself had recruited after discovering her in a soft-drink commercial. The star claimed she was the recipient of the flesh-and-blood *Psycho* who became her obsessive stalker. She appealed to Alma for help, saying, "It would take just one word from you to stop this." Alma merely walked away. She was the wife who knew too much. Hitchcock was simply adhering to Norman Bates' words: "We all go a little crazy at times." Unlike with his earlier directorial troubles, with his sexual peccadilloes he could not manage to twist the facts and put the whole blame on his wife.

Retaliation was swift and sadistic for Tippi's unwelcome protests. In *The Birds*' climatic scene, Tippi was engulfed by authentic crows rather than the plastic variety. Post spurning, she became a persona non grata and Hitchcock henceforth only referred to her as "the girl." Perhaps the truth about the adored director's allegedly deplorable actions would have come to light if in the Truffaut interview he had talked blonds rather than shop.

Miss Reville became Alma in wonderland once more when Queen Elizabeth knighted her husband, making her Lady Hitchcock. A further tribute was when Hitchcock was honored with the American Film Institute's Lifetime Achievement Award and, aged and infirm, he gave his speech from his seat, with his wife of fifty-four years by his side. "I beg permission to mention by name only four people who have given me the most affection, appreciation, encouragement, and constant collaboration. First of the four is a film editor. The second is a scriptwriter. The third is the mother of my daughter, Pat, and the fourth is as fine a cook as has ever performed miracles in a domestic kitchen. And their names are Alma Reville." Regardless of what went on in the secret recesses of Hitchcock's heart, Alma was his life's leading lady.

FILM EDITOR   MOTHER   SCRIPTWRITER   COOK

CHAPTER NINE

I DIDN'T FORGET YOU

Mrs. Simon Wiesenthal

I
f the voices submerged in the shadows of the Holocaust could speak, they would whisper of when the line separating man from beasts blurred in the atrocities the Nazis committed. Yet despite the horrors, a love story blossomed. Simon Wiesenthal and a woman from his town shared lives that rivaled the harrowing twists of a Stephen King plot.

The stranger-than-fiction story of Cyla Müller (a distant relative of Sigmund Freud) began in 1908 in the *shtetl* of Buczacz, Galicia, located in the Austro-Hungarian Empire. The town's Jews were known as *Luftmenschen*—people who live on air—because their economic prospects were so dire. Growing up in a loving family, little did Cyla know that Galicia would vanish when it became a chess game played by two of history's most heinous dictators. Buczacz was also a hazardous place for Jews because of the Cossacks who slaked their thirst for bloodletting through pogroms.

At fifteen, Cyla was studying at the gymnasium when she first met Simon Wiesenthal and fell in love. Alison Leslie Gold recounted in *Fiet's Vase and Other Stories of Survival,* "Everyone who knew them at seventeen had no doubt that the tall, dark Simon Wiesenthal and small, fair Cyla Müller—so obviously besotted with each other—would one day marry." The young couple was distraught when Wiesenthal's widowed mother remarried and planned to relocate to Dolina, close to the Carpathian Mountains. He succeeded in his plea to remain in Buczacz and boarded with the Müllers. Although Wiesenthal was serious and studious, Cyla awakened his light side, and he entertained her with funny stories, communicated in their amalgam of Polish-Yiddish. He sketched her in pencil, capturing the image of a fair-haired girl, her face a study in melancholy. Her somber mood was the result of her brother's immigration to Palestine and her fear she would never see him again.

A four-year separation came when Wiesenthal left to pursue a degree in architecture at the Technical University in Czechoslovakia. He promised upon his return as *Herr Ingenieur* he would build a fine house where they would raise children. Cyla suggested they start their marriage in Palestine to be near her brother and escape the hovering anti-Semitism. Wiesenthal declined as he would not leave his mother, especially after the accidental death of his brother Hillel. When he had attained his degree, he and Cyla wed at a rabbi's house on September 9, 1936, and moved to Lwów, Poland.

The Wiesenthals were earmarked for an unremarkable middle-class life when world events deemed otherwise. Within a few years, the Soviet Union overran Poland and instituted the "Red Purge" of the Jewish bourgeois. Wiesenthal saved himself and Cyla from deportation to Siberia by bribing a Russian commissar. Then the Nazis absorbed Poland into the Third Reich and rounded up the Jews. Wiesenthal watched as soldiers, swigging liquor, shot half the prisoners in his group. His life was spared when the church bells pealed and the Nazis retreated for evening mass. In the liquidation of the ghetto, Cyla's mother was shot by a Ukrainian policeman and Wiesenthal's mother was executed at Belzec. Wiesenthal and Cyla were deported to a labor camp where they were forced to work in a nearby railway repair shop. She was ordered to polish brass; Wiesenthal was compelled to paint over the hammer and sickles emblazoned on the railroad cars with swastikas.

Fearful of transportation to the new SS concentration camps, Wiesenthal cast about for a means of saving his wife. He struck up a bargain with the Polish Underground, Armia Krajowa (AK); he agreed to furnish maps the partisans needed for sabotage in return for forged documents showing Cyla was Aryan. In this fashion, the Jewish Cyla Wiesenthal became the Christian Irena Kowalska. On a wintery night, a member of the AK smuggled her out of the camp to Warsaw, where she was provided shelter by an architect in exchange for serving as a nanny. To those who questioned, she explained she was the wife of a Polish officer, prisoner of war of the Russians. Her blond hair and gray-blue eyes, coupled with fluency in Polish, lent truth to the lie.

By June 1943, conditions deteriorated in Warsaw as the Gestapo subjected nonpermanent residents of the city to arbitrary arrests. Desperate to elude capture and to see Wiesenthal, Cyla took a train to Lwów, where she hid for two days and nights in the ladies' toilet stall of the train station. One evening, Wiesenthal was called to the camp fence and discovered Cyla on the other side. The Polish Underground helped once more, and they arranged passage for her to a small apartment at 5 Topiel Street in Warsaw, where she was given a bed in a kitchen, which she shared with rabbits.

Wiesenthal, desiring death on his own terms, slashed his wrists. The Nazi in command saved him with the words, "A Jew should never die when he wishes. Only when we wish." Cyla was contacted by a member of the Underground who mistakenly informed her Simon had perished. Shortly afterward, she was deported, as a Pole rather than a Jew, to forced labor in a munitions plant in the Ruhr. Had she been identified as a Jew, she would have been sent to a death camp. In 1945, Wiesenthal, who had been deported to the notorious Mauthausen concentration camp in Austria, encountered an inmate from 7 Topiel Street who informed him no one had survived the street's destruction during the Warsaw Ghetto Uprising. Not wanting Wiesenthal to harbor fool's hope, he explained, "There is no hope. Topiel Street is one big mass grave." Later Wiesenthal recalled, "That night I went to sleep a widower."

The British liberated Cyla on April 11, 1945, and she returned to Poland; a few weeks later, the Americans liberated Wiesenthal and he traveled to Austria. As soon as he had regained his health, his six foot frame under a hundred pounds, he wrote to the Red Cross in Geneva to inquire about his wife and was informed she was deceased. In a nod to fate, he was perusing the lists of survivors when he saw the name Dr. Biener, who had attended school with Wiesenthal and Cyla, was living in Kraków. He wrote the physician a letter, requesting he search for Cyla's remains in the rubble of Topiel Street so he could arrange a proper burial. In the meantime, Cyla was also in Kraków and bumped into an acquaintance from Buczacz who told her Dr. Biener was also living there, in an apartment a few streets away. The physician had just received Wiesenthal's letter when his doorbell rang. When he saw Cyla on the other side, he gasped, "But you're dead!"

When Wiesenthal learned Cyla was alive, he desired nothing more than to be Orpheus and deliver his Eurydice from the

Underworld. And he knew that, unlike the mythological musician, neither he (nor Cyla) would look back. Too ill to travel, he enlisted Felix Weissberg to escort his resurrected spouse. However, just before crossing from the American to the Russian zone, Weissberg, fearing interrogation by the Soviets, destroyed Cyla's papers. When he arrived in Kraków, he could not inform Cyla of what had transpired as he had inadvertently shredded her address as well. Through a whim of serendipity, a few days later, Cyla saw a note posted on a Jewish Committee's bulletin board: "Would Cyla Wiesenthal please get in touch with Felix Weissberg who will take her to her husband in Austria." Desirous of escaping the Communists before the Iron Curtain descended, three women answered the ad, all claiming to be Mrs. Wiesenthal. Felix had no idea which one was telling the truth. After obtaining forged papers on the black market, aware he was not Solomon, he randomly chose one of the three Mrs. Wiesenthals. It turned out to be the real one, and Simon and Cyla christened their reunion a miracle. Nine months later, the product of that miracle was the birth of their only child, Paulinka.

Cyla wanted to put the terrible past behind and resume the life they would have led if a world war had not interfered: Wiesenthal would work as an architect and build a home where they could find the peace in the second part of their lives that had been denied them in the first. However, Wiesenthal said the old way was over—his life's task now was to be a Nazi nemesis and bring the butchers to justice. Refusing to immigrate to America, he moved his family into a cramped three-bedroom apartment on Salztorgasse No. 6 in Vienna. Cyla acquiesced, perhaps feeling, as Ilsa did in *Casablanca*, the cause of righteousness was more important than personal happiness. Or perhaps after losing her husband once, she was not willing to do so again. However, her one unshakable caveat was he was never to speak of the unspeakable. If she did, like Lot's wife, she would turn to a pillar of salt. Her husband, on the other hand, was mired in his yesteryear and felt it his duty to be a deputy for the dead for his six million "clients," as he called those who perished in the Holocaust. Wiesenthal said of his wife's request, "I have never discussed with her what goes on in the office. But it was tough to carry this load on your own especially in the early days." Cyla felt she was not just married to a man, but to "thousands or maybe millions of dead."

Despite their different ways of coping with the past, their marriage lasted for sixty-seven years, even in the light of postwar horror. Wiesenthal was the constant target of death threats, their home was bombed, Paulinka was threatened, and the Viennese postal service maintained a bulletproof room in which to examine his packages. Despite all his vicissitudes, what remained was his love for Cyla, his dignity, and his sense of humor. The latter was displayed when he was accused by a detractor of dining on Nazis for breakfast, lunch, and dinner. Wiesenthal retorted, "You are mistaken. I don't eat pork."

Despite Cyla's opposition to Wiesenthal's self-imposed quest to be an avenging archangel, she was proud of his singular accomplishments: creating the eponymous Los Angeles Museum of Tolerance; the uncovering of Karl Silberbauer, who had arrested Anne Frank, which eventually led to her death; the capture of Adolf Eichmann, main architect of genocide; receiving the Presidential Medal of Freedom; and film portrayals of him by Ben Kingsley and Sir Lawrence Olivier. Sadly, Cyla did not experience being Lady Wiesenthal when Simon was conferred with a knighthood by Queen Elizabeth II in 2004. She had already passed away at age ninety-five. She was interred in Herzliya Cemetery, Israel, where her daughter lives with her three children. Upon Cyla's death, Wiesenthal retired, stating his job was done.

Wiesenthal once described attending a Sabbath service with a fellow survivor who had become a wealthy jeweler. The man inquired why Wiesenthal had not resumed architecture, which would have made him rich. The self-appointed justice seeker responded, "When we come to the other world and meet the millions of Jews who died in the camps and they ask us, 'What have you done?' there will be many answers. You will say, 'I became a jeweler.' Another will say, 'I smuggled coffee and American cigarettes.' Another will say, 'I built houses.' But I will say, 'I didn't forget you.'" The same words he had said to Cyla on their long-ago rendezvous from the dead.

CHAPTER TEN

THE WHITE HORSE GIRL AND THE BLUE WIND BOY

Mrs. Frank Lloyd Wright

Frank Lloyd Wright, the world's most famous architect, observed, "Less is more." When it came to romance, however, his maxim was "more is more." Unfortunately, he was never able to achieve in his relationships the transcendent beauty of his buildings—until Wright finally met, well, Mrs. Wright.

Olgivanna Ivanovna Lazovich had about as interesting a life as someone who began a religion or rode at the head of an invading army. She was born in Montenegro in 1897, the youngest of nine. Her mother, Militza, had served as a general in Serbian battles and postwar thought nothing of throwing rocks through irritating neighbors' windows. This animosity extended to maternal skills and left her brood devoid of nurture.

When Olgivanna was eighteen, she moved to Moscow, where she met architect Vlademar Hinzenberg, ten years her senior. Although she did not love him, she adored his mother, and when the older woman begged her on her deathbed to marry her son, Olgivanna agreed. The ceremony took place on January 31, 1917; the bride cried throughout—and not tears of joy. The year coincided with the onset of the Russian Revolution and the birth of daughter Svetlana. In the tumult of the uprising, life became a treadmill of torture, and Olgivanna was reduced to trading her diamond earrings in order to obtain milk for her baby.

Olgivanna's life took another drastic turn in 1919 when she

went to see a visiting Armenian-born mystic, Georgi Ivanovich Gurdjieff. The charismatic guru claimed his eyes could not only penetrate a man's psyche but bring a woman to orgasm from across a room. The general consensus: he was mad. Olgivanna was smitten. She became an ardent follower and learned his sacred dances, which the master claimed were the path to enlightenment. When the Bolsheviks tightened their grip, Gurdjieff fled to Paris where he founded the Institute for the Harmonious Development of Man. Olgivanna and her daughter joined him while Vlademar immigrated to the United States. Gurdjieff, who advocated voluntary suffering, required she relinquish her daughter, and five-year-old Svetlana was sent to America with Olgivanna's brother Vlado. One of Olgivanna's main patients at the Institute was New Zealand writer Katherine Mansfield who had come in a last-ditch effort to cure her tuberculosis. Despite the healing powers of Gurdjieff, Mansfield passed away. (Another famous writer who fell under the Muscovite's spell was British P. L. Travers, author of Mary Poppins. In her unending quest for spiritual fulfillment she saw him as a visionary mystic leader; to others, he was an oversexed con man who had fathered seven children with seven different disciples. Travers became so besotted with her pot-bellied guru that she urged her adopted son to call him "father.")

In 1924, Gurdjieff decreed Olgivanna should journey to Chicago to preach the Institute's philosophy; although she was devastated to leave her master, she was eager to be reunited with Svetlana. Mother and daughter moved in with Vlademar, and though he wanted to resume their marriage, the romantic feelings were once again one-sided.

On November 30, Olgivanna entered the Eighth Street Theater just as the great Russian ballerina Thamar Karsavina began her performance. For the first celebrity architect, Frank Lloyd Wright,

who had the seat beside the exotic woman, her
arrival upstaged the ballerina. The two non-
conformists succumbed to the clichéd love
at first sight. Olgivanna spoke of their connection as "two powerful magnets being drawn
together." Wright later recalled, "This strange chance meeting, was
it poetry? I was a hungry man." Considering Wright's history, it
was surprising he was still hungry. His first wife Kitty had married
Wright when she was seventeen and had raised their six children.
He transitioned from home-builder to home-wrecker when he fell
for neighbor Mamah Cheney, whose husband had commissioned
the architect to design a residence. The couple fled to Frank's native
Wisconsin where he built Taliesin (from the Welsh "shining brow")
as refuge from the public glare. On its tranquil site overlooking a
river, tragedy triumphed over scandal. While Wright was out of town,
Mamah and her two children (whom she had custody of one month
a year) were at lunch when a worker from Barbados, Julian Carleton,
set the building on fire. Murder followed arson when he took an ax
to Mamah, her children, and three workers. The indefatigable Wright
rebuilt Taliesin, determined "to wipe the scar from the hill."

In the wake of the massacre and lurid headlines, Frank received
a letter from Maude "Miriam" Noel, who offered surprisingly welcome condolences rather than condemnation. They began a relationship after she addressed another missive, "Lord of My Waking
Dreams." She turned out to be psychologically imbalanced, a condition exacerbated by a raging morphine addiction, which led to their
separation. Despite his rather rocky romantic résumé, Wright was
still willing to take another chance on love. Like many other great
men, he too needed a woman at the center of his life, to feed his
ego, to be his sexual and loving partner, and to serve as intellectual
sounding board.

Despite Olgivanna's magnet metaphor and Wright's hunger, there were two viable spouses—Vlademar and Miriam. However, the couple always followed the dictates of their hearts rather than societal mores, and Olgivanna was soon ensconced in Taliesin—purportedly as the housekeeper. Her domestic role was immediately suspect as she arrived in a chauffeur-driven car; this claim did not hold up to further scrutiny when she became pregnant. The fifty-eight-year-old architect was devoted to the twenty-six-year-old exotic dancer, and the feeling was reciprocal. Olgivanna had transferred her passion from Gurdjieff and the Institute to Wright and Taliesin. One evening, Wright read to her from a book by his friend Carl Sandburg. It related how two lovers disappeared, leaving behind only a brief note: *We have started to go where the white horses come from and where the blue winds begin. Keep a corner in your hearts for us while we are gone. The White Horse Girl, the Blue Wind Boy.*

Despite the romantic lullaby, the cradle soon dropped, pushed by the wife scorned: Miriam Noel. She was infuriated when Wright asked for a divorce so he could marry his Montenegrin dancer. Her first rather unoriginal tactic (though circumstantial as the real culprit may have been faulty electrical wiring) was to burn down the rebuilt Taliesin, à la Carleton. She then contacted the Bureau of Investigation to deport Olgivanna for violating immigration law. That didn't work either. With thirst for vengeance still unquenched, when Olgivanna gave birth to second daughter Iovanna, Miriam—perhaps fueled by morphine—barged into the hospital room demanding to see her husband's baby. The new parents fled, dodging the flurry of reporters in a maneuver worthy of

Wright's Wisconsin contemporary, Harry Houdini. They holed up in Minnetonka, Minneapolis, under an alias, hiding from arrest for violating the Mann Act (a law enacted to prosecute men who took women across state lines for sexual purposes) and a lawsuit from Noel for alienation of affection. It did not take long for them to be discovered, what with Wright's trademark beret, cape, and cane floating about town with an exotic partner with a thick accent. When a man overheard the couple call a child Svetlana, he contacted the police for the $500 reward and the fugitives were arrested. They were held in different cells with Olgivanna staying with baby Iovanna while the eight-year-old sobbing Svetlana was in the adjoining cell (to keep her isolated from the criminal element). Throughout the night, her mother kept up a constant cry of "Svet, Svet, it's all right."

Eventually Miriam, the douser of Wright's flame, disappeared and Wright and Olgivanna were free to carry on their unconventional lives. They married on August 25, 1928, in Rancho Santa Fe, a wealthy enclave of San Diego. At age sixty-one, the great man had finally obtained the great love of his life. He expressed his appreciation in his memoir: "Understanding and ready for any sacrifice... came Olgivanna. A woman is, for man, the best of true friends, if man will let her be one." In his seventh decade, it appears Wright's emotional IQ had finally caught up to his intellectual counterpart.

In 1932, the couple hit upon the grand notion to found the Taliesin Fellowship in Arizona, a school for architects. The game plan was that while the students would reap from the reservoir of Frank's genius, the Wrights would sow their own rewards. They set it up as a "commune" and charged their protégées a sum that exceeded tuition at Yale and Harvard—despite delivering nothing close to a legitimate diploma upon completion. To whet the appetite of the aspiring acolytes, the school came with a brochure, an inspired advertisement for Wright, with an impressive list of Friends of the Fellowship on the back: Albert Einstein, Dorothy Parker, and Carl Sandburg to name a few. For the ensuing three decades, Taliesin became a place where the Wrights received free labor in exchange for the students benefiting from their exposure to the renowned architect. In addition, Olgivanna had complete control over the young men who fell under her jurisdiction. Wright thereby gave his wife the ultimate gift—her own live-action dollhouse, to manipulate her charges who had to attend to her every whim. Brendan Gill, in his biography of Wright, stated that in the Fellowship, Wright became something of a deity. Indeed, according to Gill, "Wright was obliged to share Christmas and Easter with his Christian predecessor…Jesus Christ."

The Wrights' marriage lasted thirty-one years until Frank's death at ninety-one, during which period, with the inspiration of his beloved Olgivanna, his work reached its zenith: Fallingwater and one of America's crown jewels of architecture, the Guggenheim. In his autobiography, Wright praised his spouse, saying, "Just to be with her uplifts my heart and strengthens my spirits when the going gets hard or when the going is good."

Taliesin's penchant for the unusual continued past its founder's death. Svetlana and her infant son were killed in a car crash. At the time of her death, she had been married to William Peters, Wright's heir apparent. When Josef Stalin's daughter, Svetlana Stalin, immigrated to the United States, Olgivanna felt her arrival and her name held a mystic connection, and she arranged a meeting between her son-in-law and the dictator's daughter. They married a few weeks later and Svetlana, in a bid to divorce her past, became Lana Peters. Alas, the birth of their baby did not save their marriage, which foundered due to Olgivanna's constant meddling.

When Olgivanna passed away at age eighty-five in 1985, she exerted her final act of manipulation. Her will directed that her husband was to be exhumed from Taliesin East in Wisconsin and be reinterred in Taliesin West in Arizona. It further stipulated his body, along with hers and that of Svetlana (her biological daughter, that is), be cremated and that the ashes be mixed together in the walls of their home's memorial garden. The Wisconsin legislature and Wright's six children with Kitty prohibited the act that they said would amount to desecration. However, what Olgivanna wanted, Olgivanna still got—even in death.

Frank Lloyd Wright was immortalized as Howard Roark in Ayn Rand's *The Fountainhead* and in the world's most iconic structures. But the soul of the man behind the myth can be found in a memorial garden in the Arizona desert, in the comingled remains of the White Horse Girl and the Blue Wind Boy.

CHAPTER ELEVEN

WHERE LIGHT AND SHADOW MEET

Mrs. Oskar Schindler

L ike most girls brought up on the tales of her countrymen, Wilhelm and Jacob Grimm, one farmer's daughter dreamed of happily ever after. Ironically, however, because of her prince, Oskar Schindler, she became the little girl in the fairy tale whose life led to a sinister horror in the woods.

Emilie Pelzl was born in 1907 in Alt Moletein, the Sudetenland, in the Austro-Hungarian Empire. An old Gypsy woman read her palm when she was a young girl: "I see your lifeline is long. You will meet a man who you will love above all, though you will not be happy at his side. There are other things, my child, I do not dare tell you." Her words frightened Emilie, who took solace in a first of May custom of planting a tree to ward off evil. Her early sense of righteousness became apparent when she defied her local pastor who instructed her to terminate friendship with Rita Reif because she was Jewish.

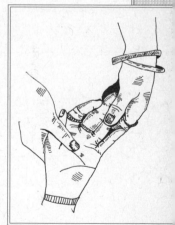

While the Grimm girls met their princes in poetic locales (a ball, a tower, a glass coffin), the twenty-year-old Emilie met her prince in a rather more prosaic place. On a Thursday afternoon, Emilie stepped out of her farmhouse and noticed two men; she took interest in the one who was slender with broad shoulders, blond hair, and deep blue eyes. While the older one tried to convince her to purchase a motor that would supply her home with electricity, another type of electricity passed between her and the young man. Soon Schindler was making frequent trips from Moravia to Alt Moletein, and Emilie surrendered her heart on a moonlit evening when he kissed her under a plum tree. Oskar Schindler was able to play on women as Antonio Stradivarius could on his violins.

After a courtship of six weeks, Emilie and Oskar were married on March 6, 1928, at an inn on the outskirts of Zwittau, Oskar's hometown. Herr Pelzl gave his daughter a sizable dowry of 100,000 Czech crowns and a warning: Schindler was a known heartbreaker. When she was dancing in her short, white wedding dress, her grandmother remarked she looked like Sleeping Beauty—one who was in for a rude awakening, as it transpired. On her wedding day, she discovered her husband's Achilles heel (a euphemism for another vulnerable part of his anatomy) was women when a vindictive former lover reported Schindler to the police on a trumped-up pretext and he was hauled in for questioning. It was not the most auspicious start to married life. Neither was his squandering of her dowry on frivolities such as outings and a luxury car.

While Emilie's life alternated between grief and happiness, the affairs of Europe were deteriorating with the rise of Hitler, who absorbed the Sudetenland into the Third Reich. Unemployed and with his get-rich schemes all resulting in failures, in 1938, Schindler joined the Nazi Party. After the invasion of Poland, he was sent to Kraków (situated thirty miles from Auschwitz) where he was in charge of an enamelware factory. He staffed it with hundreds of residents from the Jewish ghetto and workers/slaves from the nearby Plaszów concentration camp. If Emilie thought the move to Poland was to constitute a belated honeymoon, she was in for yet another rude awakening.

Oskar Schindler, who had spent his life looking for his niche, found it in Poland, the epicenter of genocide. Faced with unimaginable brutality, Schindler changed his agenda from enriching his coffers by exploiting the Jews to saving their lives. He spent his ill-gotten gains to bribe the SS to look away when he began to employ people too young, too old, and/or too ill to operate machines. Emilie, in memory of Rita who had been murdered in their hometown and as a devout Catholic, devoted her life to the same cause. She alternated between entertaining the local SS commandant Amon Göth to sumptuous dinners and feeding starving workers. This time, however, there was no tree she could plant to ward off such evil. One evening, Schindler confided in Emilie that Göth had decided to close the Plaszów Camp and send their workers to Auschwitz. Together they came up with a plan: to open a munitions factory in Brünnlitz, Czechoslovakia, and to draw up a list with the names of those they "needed." The lynchpin was acquiescence from the Brünnlitz mayor, which was highly unlikely as the local population was against having Jews in their midst. In addition, the nature of such a factory would make their town a target for Allied bombs.

Undeterred, Emilie went in the role of ambassador, and in a rare episode of serendipity in that horrible era, the mayor turned out to be Emilie's old swimming teacher from Alt Moletein. She left with priceless permit in hand. The fortunate people on the Schindlers' list, Oskar and Emilie, along with their beloved dogs Rex and Karin, relocated to the factory where life was a daily fight: against lice, typhus, and execution from the SS if their motives were discovered. In the evenings, Emilie had to switch roles and entertain the wives of SS officers.

On the day the armistice was signed, Schindler assembled his workers to listen to Winston Churchill announce the surrender of the Wehrmacht and to express his regret there was nothing more he could do. In gratitude for the list the German couple had created to save Jewish lives, the workers signed a document testifying to all the Schindlers had endured to ensure their survival. With the Soviet Army advancing, because of Schindler's membership in the Nazi Party, Oskar and Emilie were forced to flee as the document would not serve as a shield. Their lives now became a desperate struggle for survival. The Czech government had stripped the ethnic Germans of their citizenship, and after relocating penniless to Munich, Schindler could not find work. Moreover they were in constant danger from former Nazis who viewed the Schindlers as traitors of the Fatherland.

Salvation seemed to appear in 1949 when a Jewish organization provided them with two tickets to embark on the last ship transporting refugees to Buenos Aires. Emilie felt its name, "good air," was a propitious sign, and in South America they would find the happiness that had eluded them in Europe. They were accompanied by a dozen *Schindlerjuden* and Gisa, Oskar's mistress. Her husband had dropped this tidbit while they were packing; however, Emilie no longer had the energy for reproach. The couple settled on a farm in San Vincente, which reminded Emilie of her childhood home. She ran the farm on her own, raising hens while her husband raised hell in the capital, carousing and finding solace in the arms of Gisa.

After eight years, Schindler hit on another get-rich-quick scheme: to raise minks for their furs, which he joked was the origin of his wife's maiden name Pelzl. Emilie tried to dissuade him, arguing she knew nothing about raising them and knew the work would fall on her when he got bored. He assured her of its success by explaining all women loved furs; she bit her tongue from responding the only time she had ever seen one was on the shoulders of his lovers, a present from him. Of course, Emilie took over the responsibility of the minks while Schindler took to drink. In 1957, Germany passed a law offering restitution to victims who had suffered financial loss as a result of the war. They decided Schindler would return to the Fatherland to collect reparation for their confiscated Brünnlitz factory. With the money, they would try to recoup their losses from the mink business, which had drained the last of their resources.

Emilie had met Schindler on a Thursday, married him on a Thursday, and on a Thursday accompanied him to the airport. As they drove, there was silence in the car and Emilie wondered how it was possible that after sharing their lives for thirty years, they were at a loss for words. She was bewildered that after all their horror, the link between them had severed. As she watched her husband walk away, she realized he had become a stranger and at the same time, someone with whom she would be irrevocably tied. Schindler was never to see Emilie (or Gisa) again, a fact to which only he was privy at the time.

In Kraków, Emilie had been in an unfamiliar environment without knowledge of Polish and bereft of family, but she had youth and the man she loved. Now she was once again in a foreign country; however, this time she was approaching old age, financially destitute, and bereft of company other than her dogs, cats, chickens, and minks. One can easily envision Emilie looking upward with the words, "You know, *Gott*, there are other people." Of the hundred thousand marks of reparation money, Schindler sent her two hundred German marks along with a copy of *The Diary of Anne Frank*. The enclosed letter gave news of how he was putting on weight from his windfall as he was eating a lot of lobster and drinking a lot of good wine. She threw it in the fire and never opened another one from him, appalled she had wed the ultimate narcissist. Whenever asked about her absent husband, conflicting emotions of love and bitterness were revealed when she referred to him as a *Saufkopf*, "drunk," and *Weiberheld*, "womanizer," but then added, "If he'd stayed, I'd have looked after him."

Emilie Pelzl Schindler emerged from her Argentinean shadow in 1993 when she received a letter (one she did not burn) from Steven Spielberg inviting her to Jerusalem. The famed director wanted to shoot the final scene of *Schindler's List* in Israel and wanted to include her and the survivors in its closing scene. Although she felt his film should have been titled *The Schindlers' List*, and although she took exception to Oskar's portrayal as a flawed hero (she only saw him as flawed at that point), she agreed to go. She expressed her resentment when she stated, "The Jews he saved. Me he abandoned." But the reunion with her former workers whose lives she had saved was emotional, as was her visit to the cemetery where Schindler had been interred in 1974. In keeping with Jewish tradition, she placed a pebble on his grave, dismayed it was covered with sand rather than a cross. As she stood there, she said her farewell to the man who had been the architect of her singular destiny.

> *Well, Oskar, at last we meet again, but this is not the time for reproaches and complaints. It would not be fair to you or to me. Now you are in another world, in eternity, and I can no longer ask you all those questions to which in life you would have given evasive replies…and death is the best evasion of all. I have received no answers, my dear. I do not know why you abandoned me… But what not even your death or my old age can change is that we are still married. This is how we are before God. I have forgiven you everything, everything.*

The Hollywood epic had made her husband's name a part of Holocaust history and their list a valuable document. In 2013 one of the four existent copies was placed on eBay for three million dollars. Before she returned to Argentina, Emilie met with President Clinton and Pope John Paul II, who had spent his youth in Kraków, and became a heroine in her adopted homeland. She was affectionately dubbed Mutter Courage. In 1994, she was declared a Righteous Gentile by Yad Vashem in Jerusalem, and two carob trees were planted side by side alongside a plaque bearing the couple's names.

Emilie returned to Germany and settled into retirement in Bavaria where she passed away in 2001 at age ninety-three, fulfilling the last of the Gypsy's predictions. She never stopped wearing her wedding ring and said, "If I could choose again, I would pick Oskar." Her tombstone contains a large cross and a verse from the Talmud in German, "*Wer einen Menschen rettet, rettet die ganze Welt*" (Whoever saves a single life saves the world entire). In her bid for remembrance, she published her memoir, whose title was a metaphor for her tumultuous relationship with Oskar, *Where Light and Shadow Meet.*

CHAPTER TWELVE

◇◇◇◇◇◇◇◇◇

TRISTAN UND ISOLDE

Mrs. Salvador Dalí

The iconic image of the grand master of surrealism, Salvador Dalí, is as recognizable as his paintings: the manic staring eyes, the upturned waxed mustache, the outlandish clothes. However, what is relegated to the shadows is the woman who melted the heart of the man who melted the clocks.

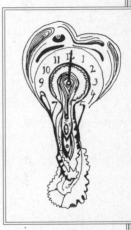

Elena Ivanovna Diakonova's childhood did not augur she was to become the lover of three brilliant men. She was born in Kazan, in the Russian Empire, in 1894. Her father, Ivan, disappeared or deserted the family while prospecting for gold in Siberia, which left wife Antonine and four children destitute. Either love or necessity led Antonine to cohabit with a Jewish lawyer, as the Russian Orthodox Church would not sanction their marriage. Elena, academically gifted, was barred from college because of her sex and enrolled in a finishing school in St. Petersburg. Her destiny as a teacher was derailed when she fell ill with consumption and her stepfather arranged a stay at a sanatorium in Switzerland.

In the tuberculosis ward, she met fellow patient, French poet Paul Éluard. They began an affair, fueled by poetry and Russian literature. Gala, as she called herself, was quick to appreciate his artistic talent—she had a built-in Geiger counter to discern genius in men before it became manifest to others. A year later, Gala returned home then made her solitary way across war-torn Europe to France to reunite with Éluard. In 1917, the two married and became parents of her only child, Cécile. Although Gala doted on her husband, she did not do likewise with her baby, viewing her as an accidental casualty of carnality. She considered children (and members of her own sex) boring. Paul prided himself on his sexual prowess but failed to satisfy Gala's gargantuan appetite, so she took husband-sanctioned lovers on the side. As Gala was endowed with striking Slavic looks, a lithe body, and unlimited libido, she had no difficulty finding them. One of these was the German Dadaist Max Ernst, who soon shared the marital bed in a ménage à trois that delighted Gala, who viewed it as exciting anatomical potential. Frau Ernst, mother of his son, did not share Gala's enthusiasm, and detested Gala, a feeling shared by the other Surrealists. Amused, she would smirk; angered, she became a Siberian tiger.

In 1929, the Éluards—along with René and Georgette Magritte—vacationed in Cadaqués, Spain, an interlude that altered their lives—and the history of art. It was in the picturesque fishing village Gala met Salvador Dalí, the embodiment of surrealism: shaving his armpits, painting himself blue, cutting up his shirt, smearing his body with goat dung. Most viewed him as a screwball; Gala viewed him as her soul mate. The connection was mutual, and Dalí, in a bid to impress the woman ten years his senior, stuck red geraniums over his ear. Gala's Parisian reputation had preceded her, and he saw in her the exciting embodiment of a demonic dominatrix; she saw in him the potential for another celebrity husband. Initially his family was relieved to see Dalí in the company of a woman; formerly he had kept company with famed homosexual poet Federico García Lorca.

However, as with all else, to know Gala was to hate her. Dalí's family soon voiced extreme displeasure that he was with an older married woman who had a child. They also believed there would be no taming of such a shrew. Dalí's father, who furnished his son with a lifetime of oedipal issues, gave him the ultimatum: the Russian adulteress or him. After he was disinherited, Dalí did what to him was the only logical thing: he shaved his head and buried his hair in the sands of Cadaqués.

As inexplicable as the images on a Dalí canvas was the artist's enigmatic sexuality, which may have been core to his erratic behavior. He denied consummation with Lorca, only because homosexual intercourse was too painful. On the other hand, he had a lifelong phobia about female genitalia and thus became, by his own admission, "one very fantastic voyeur." In Gala he discovered the perfect sexual cocktail: he achieved gratification by watching her perform with other men, including interludes with her husband Paul. Eventually Éluard was excised from his wife's life, a fact he accepted. The eleven-year-old Cécile later recounted, "After she met Dalí, she was not interested in me anymore. She was never warm, even before. She was very mysterious, very secretive. I never got to meet my Russian family."

Exiled from family, Dalí and Gala went to Paris where Dalí became the sun around which surrealism revolved. As his mistress, she also enjoyed celebrity status, and Elsa Schiaparelli and Coco Chanel vied to outfit her slim-hipped body. Gala, master opportunist, played the two designers off one another to get free designer clothes. Eventually, she became Mrs. Dalí in a civil ceremony in 1934, and his consummate Svengali—in

this case, his Sven-gala. She held the purse strings to his burgeoning financial empire and read to him as he created, often dictating what to paint (which several times included herself as the Madonna). In tribute to his manic muse, he signed his works *Gala-Salvador Dalí*. Although she did not contribute to the actual work, he explained, "It is mostly with Gala's blood that I paint my pictures."

The art historian Elliott King wrote, "There is a great mystery around her. She let Dalí be the showman—but she was the person behind the screen, making a lot of the decisions." In a lecture at the Sorbonne, he stated, "Without Gala, divine Dalí would be insane." (There is little doubt about how the students weighed in on this autobiographical tidbit.) When not in their studio, Dalí held court to fellow surrealists; Gala only made brief appearances, mainly occupied with two insatiable passions: men and shopping.

When World War II broke out, the couple sought refuge in the United States, which gave them the opportunity to schmooze with the beautiful people on both coasts: Alfred Hitchcock, Clark Gable, Walt Disney. As international celebrities, they were house-guests of the rich and famous. On one occasion, they stayed with Caresse Crosby (credited with inventing the modern brassiere) in her palatial Virginia estate, Hampton Manor, where Henry Miller and Anaïs Nin were also guests. The divine Dalí, as he referred to himself, was not so divine to Miller, and the New York writer fled the Spanish artist after a wild shouting match at dinner. Later Miller wrote on a book of Dalí illustrations, "S.D. is a prick of the first water." Caresse Crosby dropped the Dalís from A-list to Z-list.

Nevertheless, in New York City, the couple cultivated their own theater of the absurd in their suite at the St. Regis where their pet ocelot roamed the halls and entertained guests such as Andy Warhol. However, while Dalí gave endless interviews as he delighted in self-promotion, Gala kept to herself. She was never interviewed and when Warhol attempted to do so, she dropped his tape recorder in a vase of water. Among the roster of the illustrious the Dalís encountered was Sigmund Freud, whom Dalí met when he went to London to sketch the eighty-two-year-old psychoanalyst. Freud was the best candidate to put a psychological spin on the bizarre dream elements inherent in the artist's work. While sitting for his portrait, the doctor whispered to a bystander, "That boy looks like a fanatic." Dalí and Gala took it as a compliment.

In the late 1940s the couple returned to Spain, and Dalí made his home his canvas. Some of its highlights were the iconic Mae West sofa and a huge phallic-shaped swimming pool in which frolicked guests such as the Beatle George Harrison, the actors Kirk Douglas and Yul Brynner, and model Verushka. Holding the reins of their court was the artist with his upturned mustache and his dragon-like wife, whom he referred to as his lionette. At this time, Dalí reconnected with his religion, and he and Gala were married once more, this time in a Catholic ceremony.

Shakespeare stated age could not wither Cleopatra's infinite variety, but the same did not hold true for Dalí. In his later years, his hand shook so badly he could hardly hold a brush, and one detractor dubbed him "the Wizard of Was." Although the great talent was no more, Gala's avariciousness remained. It was estimated the couple's lavish lifestyle required $500,000 a month. Immortalized as a beauty on canvas, she appeared a caricature of her younger self in her seventies and wore a jet-black wig adorned with a Minnie Mouse bow. When dealing with potential buyers, she berated and bullied, employing knuckles and elbows: "Dalí need more money!"

Time did not mellow their relationship either; after one incident, he whacked her with his rhinoceros cane and she retaliated by giving him a black eye, a frame for his manic stare.

After a half century of almost constant togetherness, Gala demanded he purchase a twelfth-century castle, Púbol, as a hideaway/ love nest for her. The couple, devotees of the opera *Tristan und Isolde*, placed busts of Wagner alongside their pool. A personal effect amid the splendors was a cross-legged mannequin, clad in Gala's velvet tiger-print jacket, her back turned away from any onlooker. The artist was not allowed to visit unless he had a written invitation from its chatelaine. Ensconced in the fortress, she worshipped Jesus, but not the religious savior. Instead, it was actor Jeff Fenholt, who had played in *Jesus Christ Superstar* on Broadway, who now captured her adulation. She lavished on him Dalí paintings and transformed a room into his recording studio; he rocked away all night to the irritation of his paramour, who wanted him in bed. When he stayed in his million-dollar Long Island home (Gala's gift), she once received a pleading telegram: "Must have $38,000 or will die." Despite all her largesse, Fenholt showed little gratitude; his impersonation of Jesus apparently had not engendered any redeeming qualities in himself. However, his role later came in handy when he became a California televangelist.

Another of her menagerie was William Rotlein, a twenty-two-year-old junkie she had picked up on a New York City street. She took him to Italy where she made him vow eternal love on the tomb of Romeo and Juliet. She boasted that next to Éluard, he provided the best sex she had ever had. The liaison ended when Rotlein failed a screen test for a walk-on part in a Fellini movie. Gala despised failure, and she gave him a one-way ticket back to Manhattan, where he died of a drug overdose.

Gala's protracted absences reduced Dalí to abject depression, so she hit pause on her extravagant lifestyle to play one more role for him: private physician. To alleviate his sorrow, she administered excessive doses of valium, which reduced him to a state of lethargy. In one visit, angered by something, it was rumored she made a dent in his skull with a whack from her shoe.

Gala eventually became ill, and Dalí took her to his home, where he lavished on her his constant care. On her sickbed, they became *Gala-Salvador Dalí* once more. She passed away on June 10, 1982. Devastated by his loss, Dalí, as always, followed her wishes, her final one requesting interment in her castle. He broke a plague law enacted in the 1940s that prohibited moving the dead without official permission. He wrapped her body in a blanket and, aided by his nurse, her corpse was placed in the backseat of their 1969 Cadillac de Ville where they took a surrealistic last ride together. The driver, Gala's personal chauffeur, worried her ghost would be angry with him as she had always insisted on taking the front seat. Dalí's muse was as intimidating in death as she was in life.

Gala was embalmed and laid to rest in her favorite red Dior evening gown in a crypt watched over by mythical carved animals. Dalí spent the following nights by her final resting place on his knees, convulsed with sobs.

The tragedy of Dalí's final years was living on after Gala's demise. For the last five years of his own life, he was an invalid from hell. He lunged at his nurses, clawed them with his nails, and purposely soiled his bed. After suffering burns, he was visited by his sister on whom he rained obscenities and threats to disinherit her. She took this as a sign he was on the mend. Despite his plans to have his body refrigerated after death with the hope of resurrection, he, like Gala, was embalmed, pacemaker and all. Dalí passed away of heart failure while listening to his favorite recording of Wagner's ancient retelling of aborted love, *Tristan und Isolde*.

CHAPTER THIRTEEN

HERR WOLFF

Mrs. Adolf Hitler

Lord Byron wrote, "Man's love is of man's life a thing apart/'Tis woman's whole existence." This sentiment epitomized Adolf Hitler's relationship with his consort, who had the rather unenviable distinction of being the partner of the man history has dubbed evil incarnate.

Friedrich "Fritz" and Franziska "Fanny" Braun were a typical lower-middle-class couple in Munich, parents of three daughters: Ilse, Eva, and Margarete, "Gretl." Their lives, similar to most of their countrymen, were a study in survival due to the hyperinflation that crippled Germany following defeat in World War I. Nevertheless, they did their best for their children, who attended the local Catholic school. Their middle daughter was indistinguishable from her friends, whose lives revolved around typical teen pursuits of boys, makeup, clothes, and sports. After the lyceum, she enrolled in the Convent of the English Sisters in Simbach am Inn, where she achieved average grades and indulged in dancing, gymnastics, Hollywood movies, and romance novels. She also enjoyed the plays of Oscar Wilde (at least until they were banned when her future boyfriend came to power). In 1929, older sister Ilse obtained a job as an assistant for Dr. Martin Levy Marx, and their relationship moved from professional to intimate.

In September, Eva answered an ad in a Munich newspaper for a trainee position and began working as an assistant to Heinrich Hoffman, the photographer instrumental in the making of Hitler's official image as a demigod. Eva, an eager apprentice, developed a passion for the camera and became adept at taking and developing pictures.

She would no doubt have lived and died an unknown hausfrau except for an October 1929 encounter when the forty-year-old leader of the National Socialist German Worker's Party paid a visit to his personal photographer and saw a blond seventeen-year-old girl. As the door opened, Eva was standing on a ladder, which gave Hitler an eyeful of shapely legs; Eva saw the man behind the images who had a funny mustache. Hoffman introduced the visitor as "Herr Wolff," Hitler's childhood nickname and one used only by members of his inner circle. Hitler did not pursue Eva as he was involved in a romantic relationship with his young niece Geli Raubal, with whom he was obsessed. When Geli committed suicide in their home with her Uncle Alf's gun, the miniscule part of Hitler's DNA that was still human was devastated. Months later, he remembered the pretty girl he had met two years earlier who bore a striking resemblance to Geli; she was to serve as the classic rebound.

Heinrich Hoffman then played a new role for his Führer—matchmaker. However, before Hitler agreed to go on a first date, he had Martin Bormann scrutinize her background in case she had any Jewish blood hidden among her family skeletons. When she was deemed of undiluted Aryan stock, dates at the cinema and opera and drives in his Mercedes followed, heady fare for a girl to whom luxury was a stranger. The appeal of Hitler to Eva was getting attention from Germany's leading alpha male; Eva's appeal was she was an impressionable girl who would allow him to serve as Svengali. He explained his philosophy, saying, "A highly intelligent man should always choose a primitive and stupid woman." The comment—which could have proved a relationship buster—was taken with the proverbial grain of salt. After all, of all the German

volk, she had been chosen by the world's most powerful man as his lover. Within a year, she had lost her virginity in Hitler's home, on a couch filled with fluffy pillows. On the walls were two photographs: one of Klara Hitler (his mother) and the other of Geli Raubal.

Though no definitive knowledge exists of what really happened behind the closed doors of the Führer's bedroom, historical speculation has ranged from homosexuality to abstinence. The sole peephole into Hitler's sex life is he liked Eva to sport chamois leather underwear. (Fortunately for mankind, she never got pregnant.) Whatever transpired behind that curtain, he became the sun around which Eva's life orbited. Hitler, however, had a different agenda. He was committed to his public persona and thus presented himself as the husband of every German woman, saying, "Germany is my only bride." He elaborated on this to Reich architect Albert Speer: "It's just like an actor when he marries. For the women who have worshipped him, he is no longer their idol in the same way." Although he refused to get married to preserve his elevated status, a secret girlfriend was another matter.

Hitler was immune to the tears of his lonely lover as he did not have much time for her during the Nazi rise to power; there were the Reichstag elections to win, the chancellorship to obtain, the masses to whip up, the Jews to persecute. In despair or as a bid for attention, Eva shot herself in the neck; when she recovered, she claimed she had been symbolically aiming at her heart. This suggests she was either a remarkably bad shot or she had manipulated the master manipulator. As a variation on a theme of her favorite playwright Oscar Wilde: to lose one girlfriend to a self-inflicted gunshot wound may be regarded as a misfortune; to lose both looks like carelessness. Hitler told Hoffman that he now recognized that "the girl really loved him," and he bought her a phone for her home so that she no longer had to sleep on a bench at the photography shop, waiting for his call. He further placated Eva by installing her in a villa near his own Munich home, one replete with a maid, Mercedes, and chauffeur.

With excess funds for the first time in her life, Eva filled her emotional vacuum with acquisition of material goods and changed her outfits several times a day. Although she had an opulent lifestyle, she remained depressed because she was deprived of the one thing she coveted, her lover's constant company. When the affair cooled off again in 1935, Eva confided to her diary of her commitment-phobic Hitler, "Love seems not to be on his agenda at the moment." In response, she staged a second suicide attempt when she overdosed on the sleeping pill Phanodorm. Her inert body was discovered by her sister Ilse, who immediately contacted Dr. Marx. In his official report, he employed the euphemism "excessive fatigue." Twice proved a charm, and Hitler agreed to meet her suitably star-struck parents. Moreover, proving he knew how to show a girl a good time, he allowed her to attend the Nazi Party rally at Nuremberg. Eva understood the psychology that the way to a dictator's heart was through self-violence. He also installed her at Berghof, his mountain retreat in the cloud-swirled Bavarian Alps (from which he could nostalgically view his native Austria), which he had purchased with funds from *Mein Kampf* (My Struggle). In a nod to propriety, she had her own apartment next to her lover's, but it was general knowledge to his intimates she was the mistress of the unique manor. Evenings would find them in the study, adorned with Hitler's watercolors, where she would sip wine while he drank tea. Their favorite song was "*Blutrote Rosen*" (Blood Red Roses).

In the magnificent chalet on the hill, Eva and Gretl, two Catholic girls from the lower-middle class, got to meet the highest-ranking Nazis and foreign dignitaries, including David Lloyd George, the Aga Khan, the Duke and Duchess of Windsor, and Benito Mussolini. Although Hitler demanded she remain circumspect about their relationship, Eva giggled when she saw a photograph of Neville Chamberlain sitting on the sofa in Hitler's Munich home, saying, "If only he knew what goings-on that sofa has seen." Eva was not permitted to attend the meetings of the top brass (she was so disinterested in politics she never joined the Nazi Party), but was nevertheless Berghof's acknowledged hostess. At meals, she sat at Adolf's left and felt unassailable enough to rebuke him for being late for dinner and to shush him when he monopolized the conversation. She was also the only one who was able to challenge his high will: although it infuriated him, she refused to stop habits he found anathema, such as eating meat, nude swimming, and wearing makeup. On the other end were his aides who were too nervous even to awaken him with news of the D-Day invasion.

Eva most truly came into her own when she could record her world through the eyes of the lens, and she captured the secret life of the Nazis when they allowed themselves to take a break from world domination, catching in intimate close-ups, as in the

German-American writer Hannah Arendt's phrase, "the banality of evil." These images serve as a visual diary of the henchmen: relaxing on the terrace of the chalet, drinking coffee and eating cakes, Hitler patting the head of his adored Alsatian Blondi or walking Eva's two Scottish terriers, Negus and Stasi. When he first saw Eva's black puppy, he quipped, "My God, what is this? Racial mixing?" The candid pictures are in sharp contrast to Hoffman's idealized ones and make for the world's most macabre photo album. Although Hitler continued in his refusal to marry Eva, he spoke of spending his life with her. In the Berghof retreat was a model of Linz, his native city that he dreamt of turning into the artistic capital of the Reich. He stated, "Aside from Fraulein Braun, I'll take no one with me." It was under its sacred soil he wished to be buried by the side of Eva.

Another token of his affection, one given on the occasion of her twenty-seventh birthday, was an Eszeha wristwatch; on its back was engraved *Zum 6.2.1939 herzlichst A. Hitler* (most affectionately). He also made a provision in his will providing her with 12,000 Reichsmarks annually. However, there were limits to what he was willing to do. Eva futilely tried to intercede on the behalf of her sister Ilse and Dr. Marx, whose sexual liaison was criminalized under the Law for the Protection of German Blood and German Honor, which carried the charge of "defiling the race." The physician eventually escaped to New York in 1938, and Eva found Ilse a job as a receptionist for Speer. Eva also pleaded the case for her other sister, Gretl, who had married SS Gruppenführer Hermann Fegelein and was nine months pregnant when Hitler executed her husband for desertion in the garden of the Reich Chancellery.

The treatment of her two sisters would have been a deal-breaker for most women, but Eva never faltered in her devotion. She comforted Hitler in the 1936 Berlin Olympics when African American

Jesse Owens defeated his Aryan athletes, the 1943 German debacle in the Battle of Stalingrad, and the 1944 assassination attempt by Claus von Stauffenberg. Upon learning of this, Eva wrote, "From our first meeting, I swore to follow you anywhere even unto death. I live only for your love." It was her unerring loyalty that led him to say, "Only my dog and Eva are faithful to me and belong to me."

The true litmus test of fidelity came in the spring of 1945 when the Red Army was reaching the Reichstag; Eva rushed from Munich to Berlin to be with Hitler in the squalid *Führerbunker*. At midnight on April 28, Eva Anna Paula Braun finally got her wish without even a further suicide attempt—to become Frau Hitler. However, it was a wedding like no other. The bride wore a black dress, one that her lover had always admired, accessorized by Italian shoes and her diamond watch. The groom was in the throes of madness and kept muttering, *"Es ist alles verloren, hoffnungslos verloren,"* (All is lost, hopelessly lost). The only guests were Bormann and Goebbels, who toasted the new couple with champagne. Goebbels quickly absented himself to join his wife, Magda, in order to poison their six children before following suit. In a nod to romance and their impending doom, the song on the Victrola was "Blood Red Roses."

Their marriage, for which Eva had waited for fourteen years, was only of forty hours' duration. The honeymoon consisted of Hitler testing out a cyanide capsule on Blondi before Eva ingested her own; two minutes later, Hitler died with a pistol shot to his temple. The Hitlers' final burial was 290 miles away from his dream city of Linz; their cremated bodies were buried in the Reich Chancellery Garden above the bunker. In 1970, the KGB reburned the remains of husband and wife and scattered their ashes on a river near Magdeburg.

Hitler had once remarked, "There are two ways of judging a man's character. By the woman he marries and by the way he dies." History judges the dictator on far more, but the quote says a great deal about Eva based on her choice of spouse. Pinning her life to such a man led to her own *kampf*. Eva was just one of Hitler's millions of victims; what made her unique was she was a willing one.

Othello's words, after smothering his wife Desdemona, before taking his own life, can serve as Eva Braun's own *mea culpa*: "When you shall these unlucky deeds relate, Speak of me as I am. Nothing extenuate, Nor set down aught in malice. Then must you speak of one that loved not wisely, but too well." A chance encounter at a photography studio destined Eva Braun to become the real-life Little Red Riding Hood, devoured by Herr Wolff.

CHAPTER FOURTEEN

FADE AWAY

Mrs. Douglas MacArthur

John Milton wrote in "On His Blindness", "They also serve who only stand and wait." Ever since Penelope steadfastly wove on her loom waiting for Odysseus to return, the warrior's wife has served in the typical role of the woman who worries at home in shadow, waiting for her man to come back. In contrast, a twentieth-century warrior wife accompanied her general, Douglas MacArthur, humanizing the man behind the five stars.

If ever there was a man born for the military, it was MacArthur, son of a prominent Civil War general. He distinguished himself at West Point via eight engagements to different women in his senior year. His offer of alimony was the bait to bedding a bevy of beauties; his method of ridding himself of romantic entanglements was his mother, nicknamed Pinky, who explained her son would never marry as he was wed to the army.

On February 14, 1922, he finally tied the knot with fabulously wealthy socialite Henrietta Louise Cromwell Brooks, sister-in-law of tobacco heiress Doris Duke. William Manchester, in *American Caesar*, described her as on the prowl for Gatsby's "gold-hatted, high-bouncing lover." She thought she had found him in the gold-embroidery-hatted MacArthur. Cracks soon appeared: she told her brother that while MacArthur may have held a high rank in the army, "he's a buck private in the boudoir." A further fissure was MacArthur's transfer to the Philippines; she hated its steaming heat and lifestyle. After the divorce, she married British actor Lionel Atwill, which led her to quip, "It looks like I traded four stars for one."

Generals and their mistresses are a tale as old as time—Mark Antony had Cleopatra and Douglas MacArthur had Isabel Rosario Cooper, a teenaged Eurasian actress nicknamed "Dimples" (though none were visible). When he returned to Washington, Isabel was ensconced in a love nest near Douglas's office adjoining the White House. He bought her many lacy tea gowns, but no raincoat; his gifts made it manifestly clear her role was an indoor accessory only. After a *Washington Post* gossip columnist uncovered the clandestine affair, rather than falling on his sword—à la Antony—Isabel was given a $15,000 payoff via aide Dwight D. Eisenhower. The cast-off mistress used the money to open a hair-dressing salon in the Midwest; she ended her days through suicide.

MacArthur, twice having met his romantic Waterloo, felt consigned to a life where his only significant other was the army. In later years, a news correspondent asked about the general's nonpareil military success; after puffing on his corncob pipe, the great man responded, "I believe it was destiny." But romantic destiny wasn't going to take that for an answer.

Jean Marie Faircloth was born in Nashville, Tennessee, on December 28, 1898, in a white-pillared home that could have served as a stage design for *Gone with the Wind*. At age eight, her wealthy parents divorced and her mother took daughter and sons to her native Murfreesboro. The head of the new household was her grandfather, Captain Richard Beard, who raised the children to view the Confederate uniform as a badge of honor. Little Jean became known as "the flag-wavingest girl" in town, and her Pied Piper was the sound of a bugle. A member of the conservative group Daughters of the American Revolution recalled, "Every time Jean

Faircloth heard a 4th of July firecracker go off, she jumped to attention and saluted."Young men were advised if they wanted to win the heart of the diminutive, raven-haired beauty, they had better don a uniform. When her father died, he left her a substantial fortune and she took trips around the world.

Jean was aboard the SS *President Hoover* on the way to Shanghai when she met MacArthur, who was en route to Manila to become military advisor to the Philippines. They were introduced by Pinky, who felt a kinship to the genteel Southern woman and considered the fact she was eighteen years younger than her son no impediment. Jean and MacArthur had dinner together, and the next day the smitten suitor sent flowers. Later Jean recalled of their shipboard romance, "And that was that." She disembarked in Manila and remained for the next year and a half, whenever possible by the side of her man in uniform.

AND THAT WAS THAT.

They were married in a quiet ceremony in the chapel of the Municipal Building in New York on April 30, 1937. Reporters who gathered at the news of their nuptials were told by the fifty-six-year-old MacArthur, in reference to his marriage, "This job is going to last a long time."

The bride was not to return to the United States for fourteen years; however, this did not bother her as Jean felt home was her husband. The MacArthurs lived in a penthouse in the luxurious Manila Hotel with a distant view of the island fortress of Corregidor. In the presence of others, Jean addressed her spouse as "General"; in private she called him "Sir Boss." In turn he referred to her as "Ma'am" or as "my finest soldier." Their family was completed with the birth of their only child, Arthur MacArthur IV. Jean and Douglas didn't care about the redundancy; they'd christened him after his grand-father whose legacy came above any future embarrassment such a repetitive name might bring their child. His adoring parents saw each of his waves as a salute and never doubted he would become a third-generation general. When the baby was four days old, Jean hired a Cantonese nanny, Ah Cheu, who could look after her son, which enabled Jean to look after his father. MacArthur later wrote in his memoir, "With my little family, I would be lonely no more."

The catalyst that altered the trajectory of the couple's fate was the bombing of Pearl Harbor. With the Japanese poised for an attack on the Philippines, American families fled to the States, but Jean was adamant to stand—or fall—with her man. They evacuated to an underground command center on Corregidor, and as bombs shook its walls, Jean still refused to leave or send three-year-old Arthur from harm's way. For comfort, the child clutched his stuffed rabbit he had named "Old Friend." She said, "We have drunk from the same cup. We three shall stay together." Three months later, upon President Roosevelt's orders that MacArthur leave for Australia to take over the American forces there (he could not let his most famous general fall to the enemy), the family fled on a torpedo boat. Before he stepped off the dock, the general made a promise to the Filipino people: "I shall return."

For nights, the commander in chief of the United States Armed Forces and his family sailed on the Pacific, prize targets of Imperial Japan. But they escaped down under to free-dom. After settling in a Melbourne hotel, to commemorate his wife's devotion, MacArthur presented Jean with a platinum-and-diamond wristwatch inscribed, "To my bravest. Bataan-Corregidor March 1942 MacArthur." When military matters kept them apart, he still found time for letters that he always began with the salutation "Dearest Jeannie" and signed, "Sir Boss."

Just as the bombing of Pearl Harbor led to the MacArthurs' departure from the Philippines, a second bomb occasioned another move toward the end of World War II. After the devastation of Hiroshima and Nagasaki from the atom bombs, President Truman appointed MacArthur as the Supreme Commander of the Allied Powers, with the approval of Britain's Attlee, Russia's Stalin, and China's Chiang Kai-shek, to provide stability to occupied Japan. The family arrived in Tokyo and moved into their new home, in disrepair after the atom bomb, which had been the American embassy prior to the war. The general accepted the formal surrender of Emperor Hirohito in Tokyo Bay aboard the USS *Missouri*.

The end of the "emperor" general's reign came when Truman relieved him of his fifty-one years of service due to insubordination in the Korean War. The general's encroachment on the Chinese border triggered the entry of Mao's communist Chinese, a major miscalculation. Upon reading of his dismissal, a grim-faced MacArthur turned to his wife and said, "Jeannie, we're going home at last." For thirteen-year-old Arthur, home was a place where he had never set foot. The family was deeply moved when a quarter of a million Japanese lined the route to the airport where the army played "Auld Lang Syne." In the same vein, only the second coming would have upstaged the MacArthur arrival in America: they were greeted with a tickertape parade with thousands of citizens lining the family's motorcade.

The mythical military hero was invited to deliver a radio-covered speech to Congress that was anticipated as eagerly as the Sermon on the Mount. While a teary-eyed Jean listened from her reserved seat in the front row of the visitor's gallery, MacArthur gave an emotional farewell address that concluded, "Old soldiers never die—they just fade away. I'm an old soldier who tried to do his duty as God gave him the light to see that duty. Good-bye."

Douglas, Jean, and Arthur MacArthur moved into their final residence, the thirty-second floor of Manhattan's elite Waldorf Astoria. There, the great man devoted his time to writing about his great life. He wrote of his marriage to Jean, "It was perhaps the smartest thing I have ever done. She has been my constant friend, sweetheart, and devoted supporter ever since. How she has managed to put up with my eccentricities all these years is quite beyond my comprehension."

With MacArthur's passing in 1964, millions mourned, but none so deeply as his widow. Ironically, it was his father's death that allowed Arthur to escape the MacArthur shadow under which, unlike his mother, he was not content to remain. Unlike his illustrious forbears, he bypassed West Point for Columbia and devoted himself to music rather than the military. He changed his name and virtually disappeared from public view. Posterity would have no Arthur MacArthur V.

Jean remained a public figure, believing this was in keeping with the role of the general's wife. At age ninety-one, with her friend Barbara Bush at her side, President Ronald Reagan presented her with the Medal of Freedom, and the government of the Philippines honored her with its Legion of Merit. She was one of the few private citizens to receive a visit from the emperor and empress of Japan during their American visit.

The diminutive Jean was feted by high society (one of her admirers was Prince Albert of Monaco), and publisher Malcolm Forbes threw her a ninetieth birthday party attended by Frank Sinatra, Barbara Walters, and other luminaries. In response to their praises, she said with her self-effacing reply, "People are so good to me."

Jean remained a symbol of white-gloved propriety though she never lost her adventurous spirit. Columnist Liz Smith recounted when she attended Malcolm Forbes's hot-air balloon expedition in France, Mrs. MacArthur was a member of the party that included guests Walter Cronkite and the king of Romania. The ninety-one-year-old Jean gamely let Forbes help her into the balloon, which led the journalist to remark, "There won't be any more grand old ladies like her." After a life as the helpmeet of MacArthur, it would take a lot more to intimidate the general's lady.

MacArthur ultimately kept his promise to the Filipino people to return; he did and he freed them from Japanese control toward the end of WWII. However, his famous farewell quotation proved false in one aspect. For the American public—and for his widow—the memory of the old general would never fade away.

CHAPTER FIFTEEN

MADAME BUTTERFLY

Mrs. Julius Rosenberg

A s Jell-O conforms to its mold, children often adhere to the values of their parents. However, in a 1950s love story that involved Julius Rosenberg, it was a Jell-O box and a Remington typewriter that made a woman's path stray far afield from what her family, or anyone else, ever envisioned.

Ethel Greenglass, born in 1915 in New York's Lower East Side on Sheriff Street, was the daughter of Russian Jewish immigrants Barnet and Tessie. Her father was barely able to support his family through his sewing machine repair shop, and they lived in a cramped, unheated tenement. Ethel attended the Downtown Talmud Torah, followed by Seward Park High, which she completed at fifteen. As college was usually not in the horizon for females, especially destitute ones, she worked at a shipping company. However, Ethel's dream was to have a career in the arts, and the highlight of her youth was when her vocal group performed at Carnegie Hall and the Metropolitan Opera House.

Ethel was exposed to fellow workers who encouraged her to join the Communist League where she could fight for economic equality and against European fascism. When her union organized a strike, she was one of four members of its committee. Her mother, Tessie, disapproved, but Ethel felt her rebel nature had found its cause.

In 1936, Ethel was invited to perform at a New Year's Eve

party for the Seaman's fund-raiser; very shy, she was agitated as this time she was not singing as part of a group. A young man there sensed her fear and, introducing himself as Julius Rosenberg, inquired why she looked upset. They retreated to a private room where he bolstered her courage and won her heart when he told her to imagine, while on stage, she should sing for him only. Before the evening was over, they were a couple and she had promised she would support him while he completed his electrical engineering degree, a career his father disapproved of, preferring he attend rabbinical school. This innocuous meeting of boy meets girl would lead to a notorious end.

In 1939, when Rosenberg graduated from City College in New York, Ethel became Mrs. Rosenberg. When she was fired from the shipping company because of her part in the strike, she was enraged, but with her new role as wife and later as mother to sons Robert and Michael, she devoted herself to family, abandoning any interest in music, jobs, or the sickle and hammer. Ethel and Julius doted on each other and their children. Rosenberg's position at the Army Engineering Laboratories in New Jersey provided a steady, comfortable income for the young family. Photographs from their first years as man and wife show an ordinary-looking Lower East Side couple idling on the grass in Central Park and carrying their boys on their shoulders at the beach.

The first rung in the ever-ascending ladder of horror came in 1945 when Rosenberg was fired after his membership in the Communist Party was discovered (his subscription to the paper, the *Daily Worker*, did not help matters). Ethel was frantic since both of them had now been branded as red and thus would be unable to obtain employment. As their savings dwindled and with two young boys to support, she felt things could not get worse.

On July 15, 1950, as the couple was watching television with their sons, FBI agents filed into their apartment and clapped handcuffs on Rosenberg in front of his terrified family. With the boys crying hysterically for their father, Ethel was beside herself.

Her husband was charged with leaking atomic secrets to the Soviet Union, which was the ultimate "Et tu, Brute"—cooperating with America's Cold War archenemy. In prison, Rosenberg was steadfast in his refusal to name names. His stoicism led to a journalist likening him to the Lone Ranger, the masked ex-Texas Ranger who was a self-appointed fighter against injustice in the Old West. When incarceration did not break him, the head of the FBI, J. Edgar Hoover, issued a memorandum to the Attorney General that by taking action against Rosenberg's wife, it "might serve as a lever in these matters." Accordingly, Ethel was arrested the following month as she walked to catch a subway after spending the afternoon testifying before a grand jury. She was denied the opportunity to arrange care for her sons, who had been left with a babysitter. Metaphorically the prosecution put a gun to Ethel's head and said, "Talk or we kill her." She was incarcerated in the Women's House of Detention, but her husband gave no indication his wife's threatened prosecution would make him cooperate. Although the lever did not work, the government was now committed to the prosecution of Ethel as an equal partner in espionage.

The state versus Julius and Ethel Rosenberg was dubbed "the trial of the century," and the eyes of the world were riveted on the proceedings taking place in a Manhattan courthouse. From the beginning, the deck was stacked against the defendants: it occurred against the backdrop of Americans frantically building bomb shelters in case of Soviet attacks and the popular catchphrase of the times, "better dead than red." The trial, which began two years after the Soviet Union had exploded its first atomic

bomb, posed the question of whether the Rosenbergs had accelerated by five to ten years the end of the American nuclear monop-
oly by providing critical secrets to the Russians. The courtroom
drama was played out against the backdrop of the Iron Curtain,
behind which the Soviet Union was supporting North Korea in
its nuclear efforts. The pieces of the chessboard were in place. The
outcome? The fate of the world.

The star witness for the prosecution was ironically Ethel's
brother, David Greenglass, who had worked as a machinist for
the Manhattan Project and who provided the eleven male and
one female jury (none of whom were Jewish) with incriminating
evidence implicating his brother-in-law. He claimed Rosenberg
cut a Jell-O box in two for use as a signal so he could be recognized by other Soviet agents. In a moment of courtroom drama,
Greenglass was given a Jello-O box to demonstrate how it had
been used. (The box, imitation raspberry flavor, is now housed in
the National Archives.)

Ethel's brother became the 1950s counterpart to the Bible's
Cain when he implicated his sister, providing the prosecution
with the only evidence against her. Greenglass testified he and
his wife, Ruth, had visited the Rosenberg home in Knickerbocker
Village where he provided Ethel with his handwritten notes concerning secrets from the Manhattan Project that she transcribed
on a Remington typewriter intended for transmission to Moscow.
Rosenberg then burned the original notes in a frying pan. The reason
behind Greenglass's damning testimony was self-aggrandizement;
for the first time, the unassuming man had garnered the spotlight.
He also named names to save Ruth (who was also charged), from
prosecution and himself from a lengthier prison term or even a
death sentence. To add insult to injury, he exaggerated Rosenberg's
role as a Soviet spy to cover up his own.

In contrast to her brother who had no problem pointing fingers at everyone but himself, Ethel invoked the Fifth Amendment and refused to testify. It was a move that precluded implicating others; however, it was also a move that did not garner sympathy from the jury. Had she presented herself as she was in actuality, a mother who spent her days baking cookies (not making Jell-O), she might have convinced them she was merely a typical '50s housewife caught in a sinister web.

In jarring juxtaposition to her silence, the prosecutor delivered a thunderous denunciation. "She sat at that typewriter and struck the keys, blow by blow, against her own country," he stated. The jury made no recommendation for mercy; the judge showed none. The judge said that by handing over America's mightiest weapon—the atomic bomb—to the Soviets, the Rosenbergs had precipitated the Korean War, which had claimed 50,000 lives. As he spoke, the church bell of nearby St. Andrew's Roman Catholic Church tolled the hour of noon, its longest toll of the day. Rosenberg swayed slowly back and forth on the balls of his feet. Ethel, five feet tall and one hundred pounds, stood at his right. When the judge described her as a full-fledged partner, her right hand clamped the chair in front of her in a white-knuckled grip. Tessie Greenglass sobbed when she heard her daughter's death sentence and her son's fifteen-year sentence (his testimony spared his life). Tessie told the press, "I blame the Russians for poisoning my children."

The verdict did not mean an end to the love story of the Romeo and Juliet of the Lower East Side. Ethel and Julius were sent to Sing Sing Prison, an ironic name considering singing had led to their introduction. On the evening after they had received their duel date with the electric chair, when confined in adjoining cells, Ethel sang to her husband from the operatic tale of the geisha who had stabbed herself with a dagger, preferring death to a life lived in shame. Rosenberg responded, though not as well nor as romantically, with "The Battle Hymn of the Republic." On another occasion, locked in a police van, separated by a mesh screen, they locked lips in a stolen kiss. When they were moved to separate detention facilities, their letters bespoke their love: "Dearest Julie, they'll be putting out the lights soon and then I'll be alone with you. So I pretend, anyway. Oh, how I miss you and long to be in your arms where I belong. Good night darling." In the death house where two of their three years in jail were spent, they were permitted to see each other, behind a visitor's screen, every Wednesday—"wondrous Wednesday" as Ethel referred to it. On one of these occasions, they were permitted a face-to-face encounter in which they rushed into each other's arms and Rosenberg's face was so covered with lipstick it looked as if he were bleeding. The guards wrestled them apart and Ethel took her seat, weeping. The photographs from this time were in marked contrasted to the earlier family albums: Ethel and Julius in a jail van, their sons ambling along the walls of Sing Sing.

The Rosenberg trial was one that polarized the country: one camp contended they should be fried immediately, the other claimed the couple was a victim of a witch hunt. Jean-Paul Sartre called the sentence "a legal lynching which smears with blood a whole nation." Thousands of Rosenberg supporters demonstrated, among them Robert and Michael holding signs that said, "Don't kill Mommy and Daddy." An avalanche of letters asking for clemency poured into the White House, including ones from Albert Einstein, Bertolt Brecht, Dashiell Hammett, Frida Kahlo, Pablo Picasso, and Pope Pius XII.

At the end, there was one last chance for physical intimacy, albeit a painful one. On the evening of their execution, Julius and Ethel were once again on opposite sides of a mesh screen. Before he was led away, Rosenberg touched his finger to his lips and pressed them through the opening as Ethel did the same. In the moments following his death, the prison rabbi implored Ethel to save herself, at least for her children's sake, by giving last-minute testimony implicating her husband and others. She replied, "No. I have no names to give. I cannot wrong my conscience." By her refusal, Michael and Robert became the country's most infamous orphans. When strapped in the electric chair in Sing Sing, perhaps she found courage, once again, by conducting her final performance with dignity for Rosenberg's memory.

In later years, Greenglass recanted his testimony, saying he condemned his sister in order to cut a deal to save Ruth, the one who had typed his notes. He explained rather callously, "My wife is my wife. I mean, I don't sleep with my sister, you know." His confession sealed his reputation as Rat Rosenberg. For Woody Allen fans out there, it also explains the allusion from Allen's character in *Crimes and Misdemeanors* musing about an odious relative, "I love him like a brother—David Greenglass." Greenglass was released in 1960 after serving a decade in prison, changed his name, and vanished into the New York night. Then he agreed to be interviewed for *60 Minutes*, perhaps in a bid to recapture the spotlight. He stated, "I sleep very well… Every time I'm haunted by it, my wife says, 'Look, we're still alive.'" He also stated if he ever met his two nephews—orphaned by the state and their uncle—he would tell them he was sorry their parents had been executed.

On the fiftieth anniversary of the Rosenbergs' execution, journalist Clyde Haberman visited the couple's adjoining graves at Wellwood Cemetery on Long Island. A groundskeeper, observing the interred had died on the same date, asked, "An accident?" The answer to his question is no. Ethel was doomed because of her name, her beliefs, and her steadfast decision to prefer death to a life lived in shame—the American Madame Butterfly.

CHAPTER SIXTEEN

THE MAN WITH THE GOLDEN PEN

Mrs. Ian Fleming

B ond. James Bond. This was the classic greeting of the most dashing member of Her Majesty's Secret Service. However, if people knew the biography of his creator, Ian Fleming, they might have thought of him as Bondage. James Bondage. And he was met, lash for lash, by his ladylove.

When one thinks of the British peerage, the image is often of impeccably dressed aristocrats conversing in the Queen's English. The customary term to describe this breed is "stiff upper lip," but stiff, when it came to Ian Lancaster Fleming, only referred to an overworked part of his anatomy. His father was Valentine Fleming, killed on the Western Front when his son was nine. The former Member of Parliament was held in such high esteem his obituary was penned by Sir Winston Churchill. Ian was raised by his über-domineering wealthy mother, who constantly humiliated him and whose clutches left such an imprint he equated a walk down the aisle with one down the green mile. He quickly bored of his lovers, chiefly those married to other men (his pick-up line was asking if a woman cared to sleep with him), confiding to a friend that females were like pets, men the only real human beings. However, he changed his mantra when he met a fellow member of the peerage who shared his sexual persuasion; it was a union made in sadomasochistic heaven.

Ann Geraldine Mary Charteris was born at Stanway, Gloucestershire, on June 19, 1913, but after the death of her mother, she lived with her grandparents in the Cotswolds. In the upper-class milieu, plays were penned for her and her siblings by the author of *Peter Pan*, Sir James Barrie. In 1932, Ann married her first suitor, Baron Shane Edward Robert O'Neill, a wealthy man with a position in the capital. She subsequently became London's leading hostess. However, despite her marriage and children, Raymond and Fionn, she was not satisfied with a life of servants and baronial halls and began a love affair with Esmond Cecil Harmsworth, heir to Lord Rothermere, owner of the *Daily Mail*. She was not the least bit ruffled when her two men played bridge together.

When her husband went to war in 1939, bored with only one sexual partner, she simultaneously began seeing Ian Fleming, an influential assistant to the director of naval affairs whom she first met at a swimming pool in the chic French seaside resort of Le Touquet. She was immediately drawn to the twenty-eight-year-old whom she described as a "handsome, moody creature" with his Greco-Roman profile and crooked nose, a result of a football injury. After living on the continent, Fleming could seduce women in four languages, something that delighted Ann. When her husband was killed in Italy in 1944, she wanted to become Mrs. Fleming, but as Ian explained, marriage was not on his radar.

Ever practical, she became the wife of Harmsworth, now Viscount Rothermere, instead, with whom she lived in great luxury at Warwick House, off Green Park. In their mansion, she battled postwar austerity by throwing sumptuous parties whose guests included Sigmund Freud's artist grandson, Lucian. She also busied herself as the power behind the throne of the *Daily Mail* and serving as mother to her children. However, the multitasking and free-thinking Ann continued her affair with Fleming, who had become a journalist at the *Sunday Times*. Independently wealthy, he spent three months a year at his beloved seaside home in Jamaica, Goldeneye, christened after the codename of his wartime intelligence project. When he was gone, they wrote letters of yearning to each another; in one, Ann declared, "I long for you to whip me because I love being hurt by you and kissed afterward. It's very lonely not to be beaten and shouted at every five minutes." Equally sentimental, Fleming responded, "All the love I have for you has grown out of me because you made it grow. Without you I would still be hard and dead and cold and quite unable to write this childish letter, full of love and jealousies and adolescence." Desperate for Fleming's company—or flagellation—she told Esmond she was leaving for a vacation in Jamaica to visit her friend Noel Coward, and Fleming and Ann resumed their affair against a Caribbean backdrop. What put a crimp in their passion was Ann's pregnancy (fathered by Fleming). Baby Mary passed away after eight hours. Upon learning of the affair, Rothermere magnanimously forgave his errant wife with the caveat she never see Fleming again. For Ann, that was akin to telling Niagara's waters not to fall; she left home and estate and became the mistress of Goldeneye.

Their home became a Mecca to esteemed guests such as Truman Capote, Graham Greene, and Evelyn Waugh, who often walked down the steps to the beach where they speared their lunch. Visitors were surprised how their hosts managed to go through so many wet towels, always piled Babel-fashion in the laundry room. If those sodden towels could speak, what a tale they would tell. They were used to relieve the stinging burns of whips, slippers, and hairbrushes with which the lovers routinely beat one another, Fleming inflicting pain more often than Ann.

Their guests began to get an inkling of the usage of the towels when they noticed an abundance of books strewn about whose spines were emblazed with the word "flagellation," replete with illustrations of men and women standing over one another, whips posed. The sadomasochism came to a grinding halt when Ann once more became pregnant and her long-suffering spouse finally filed for divorce. Fleming decided to bite the bullet and do the chivalrous thing by asking Ann to be his wife. After all, she was carrying his child and could match him lash for lash. They were married in 1952 in Port Maria's town hall; Noel Coward served as best man.

It was the impending baby that also gave birth to the most dapper spy since Sherlock Holmes. Fleming, a commitment-phobe, was wary of his impending nuptial and yet desired to do right by marrying the woman he loved. In order to stave off his angst, he took Ann's suggestion he write a novel. He later recalled, "I was just on the edge of getting married and I was frenzied at the prospect of this great step in my life after having been a bachelor for so long and I really wanted to take my mind off the agony and so I decided to sit down and write a book."

He ordered a gold-plated typewriter from London, and his first order of business was to name his protagonist. As he pondered the moniker, his face was wreathed in smoke from his personalized cigarettes—a Balkan and Turkish mixture made especially for him, ensconced in a Dunhill holder. He brushed aside his original impulse of calling his fictional creation something upper class and stuffy, like "Peregrine Carruthers." Exotic things would happen to and around his high-living spy, so in contrast, he wanted his name to be as dull as possible.

It was at this point his eye was caught by a book, *Birds of the West Indies*, penned by his American neighbor, James Bond. The idea behind "007" came from a prefix that appeared on British intelligence files during the war. The character was the wish fulfillment alter ego of the author though they shared similarities: love of scrambled eggs, gambling, golf, and women. His opening line of *Casino Royale* set the tone for the rest of its pages: "The scent and smoke of a casino are nauseating at three in the morning." As with his relationship with Ann, sex and cruelty went hand in hand in his novels.

Before shipping it off for hopeful publication, Fleming offered to dedicate it to Ann; she refused as she said her name was too aristocratic to be associated with a work she deemed pornographic. Fleming threw himself into the marketing of his fictional child, but the key to its success was when America's new president, John F. Kennedy, announced it was among his bedside books. He was said to have been reading Bond the night before he was assassinated, as was his killer. The novel became wildly successful—but the same could not be said of the Fleming marriage.

It was not Goldeneye's transformation from a haven of S&M to a haven for a child (whips replaced by nappies/diapers) that curbed Fleming's lust for Ann, as he doted on son Caspar, nicknamed 003-and-a-half. Indeed, he was the inspiration behind Bond's childhood classic *Chitty-Chitty-Bang-Bang*. Rather, it was Ann's caesarean, which left

disfiguring scars on her stomach, that cooled Ian's ardor. He had a horror of physical abnormalities. Ann admitted it put the death knell on intimacy. And soon other cracks appeared on the marital horizon.

While Bond found a casino at three in the morning nauseating, Ann began to feel a similar sensation after extended periods in Jamaica and began spending time in their Regency house in Victoria Square, London, where she again became the nucleus of the glitterati such as Evelyn Waugh. Fleming felt these events stuffy and preferred dinner and bridge at Boodle's Club when he was in London promoting his series of books and stayed at another of their homes in Sevenhampton, near Wiltshire. A 1962 letter from Fleming depicts their mutual misery: "In the present twilight we are hurting each other to an extent that makes life hardly bearable." Their increasingly separate lives led to a series of affairs, Ann with Labor Party leader Hugh Gaitskell and Fleming with innumerable women. Apparently his habitual pick-up line was even more potent when he became the writer with the golden arm. However, while Ann was comfortable with her husband's foray into infidelity, she felt entirely different when the physical adultery became an emotional one.

Fleming, who had always served as a sexual magnet, became the one smitten when he met Blanche Blackwell, scion of an old Jewish Jamaican family. His habitual pick-up line was altered upon their first encounter when he inquired if she were a lesbian. The answer became apparent when they embarked on a love affair sprinkled with affection rather than blows. Ann was devastated when the spy who loved her began to love another. In tribute to his new dark-haired muse, Fleming immortalized her in the character of Pussy Galore, the lesbian gang leader in *Goldfinger*. In a nod to a *mea culpa*, when the Flemings were in England, Blanche planted flowers in the garden at Goldeneye. Ann, not appreciating the neighborly gesture, tore up the shrubs and hurled them into the sea. To a visiting friend, Mrs. Fleming pointed out Blanche's estate and remarked, "On the left is the house that belongs to Ian's Jamaican wife. You may look, but I cannot."

The tug-of-war between mistress and wife ended after

Fleming's heart attack, which failed to curtail his seventy-cigarettes-and-bottle-of-gin-a-day habit. Fleming lived as hard as his fictional creation, one whose central preoccupation was a determination, as the spy had stated, "not to waste my days in trying to prolong them." The title of a John Gardner novel featuring the famous secret agent, *Nobody Lives Forever*, came to pass when Fleming died in a Canterbury hospital in 1964, on Caspar's twelfth birthday. Blanche, suffering from the ostracism of a mistress, was not welcome at his funeral services. However, she became the owner of Goldeneye, which she shared with her son Christopher, who helped make reggae music and singer Bob Marley world famous. Ann was bereft by the death of the man whose life had shadowed her own for thirty years. Caspar was equally devastated and began acting out. Ann wrote Evelyn Waugh, "Caspar hates me and talks of little but matricide. What should I do?" Caspar died from a drug overdose at age twenty-three, plagued by the same demons that had pursued his father; his mother had to be sedated when she received the news. Ann never recovered from the deaths of husband and son and became a reclusive alcoholic. In 1981, after succumbing to cancer, she was laid to rest beside Fleming and Caspar in Sevenhampton.

Although Ian Fleming and his idealized alter ego have become world-renowned icons, Ann has been lost in the shadow of the Bond beauties. However, without her, Fleming never would have become the man with the golden pen.

CHAPTER SEVENTEEN

BELOVED INFIDEL

Mrs. F. Scott Fitzgerald

F. Scott Fitzgerald pessimistically pronounced, "There are no second acts in American lives." He based this on his own freefall: from golden boy of the twenties to forgotten has-been of the forties. What eased the pain of later years was the purveyor of a poisoned pen.

Sheilah Graham was a female Gatsby who fashioned her past to fit the romantic backdrop of wishful thinking. She entered the world as Lily Shiel on September 15, 1904, in London, the youngest of six children born to immigrants Louis and Rebecca, refugees from Ukrainian pogroms. At eleven months, her father passed away from tuberculosis on a trip to Berlin and was interred in its Jewish cemetery. His death plunged his family into abject poverty and they relocated to an East London slum, where Rebecca, who hardly spoke English, found work cleaning public latrines. The Shiels boarded in a basement and subsisted on potato soup. In keeping with her Dickensian roots, when Lily was six, Rebecca placed her in the Jews Hospital and Orphan Asylum. By way of welcome, the staff cropped her thick, ash-blond hair, prevention against lice. Through the barred windows, she would watch children—those without shorn hair.

Lily remained in the institution till age fourteen when she returned home to care for Rebecca, dying of stomach cancer. Her inheritance was bittersweet—in her mother's purse, she found a faded photograph of herself as a child, dressed in a cheap apron, hand clutching a wooden spoon.

Lily obtained a position as a toothbrush demonstrator and was surprised her only customers were male. At first she assumed men cared more about hygiene, until she realized they were interested in more than a gleaming smile. She dated a millionaire who showered her with diamonds, but she could not sacrifice love for wealth. She wed Major John Graham Gillam—if not her great passion, her great friend. He served as her Henry Higgins and eased her Cockney accent. Then, as James Gatz had transformed to Jay Gatsby, Lily Shiel transformed to Sheilah Graham when she became a chorus girl.

Gillam did not mind when his dancer wife stepped out with well-heeled men, such as Randolph Churchill (Winston's son), as he was either impotent or homosexual and had married Lily to rescue her from the streets. Sheilah, under no illusion her only show biz talent was her legs, segued to journalism and was delighted when the *Daily Express* paid her two guineas.

Through Tom Mitford (brother of famed novelist Nancy Mitford), Sheilah met Charlie Chaplin, fellow survivor of London's slums. She was dazzled by his portrait of America, where one is not judged by one's lineage but by one's success. Afraid her true origins were as indelible as a tattoo, she left Gillam and the Old World for the New. In her purse, she carried the faded photograph—altered to show a little girl with lovely blue frock, wooden spoon replaced with a daffodil.

In 1933, Sheilah moved to New York where she became a professional journalist and three years later was offered a syndicated column in Hollywood. As the celluloid capital was founded on the blurring of reality, the young woman happily headed west. She became a gossip columnist, rival of Louella Parsons and Hedda

Hopper, and the ladies of the poisoned pens were dubbed the "unholy trio." They wielded the power to make or break a star's career, and chiefly did the latter. Of the three, Sheilah was the youngest and, as she was quick to point out, the prettiest.

Sheilah was ready to forego her $5,000-a-week salary and the deference of stars and studio bosses when she received a telegram—a proposal from a former British suitor, the Marquess of Donegal. Delighted with the title and fortune more than the man, she accepted. She felt no qualms about abandoning her typewriter, for she felt she merely possessed a quality that was "salable mediocre." To celebrate her engagement, writer Robert Benchley threw her a party at his bungalow in the Garden of Allah, where, among writers such as Dorothy Parker, she glimpsed F. Scott Fitzgerald—who immediately vanished in a haze of blue cigarette smoke.

Fitzgerald and Sheilah met again at the Coconut Grove, a supper club where the rich and famous dined and danced the night away under a ceiling painted midnight blue with sparkling stars strewn both on and under its firmament. Fitzgerald, recognizing her from her engagement party, whispered, "I like you." Sheilah responded, "I like you too." She asked him to dance and he agreed after the next, as it was promised to Dorothy Parker. In her memoir, she recounted the magic of floating in Scott's arms: "As we danced, the room and everyone in it faded away. It is hard to put into words how Scott Fitzgerald worked this magic, but he made me feel that to dance with me was the most extraordinary privilege for him…"

Sheilah was shocked at the intensity of her disappointment when Fitzgerald cancelled their next meeting because a family friend, actress Helen Hayes, was bringing his fifteen-year-old daughter Scottie for a visit. When Sheilah asked if she could still be included, Fitzgerald agreed. The daughter and the mistress got along, perhaps because they both carried a heavy mantle: Sheilah from the orphanage, Scottie as the only child of one of the most famous—and flawed—couples of the twentieth century. Her mother Zelda, who had been suffering from mental illness for years, was hospitalized in a psychiatric institution in North Carolina. The fairy tale couple of the '20s were to have no happily ever after. At the end of the evening, when Scott whispered, "Good night, Sheilo," she did not want him to leave. He enveloped her in his arms and she forgot he was married and a father or that she was engaged. If this were not impediment enough, the great writer's pen had dried up and he barely made enough as a scriptwriter to cover his wife's hospital bills and Scottie's tuition. This didn't deter Sheilah; she returned her diamond ring, as big as the Ritz. She would never be the wife of the Marquess of Donegal.

The years with the self-proclaimed romantic egotist provided both agony and ecstasy. Fitzgerald was in failing health, fighting an epic and losing battle with the bottle. Nevertheless, she believed in her "gold-hatted" lover. She understood the depth of his humiliation when bookstores no longer shelved *This Side of Paradise*, *The Great Gatsby*, and *Tender is the Night* (ironically bookstore staples today). Similarly, when she introduced him, there was always the inevitable embarrassment for many people meeting a man so forgotten they thought he had already died. In a painful episode, after hearing there was to be a stage production in Pasadena for "The Diamond as Big as the Ritz," they dressed in their finest and took a limousine to the theater. A tidal wave of pain rushed over them when it turned out to be a student production and they comprised the entire audience.

Sheilah persisted in her belief in his writing, and Fitzgerald began to work on a novel with a Hollywood backdrop, *The Last Tycoon*. It revolved around a love affair between Kathleen Moore and Monroe Stahr, loosely based on the romance of Sheilah and Fitzgerald. Buoyed by love, Fitzgerald traded his booze for soda and decided to douse his demons for the sake of Sheilah and Scottie. Although she could not be his wife, Sheilah felt she was far more than his mistress. Even without formal vows, she committed herself "for better or worse till God do us part."

One day in their beach house on Malibu, rented from Frank Case, manager of Manhattan's Algonquin Hotel, Fitzgerald found Sheilah struggling to read Proust's *Remembrance of Things Past*. When he showed his surprise as she had attended London's finest schools, she shared with him what she had kept locked in her secret vault—the story of Lily Shiel. In response, he became Pygmalion and Sheilah Galatea; he taught her the secrets behind literature's immortal words. Under his tutelage, Proust's madeleine became her potato soup, drawing back the curtain behind which Lily hid. Just as John had helped exorcise her Cockney, Fitzgerald designed a course of study, "College of One," to give her the education she had been denied. He drew up a list of books for her to read. Immersed in the classics, they pretended to be famous characters from novels by Dickens, Thackeray, and Tolstoy. He urged Sheilah to pen her autobiography, insisting she had the writing ability as well as a life story that surpassed most others.

The couple spent hours lying on their sofa massaging one another's feet and egos or scooping into buckets the fish that came to spawn on the beaches of Malibu. On one occasion, they took a trip to Tijuana and, in typical tourist fashion, had their picture taken. It captured a beaming Sheilah astride a donkey; beside her stood her urban cowboy, wearing a sombrero and serape. The sombrero-wearing Fitzgerald was not the gold-hatted lover of which a youthful Lily had dreamt, but Sheilah was a woman in love and did not care. It was their only picture taken together and it was kept beside the sepia-colored one of a little girl in a blue dress.

Tragically, paradise had another side, and it came out when Scott relapsed and began to drink—an evil elixir that transformed him from Dr. Jekyll to Mr. Hyde. In *The Crack-Up*, he had written of the "real dark night of the soul where it is always three o'clock in the morning, day after day." Impossibly charming when sober, he turned into a monster when drunk. Liquor provoked him into jealous rages, and during the great drinking binge of 1939, he accused Sheilah of returning the affections of men pursuing the beautiful columnist: Errol Flynn and Gary Cooper. He turned to his nurse, Miss Steffan, who was caring for him, and like a deranged Rumpelstiltskin began chanting, "Lily Shiel! Lily Shiel!" For emphasis he hurtled at her the other buried dagger, "Dirty Jew!" He then brandished a gun in front of the terrified nurse and Sheilah. In response, Sheilah said, "Take it and shoot yourself, you son of a bitch. I didn't pull myself out of the gutter to waste my life on a drunk like you."

Understandably Miss Steffan quit, but Sheilah ultimately did not give up on her Gatsby. They reconciled and the couple reunited at the top of Laurel Canyon, overlooking Hollywood, and he swore he would never drink again. If the setting had been a Hollywood script, it would have ended there, with the lovers who had been through hell finding happiness among the twinkling stars of Tinseltown.

In the epigraph of *The Great Gatsby*, Fitzgerald wrote, "Lover, gold-hatted, high-bouncing lover/I must have you." Sheilah—for better and worse—did have him until shortly before Christmas in 1940. He was reading the *Princeton Alumni Weekly* and eating a Hershey bar while Sheilah read a book on Beethoven. Suddenly he rose, clutched the mantle, and slumped to the floor. A devastated Sheilah ended up in Dorothy Parker's home, and the two women wept the loss. Later Parker would say over Fitzgerald's casket the words Nick said over Gatsby's: "Poor son of a bitch." For Sheilah, a mistress who mourned as much as any lawfully wedded wife, felt with Scott's passing all she had left was reminiscences of how tender were the nights.

Scottie gently told Sheilah it was best if she not go to the funeral. Although she was not included, Fitzgerald's Sheilo nevertheless grieved for him. His joint tombstone with Zelda applied not just to the Fitzgeralds, but also to Graham. It bore a quotation from *The Great Gatsby*: "So we beat on, boats against the current, borne back ceaselessly into the past." Thanks to her lover, Sheilah was not only able to make peace with her past, but to write about it as well, just as her lover had wished. She chose for her memoir's title the name of a poem from Scott, *Beloved Infidel*.

⬦⬦⬦⬦⬦⬦⬦

CHAPTER EIGHTEEN

ANY OTHER MAN

Mrs. Billy Graham

One of the most challenging jobs in the world is that of the evangelist: hand-wrestling the devil over souls. Fortunately, when it came to saving his own, the Reverend Billy Graham had his fellow crusader in Christ, his "soul mate and best friend."

Alexander Pope made the observation, "Just as the twig is bent, the tree's inclined," and Ruth McCue Bell's twig was shaped through a singular childhood. Lemuel Nelson Bell had sacrificed a promising career as a baseball pitcher to become a Presbyterian doctor in a ministry founded by the father of Pearl S. Buck. Bell delivered his daughter in his hospital in Jiangsu, China, in 1920, the year of the tiger. Her parents' Asian friends did not ignite firecrackers, as was usually customary at the birth of a baby, because of her gender. Mrs. Bell hired Wang Nai Nai to look after the baby; before the nanny's Christian conversion, she had been a procuress of "little flowers," a euphemism for child prostitutes.

Ruth's childhood fantasy was not falling in love with a handsome prince. Her nightly prayer was the Lord would allow her to be captured by bandits and killed for the sake of Jesus. Perhaps her parents harbored similar great notions, as outside the ministry walls, the country seethed with unrest as battles raged among warlords and rebels and thieves. At age twelve, Ruth decided her calling was to become an "old maid missionary" in Tibet. Before that, however, she joined her sister Rosa in Pyongyang Foreign School in what would later become North Korea. After graduation, her parents enrolled her in Wheaton College, near Chicago. She viewed Wheaton as a stopover on her way to the roof of heaven—the Himalayas.

The meeting that was to turn Ruth into the first lady of evangelism occurred when a born-again Southern farm boy, William Franklin Graham Jr., mustered his courage to ask out the girl studying in the school's library. She had no problem choosing her outfit—she only had one good homemade black dress that she spruced up with a string of dime-store pearls. She also wore lipstick, justifying her audacity, "It didn't seem to me a credit to Christ to be drab." Their first date was a Sunday afternoon production of Handel's *Messiah*. With her presence eclipsing the music, Graham was a bundle of nerves inside a bargain-basement suit. Fighting his urge, he did not dare hold her hand. Smitten, he wrote his mother, "I have just met a wonderful girl. She looks a little like you and even her voice sounds like you. This is the girl I'm going to marry." He later recalled he could see Christ coming out of her face. When Ruth returned to her room, she knelt down and prayed, "If You let me serve You with that man, I'd consider it the greatest privilege of my life."

The courting rituals of the young Billy Graham were far from conventional. He subscribed to the Latin quotation, "*mens sana in corpore sano*," (a healthy mind in a healthy body). Instead of sending Ruth bouquets of roses, he brought her bottles of vitamin pills. Instead of taking her dancing under the stars, he insisted she perform jumping-jacks to keep herself in peak shape. While other girls might

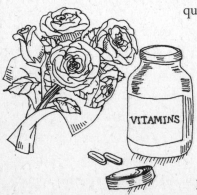

have placed a well-aimed kick at that, Ruth looked on him with eyes of adoration.

When "the preacher," as the students at Wheaton called him, brought up the topic of marriage, although in love, Ruth demurred. After she explained her commitment to her old-maid missionary goal, her suitor responded, "Woman was created to be a wife and mother." Conflicted, Ruth confided to her journal, "If I marry Bill, I marry him with my eyes open. He will be increasingly burdened for lost souls and increasingly active in the Lord's work. After the joy and satisfaction of knowing that I am his by rights, and his forever, I will slip into the background." When she told Graham she believed God would have her say yes, he used every penny of his savings to give her a yellow-gold engagement ring.

The Grahams wed on Friday, August 13, 1943, in Montreat Presbyterian Church in North Carolina. For their honeymoon, they drove to nearby Blowing Rock. When the bride awoke the following morning, she was distraught her new husband was asleep on the floor: he claimed the bed was too soft. The empty bed proved an apt metaphor for the Grahams' marriage; over the next five decades, Ruth would spend many a night alone, sleeping with Billy's tweed jacket for comfort. However, despite his world travels, the couple had five children, whose bassinets were decorated with snippets of her wedding veil. The first, born while Billy was away, was Virginia Leftwich, named after Ruth's mother, but nicknamed Gigi, Chinese for "sister." She was followed by siblings Anne, Ruth Bell, William Franklin III, and Nelson Edman. Graham spent so much time away that on an occasion when he was home, Franklin asked, "Mama, who is that in bed with you?" Ruth also took under her wing a neighbor's child, future crime writer Patricia Cornwell, after her father's desertion and her mother's nervous collapse. Without complaint, she raised her brood largely on her own, with the wifely words, "I'm assuming home responsibilities, to free you for your more important ones."

Ruth kept the home fires burning on the Graham retreat, Little Piney Cove, which sat atop a mountain in Montreat with a sweeping vista of the Swannanoa Valley. The missus had it constructed of thousands of logs salvaged from old cabins and barns. The workers were aghast at the choice of materials; they had been born in log cabins and their dream home was one of linoleum floors and department store furniture, so why a wealthier preacher's wife would opt for a rustic cabin was beyond them. While Ruth had a nesting nature, Graham's idea of comfort was a hotel room. Ruth used to joke, "When Bill gets to heaven and finds it's not like a Holiday Inn or a Marriott, he'll be back."

The home had a feel of an old sweater, with soft worn couches, braided rugs, innumerable family photographs, and lots of fireplaces. When construction had begun, Ruth determined it should have a lot of fireplaces; in their first home, they had been so poor that in lieu of one, she had wrapped a piece of red satin over a light bulb. Before the master of the house departed for India, he had ordered there be no more than two log-burning apparatuses; he returned to five. She demurely stated she had thought he had dictated no *less* than two. As she used to tell her children, "There comes a time to stop submitting and start outwitting." Over the main one in the living room, she had fashioned a mantel from a heavy slab of wood from what had once been the local lake's diving board. On it was carved a quotation from Martin Luther, "*Ein feste Burg ist unser Gott*," (a mighty fortress is our God). When heavyweight boxing champion Muhammad Ali visited, he declared, "It was the kind of house a man of God would live in."

Raised Presbyterian, Ruth did not subscribe to capitulating to a husband's authority the way Graham, raised in a Southern Baptist family, expected. She was once driving and accidentally hit the accelerator instead of the brake, sending her crashing through a fence. Nobody was injured, but in a call from California, Graham demanded she shred her driver's license. After all, his mother, Morrow, had never been behind the wheel. When she refused, her husband said, "I don't recall reading in Scripture that Sarah ever talked to Abraham like this." Ruth retorted, "Well, I don't recall reading in Scripture that Abraham ever tried to take Sarah's camel away."

When the Reverend Graham—the most incorruptible evangelist ever to raise a tent or a dollar—was asked how he became the greatest preacher in history, he explained it was because he was offering "the greatest product in the world." But his earthly power, the one who raised him up and yet kept him grounded, came from Ruth, as steadfast as her biblical namesake. Waving a bible overhead, the towering blue-eyed preacher, clad in a green gabardine suit ("God likes color"), pulled in millions, both in terms of converts and money. He met with twelve presidents in the White House, the queen in Buckingham Palace, Hollywood stars, and business moguls. The aphrodisiac of power and wealth might have corrupted, but Graham had a wife who punctured pretention. When rumors circulated in 1964 that he was considering making a presidential run, Ruth informed him, "If you run, I don't think the country will elect a divorced president."

There were many temptations beckoning to the charismatic leader, but Ruth was there as shield. He vowed never to be alone in a room or a car with any other woman than his wife. Members of his evangelic team would enter his hotel room, a vanguard army, to search it for any overly fervent fan or tabloid reporter. Once a society matron batted eyes at Graham and mentioned it was a shame he was not in politics. Ruth replied, "Maybe the Lord thought politics had its share and decided to give the ministry a break." Perhaps Mrs. Graham's most searing quip was when she was asked if she had ever considered divorce, to which she responded, "Divorce? No. Murder. Yes." Ruth kept her husband honest and likewise adhered to a staunch moral code of abiding by Christian ideals. One Christmas her good friend, country star June Carter Cash, gave Ruth a hooded full-length mink coat; Ruth promptly auctioned it for charity.

One of the times Ruth had need of prayer occurred during the years when Nelson and Franklin became the prodigal sons. After the teenaged Franklin refused to stop smoking, Ruth made him chain-smoke a whole pack. Similarly, when he would not stop pinching his sisters on a trip to a fast-food restaurant, she locked him in the trunk. Fellow patrons were aghast to witness her open the trunk and a child's arm appeared to take his bag of food. More serious was when they fell in love with fast cars, liquor, and girls and were no strangers to the local police.

In her twilight years, Ruth, with the exception of putting on a gown to accept the joint husband-and-wife Congressional Medal of Honor, spent most of her time at Little Piney Cove, in the warmth of a glowing fire. Gigi recounted how whenever her father returned home, it was like a honeymoon. Graham, age sixty-nine, confided to his biographer, "You know, we're still lovers."

Although Ruth had her way in the battle of the fireplaces and the driver's license, there was one she lost. She waged a campaign to

YOU KNOW WE'RE STILL LOVERS.

be buried near her beloved mountain home. Graham had another agenda when he decided their final resting place would be at the Billy Graham Library in Charlotte. She was appalled, referring to it as "a tourist attraction" and "a circus." She based this on the fact that the center was constructed in the shape of a large barn and silo—a nod to Graham's roots—and a life-sized mechanical Holstein, Bessie, greeted visitors. Large donors had their names inscribed on the concrete silo.

Ruth's favorite apron was purchased in Switzerland; it snapped on—an apron without strings. It was not symbolic of the woman who spent her life often alone, as Christ, Billy's congregation, and family always came first. However, it was a unique cross Ruth was glad to have borne. As she said, "I'd rather have a little of Bill than a lot of any other man."

CHAPTER NINETEEN

HERE'S TO YOU

Mrs. Jackie Robinson

T he most iconic jersey in baseball history is emblazoned with number 42: Jackie Robinson wore it when he dared dream the impossible dream. But the number not only symbolizes a pivotal moment in the civil rights movement—it represents an enduring love story.

Rachel Annetta Isum was born in Los Angeles on July 19, 1922. The city was infected with racism: a nearby theater required blacks to sit in the balcony, and an adjoining hamburger stand refused nonwhites service. Despite the bigotry surrounding her family, her parents provided stability: violin lessons, visits to the Huntington Museum, and attendance at the local Bethel African Methodist Church. An indelible childhood story from her father related how he had grown up in Chicago where his parents had lived in a rental for forty years after which time they were evicted. His message: "A key to one's own home provides the only key to security." They intended for her to get that key through education.

Following graduation from nearby Manual Arts High School, Rachel won a scholarship from a civic group and entered UCLA. At university, she not only became the first of her family to attain a degree; she also became the tireless teammate of a man whose shadow was to stretch far beyond Ebbets Field.

UCLA's few African American students congregated in the corridors of Kerckhoff Hall, where Rachel first laid eyes on Jack Robinson, a four-sport letterman. He favored crisp white shirts to showcase the color that he refused to view as a badge of shame. Rachel was interested—as were many girls—but felt she would never be the homecoming queen to the big man on campus. Nevertheless, in a nod to "hope springs eternal," she would arrive early in her beat-up Ford V8 to accidentally bump into him. They were introduced by a mutual friend, and Robinson was taken with Rachel's beauty and dignity. For their first date, Jack (as she called him) invited her to a Bruin football dinner at the Biltmore. She was eighteen years old and nervous—she had never been on a date or a guest at a hotel. Sheathed in her first black dress, purchased from the May Company basement, she danced the foxtrot throughout the night with her date—her destiny.

To their mutual dismay, in 1942, Robinson moved to Honolulu to play semipro football. Realizing Rachel was "the one," he wrote daily love letters and sent a weekly box of candy. Rachel declared her love but said she would not marry until she became a nurse and he obtained a position as a high school coach. Robinson left Hawaii two days before the bombing of Pearl Harbor, and true to his middle name (Roosevelt), he enlisted in the armed forces. The couple had a major spat when Rachel wrote she wanted to volunteer for the service and he replied she should be content in the role of his "personal draftee." Rachel returned his ring, though reconciliation followed. The war hit home when Rachel's brother, Chuck, a Tuskegee airman, was shot down over Yugoslavia and interred in a prisoner-of-war camp. Robinson, for his part, faced court-martial when he took a stand by refusing to sit at the back of the bus in

Waco, Texas. When a white MP used the epithet "nigger," Robinson threatened to "break in two" anyone who used that word.

After his honorable discharge from the military, the couple planned a life together; however, their best-laid plans—and American history—were irrevocably altered with a meeting with Branch Rickey, president of the Brooklyn Dodgers. Rickey was committed to his "noble experiment"—to put a crimp in Jim Crow, a tradition as American as baseball. He understood the man chosen for the fight would need to be the possessor of Samson-like emotional endurance, who would be able to keep his fists down and courage up. Robinson asked, "Mr. Rickey, do you want a ball player who is afraid to fight back?" "No," was the response. "I want a ballplayer with guts enough not to fight back."

Five years after their first meeting, Rachel and Jackie were finally married on February 10, 1946, in a black church in West Los Angeles, followed by a reception at the Isum home. While the contemporary connotation of a sports wife is a woman obsessed with diamond karats and being arm-candy for her celebrity spouse, Rachel was cut from a different cloth. She was Robinson's strength, the one who made sure the only time his fist was publicly clenched was when he grasped his bat. In February 1962, Robinson penned a newspaper column recounting his love. "Thinking about Rae always makes me want to remind women how important they are in making the world go round. It's an old saying—but a true one—that behind every successful man there is usually a woman who deserves much credit for his success."

In the theme song from *The Graduate*, Simon and Garfunkel sang of a Mrs. Robinson: "Look around you, all you see are sympathetic eyes." But this was not the case for her baseball counterpart of the same namesake when Robinson broke the color barrier on April

15, 1947. On that day, the player with the 42 jersey had to be the Artful Dodger of the Dodgers, ducking the fans who threw racial epithets, the balls pitched at his head, the cries of "Nigger go home." Mainstream America did not take kindly to an African American on the field; the reigning belief was blacks belonged in the seg-regated spectator section or hawking popcorn and Cracker Jack. Death threats targeted not just Robinson but also Rachel, some-thing that would cause many a trophy wife today to take off in her stilettos. On the contrary, through every game, Rachel Robinson was in the stands, back ramrod straight, feeling each taunt, every indignity. She had to remain strong for her husband, for her people, for their children: Jack Jr., Sharon, and David.

Nevertheless, there were some magic moments. Pee Wee Reese, from Kentucky, in one game placed his arm around Robinson's shoulder. He later remarked, "You can hate a man for many reasons. Color is not one of them." April 15 had historically proven a tragic date—Abraham Lincoln passed away from an assassin's bullet, and the *Titanic* submerged in the Atlantic—but because of Robinson and the forces that kept him from faltering, it was to become a piv-otal date in the timeline of tolerance.

In the late 1940s, the era before the multimillion-dollar con-tracts, the Robinsons diligently saved and realized their dream of home ownership. One of Rachel's cherished childhood memories was from when she was ten and her father held a solemn front-porch ceremony to burn the mortgage after his final payment. They purchased a house on Long Island, a neighborhood that included jazz musician Count Basie. It became their haven where the cardi-nal rule was not to talk about the negativity. There the main focus was their three MVPs, their children, who not only had to deal with prejudice but also a father who was at the eye of the racist storm.

Daughter Sharon recounted a favorite wintertime ritual in

which her father would test the backyard lake to ensure its safety for ice-skating. Although he could not swim, he would step onto its deepest part to make sure it was safe. The ritual could well serve as the metaphor for the man. In a newspaper entry, Robinson wrote, "In my trophy room at home, I've got lots of awards and medallions and certificates. Sometimes I think there should be two names on them instead of just mine. For Rae has been a full partner in anything I have done or tried to do ever since that lucky day in California when we decided to share our lives."

In 1956, the once-indomitable athlete, weakened by injuries and diabetes, announced his retirement in *Life* magazine. If the Fates' loom ran on karmic justice, Jackie and Rachel's later days would have been as tranquil as the earlier were tumultuous, but the sisters did not weave that pattern. Simon and Garfunkel had admonished, "Most of all, you've got to hide it from the kids," but the Robinsons were unable to do that with Jackie Jr. He had survived Vietnam and a heroin addiction only to die at age twenty-four in a car accident. Wracked with pain, Robinson stated, "You don't know what it's like to lose a son, find him, and lose him again. My problem was my inability to spend much time at home. I guess I had more of an effect on other people's kids than I did on my own." Rachel's training as a psychiatric nurse and her faith helped her cope with the devastating pain.

A year later, Robinson made his final public appearance at the 1972 World Series in Cincinnati. Rachel's worry was palpable as she gazed at her husband, enveloped by baseball dignitaries. The fifty-three-year-old was nearly blind, his eyes clouded by diabetes. Illness had slowed his energetic gait to a wary shuffle. His hair had turned as white as the crisp shirt he had worn when he caught Rachel Isum's eye—and heart—at UCLA. Nine days later, Robinson passed away from a massive heart attack at their Connecticut home.

Rachel's lifelong commitment to Robinson embodied Elizabeth Barrett Browning's sentiment, "And, if God willeth, I shall but love thee better after death." Months after her husband's passing, she became the keeper of his flame. In a nod to her father's words, "a key to one's home provides the only key to security," she began the Jackie Robinson Development Corporation that provides housing to low- and middle-income families.

Rachel, currently in her nineties, never lost her sense of humor. The Dodgers, not surprisingly, remain her favorite team, which became manifest when she attended a Saratoga race course. She had become friendly with Nick Zito, whose horse, Bellamy Road, was owned by George Steinbrenner, owner of the NY Yankees. As she passed its stall, the horse nipped her arm. She replied, "Fifty years later, and the Yankees are still trying to bite me."

Another anecdote shows she has also maintained her indomitable spirit, which assisted her husband in maintaining his own. On September 11, 2001, Rachel and Dorothy, the widow of Pee Wee Reese, were in New York City's Hall. They were there to choose one of five bronze sculptures commemorating when the Kentucky-born Reese had laid his arm around Robinson's shoulder. When the first airplane hit the World Trade Center a few blocks away, concerned city officials began to usher the two baseball widows to a secure location. Not one to accept preferential treatment, even though she was almost eighty at the time, Rachel walked alone to her apartment on the Upper East Side. Leonard Coleman, president of the National League, voiced his tribute, "If there was a flood, I'd get next to Rachel. She stands on higher ground than the rest of us."

A slew of posthumous honors keep the flame burning for the athlete who bore on his shoulders the weight of history: induction into the Baseball Hall of Fame, the retirement of the iconic 42, a movie named after his number—all of which allow Jackie

Robinson to steal home once more. And because Rachel was Robinson's anchor, it is fitting on April 15 to make a toast to Mrs. Robinson: "Here's to you."

HERE'S TO YOU, MRS. ROBINSON.

CHAPTER TWENTY

THE LADY AND THE TRAMP

Mrs. Charlie Chaplin

C harlie Chaplin's character of the Little Tramp became an immortal icon for his deft portrayal of man's tragicomic conflict with fate. The lonely fellow buffeted by life resiliently picked himself up again and again in the hope that the next encounter would turn out better. And what made the man behind the clown stop leaning on his famous cane and throw it heavenward was the love of his lady, whose story has slipped through the crack of time.

This woman, who embodied American royalty both through birth and marriage, was lost behind the giant shadows cast by two larger-than-life men. Her father, Nobel Laureate Eugene O'Neill, met her mother, Agnes Boulton, in a Greenwich Village bar, the Hell Hole, a name laden with foreshadowing of their life together. Their first child was son Shane and second was daughter Oona, born on May 14, 1925, in Spithead, an oceanfront home in Bermuda. Her unique name derived either from the anglicized version of Juno or the Irish word for lamb. Despite the couple's commonality of children, writing, and alcoholism, O'Neill deserted his second wife to marry his third, actress Carlotta Monterey, who could have served as role model for a Disney stepmother. Growing up without a father left Oona with a lingering emptiness, and throughout her life, she tried to cling to a father-daughter relationship.

O'Neill, notoriously tight-fisted, would have preferred the

removal of an impacted molar to coughing up child support. Nevertheless, he agreed to finance Oona's education at Manhattan's exclusive Brearley School. It was during these years she made the acquaintance of lifelong friends Gloria Vanderbilt and Carol Marcus. The girls had the common denominators of striking beauty and were, through death or desertion, fatherless. The charmed circle later became the muses of their friend Truman Capote and served as collective inspiration for the character of Holly Golightly in *Breakfast at Tiffany's.*

On a visit to her mother's Point Pleasant, New Jersey, home, Oona was introduced to Jerry, an aspiring young writer who became her first boyfriend. Their courtship was interrupted when he enlisted after Pearl Harbor, but he wrote letters of longing from overseas. Oona became the princess of the Stork Club and was crowned Debutante of the Year. Dazzled by the limelight, she turned down acceptance to Vassar for the silver screen. She traveled to California, accompanied by Carol, who was on her way to marriage with writer William Saroyan, whom she was to divorce and remarry before achieving lasting happiness as the wife of Walter Matthau.

Oona also acquired her own prominent escort, Orson Welles, as well as agent Minna Wallis, who thought she would be perfect for a role in Charlie Chaplin's film *Shadow and Substance.* Minna called the director, her personal friend, and asked him to her home to meet the fledging starlet. He agreed, though with the feeling that the daughter of O'Neill would be bleak and spend the evening searching for a ledge. Instead, in his quest for a screen heroine, he met his romantic one. After their fateful meeting, Oona had an inkling she'd landed the greatest role of her life. In a letter to Carol, the seventeen-year-old gushed she had just met Charles Chaplin and "what blue eyes he has!"

An impediment to their three-decade romance was that Chaplin's legendary screen persona, the Little Tramp, was his off-screen one as well. By the time of their meeting, Hollywood's most energetic actor/director had successfully batted those baby blues at half the female population of California. When this came out, the paparazzi were ecstatic and embarked on a feeding frenzy. But not everyone shared their joy. O'Neill was infuriated his daughter was considering marriage with a man the same age as her father, whose three former marriages had quick expiration dates, who was involved in a paternity suit, and who had left-ist leanings. He wrote that if she walked down such an aisle, he would end all future contact.

Another irate letter arrived, one from her boyfriend Jerry regarding her betrayal. Their courtship officially ended when Oona chose the Tramp over the creator of Holden Caulfield. It was perhaps in ire against Chaplin when Jerome ("Jerry") David Salinger published his later novel, *Catcher in the Rye*, with his pro-tagonist Holden Caulfield stating, "If there's one thing I hate, it's the movies. Don't even mention them to me."

In contrast to all the naysayers, Oona's mother, Agnes, was delighted with a marriage that could provide her daughter with enormous wealth, the company of the world's most famous, and drive a stake through her ex-husband's heart to boot.

A nuptial veteran, Chaplin knew how to elude the eye of the storm, and the couple fled up the coast to Carpinteria, near Santa Barbara, where they were wed in a private ceremony. Oona's stock reply when asked about their thirty-year age difference: "Charlie has made me mature and I keep him young." Such sentiments led to actress Joan Collins's observation that Mrs. Chaplin was an American geisha. Apparently Oona was more lamb than Juno.

When Chaplin carried his bride over the threshold of 1085

Summit Drive, she entered a magnificent six-acre estate on a hillside overlooking Beverly Hills, in close proximity to Pickfair, the mansion owned by Mary Pickford and Douglas Fairbanks. The couple initiated Sunday Open House where the glitterati were invited for tennis, dining, and company never guilty of Oscar Wilde's one unforgivable sin: to be boring. In Hollywood, an invitation to the Chaplins' was analogous to Queen Elizabeth summoning one for Buckingham Palace afternoon tea. Typical guests included Noel Coward, Thomas Mann, Evelyn Waugh, and Albert Einstein. Presiding over the court, the Tramp traded his cane for a scepter, and no one hung on to his words more fervently than his worshipful spouse. Soon the estate, serviced by a full-time staff of ten, included four adored children.

However, a storm cloud was gathering on the blue Hollywood horizon. During the witch hunts of the 1950s, the House Un-American Activities Committee turned its spotlight on the Little Tramp. Chaplin, who had grown up in the slums of London, championed leftist causes and was a vocal critic of the Cold War government. He insisted he was a comedian, not a communist, but Washington believed otherwise. In order to distance himself from unwelcome scrutiny, the director decided to attend the London premier of his film *Limelight* and to show his wife and children the city of his birth. On the second day of their sea voyage aboard the RMS *Queen Elizabeth*, the Chaplins were dining with pianist Arthur Rubenstein when Chaplin received a telegram stating he would be barred from reentry to America until he could prove "moral worth." Infuriated, Chaplin told Oona he was a political martyr and would never return to the United States, which, by extension, would make her a stranger to her own country. Oona agreed and refused to look back; her allegiance never faltered. She stated, "He is my world. I've never seen or lived anything else." In 1953, in solidarity, she renounced her American citizenship and became a British subject.

The Chaplins found their final home in Switzerland in an eighteenth-century, fifteen-room mansion on forty acres, ample space to raise their eight children—the Manoir de Ban. Its panoramic view encompassed Lake Geneva and the Alps. It became an intellectual watering hole with visitors such as Pablo Casals, Nikita Khrushchev, Jawaharlal Nehru, Yul Brynner, Carol and Walter Matthau, and Gloria Vanderbilt. The children were overawed by the arrival of Truman Capote, who was dressed toe to neck in red and managed to thoroughly irritate their father. They also entertained neighbors who comprised a who's who of exiled royalty, including the former king and queen of Italy. However, most evenings consisted only of the Swiss Family Chaplin, where the chatelaine would hold hands for hours with her husband while the children were attended by governess variations of Maria von Trapp. Chaplin stated, "My wife and children are more important than all the publicity in the world." In his eighties, the spotlight of publicity once again fell on the aged Tramp, who had bequeathed to the world humor and humanity.

In 1972, Chaplin broke his twenty-year exile from the United States to receive an honorary Oscar. The theater darkened to play clips of his classic films, and when the lights turned on and the audience saw their returned clown prince, he received the longest standing ovation in Oscar history, accompanied by cheers of "Charlie!" There was not a dry eye in the house when Jack Lemmon presented him with his iconic hat and cane—and the most copious tears were from Oona. Another great honor followed three years later when Queen Elizabeth II conferred knighthood on the Little Tramp and the couple became known as Sir Charles and Lady Oona.

There is a saying, "it is not wise to let too much light into the castle," and this held true for the Manoir de Ban. Although Oona seemed to have an enchanted life with her fairy-tale marriage, eight children who were the recipient of their mother's beauty and their father's fortune, a magnificent estate replete with honorary Oscar and title of Lady, sorrow still infiltrated. She had named one of her sons Eugene, but that still did not secure reconciliation with her father, who died without a deathbed forgiveness. In his will, he disinherited his only daughter and any of her issue. The O'Neill curse also claimed her brothers: Eugene Jr. committed suicide in his bathtub, and Shane plunged to his death from a window of a police station. Both of their deaths had been brought on by alcohol and drug addiction. Her mother, Agnes, died in squalor, her Pleasant Point home overrun with an army of cats who had soiled every available surface of Oona's childhood home.

The greatest of all heartaches came on Christmas Day 1977, when Chaplin passed away. Oona was in a realm beyond bereft and was known to sit holding his glove. The anguish of his passing was compounded when grave robbers stole her husband's corpse and demanded a ransom. If not paid, one of her seventeen grandchildren would be harmed. The response brought out Oona's Juno at last; she refused to give in to their demands, saying, "A body is simply a body. My husband is in heaven and in my heart." His remains were discovered in a cornfield, and the farmer on whose land it was found consecrated the spot with a cross and a cane. Oona declared the tribute more moving than her husband's official burial site.

After thirty years as the archetypal bird in a very gilded cage, Oona became a merry widow, trying to find escape through young lovers; one of these was David Bowie, another Ryan O'Neal. Gloria Vanderbilt's comment on the latter liaison: "Ryan wanted to marry Oona just to make her an O'Neal again."

Although that nuptial did not transpire, Oona did revert to being an O'Neill once more: she slid into the arms of alcohol. Increasingly inebriated, Oona became a recluse in Manoir de Ban where she watched endless films of Chaplin. In the silver screen, she was able to dwell once more in the golden days of the lady and the tramp.

CHAPTER TWENTY-ONE

NOT WITH MICE

Mrs. Pablo Picasso

No one used and abused women quite like the greatest artist of the twentieth century, Pablo Picasso. The painter eviscerated his models, their images twisted into tortured cubes on canvas. Yet harrowing as these depictions were, they pale beside the real-life dramas behind the palette. One of these handmaidens to creation helped rescue Picasso from the angst of his blue period, while simultaneously struggling to break free of the diminutive giant's shadow.

Françoise Gilot met the first man, painter Emile Mairet, who registered an impact on her life from the top of her grandmother's Parisian staircase. When she looked down, she was entranced with the image of a sixty-year-old stranger outfitted with a flowing black cape. When she asked his identity, her grandmother replied, *"Ah, mais oui, Il est un artiste!"* (Ah, but yes, he is an artist!) to which Françoise replied, *"Ah, moi aussi,"* (Me too). She was five years old.

The girl destined for a dual rendezvous with genius was born in France on November 26, 1921; her father, Emile, owned chemical firms that made colognes for Christian Dior, and her mother, Madeleine, was a watercolorist. Although Françoise persisted in her early aspirations, Emile entertained more pragmatic goals for his intellectual only child. According to his dictate, she became a law student at the Sorbonne but dropped out, explaining that with the Nazi Occupation, law no longer existed. Monsieur Gilot's parental advice before throwing her out of the house: "You'd better put on some lead-soled shoes and get down to earth. Otherwise you're in for a rude awakening."

On a May evening, Françoise and her friend Genevieve went for dinner at Le Catalan, a small bistro on the Left Bank frequented by painters and writers. At the next table were Pablo Picasso and his companion, raven-haired Dora Maar, the mistress he depicted on canvas as the weeping woman—most notably in *Guernica*—and who for many years had served as his tortured goddess. Dora had also met Picasso at a café, Les Deux Magots, where he had become mesmerized when he encountered her playing a form of Russian roulette: she was stabbing a knife between her splayed gloved fingers till she drew blood. The rest of the patrons were aghast; Picasso was delighted and took both gloves and girl home. When Dora noticed her lover was riveted on the girl with the smoky-blue eyes, hair wrapped in a green turban, she sent daggers of animosity in her direction. Picasso, born with an abundance of *cojones*, ignored his girlfriend's fury and made certain his brilliant discourse carried. He progressed from eye contact when

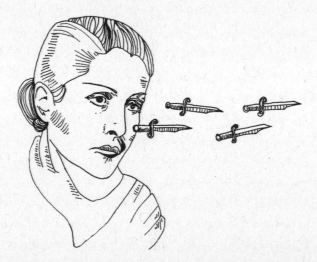

he brought over a bowl of cherries and informed Françoise she was welcome to visit his studio. Genevieve warned her against getting involved with the man who was known to be as prolific with his phallus as he was with his paintbrush, but admonition fell on deaf ears. As Françoise wrote in her memoir, an affair with Picasso was a "catastrophe I didn't want to avoid." He was the mogul of modern art, she the ingénue the randy old master was used to having for breakfast. Except Françoise was different.

Françoise's interest in the icon was not just admiration for his art but for the courage of his convictions. Unlike France's other expatriates, he did not flee with the Occupation though his "degenerate" art made him live under the scrutiny of the swastika. Françoise was familiar with the story that Picasso used to hand out postcards of his antiwar masterpiece *Guernica* to German officers. When one asked if he had made the painting, he answered, "No. You did."

Picasso was taken with Françoise's paintings, whose images of hawks symbolized the Nazi predators, and was similarly smitten with her beauty. No one was surprised when the sixty-three-year-old painter took the virginity of the twenty-one-year-old, but they were shocked when they began to live together. Dora's reaction when she was supplanted by "the schoolgirl" was a severe nervous breakdown. Her parting shot at Françoise was that her affair with Pablo would not last and that she would be "out on the ash-heap before three months had passed." Dora then turned to Picasso, "You've never loved anyone in your life. You don't know how to love."

In the beginning, Françoise was the mouse-spouse who subjugated her dreams to pleasing Picasso. She wrote of her life's great passion, "There were moments when it seemed almost a physical impossibility to go on breathing outside his presence." Another surreal byproduct of life with Picasso was sailing in a rarified circle: after a visit with Gertrude Stein, Françoise vowed never to again enter the famed salon because it meant getting terrorized by Alice B. Toklas. Simone de Beauvoir and Jean-Paul Sartre were regular visitors. And she once caught Matisse in his garden, playing hide-and-seek with his secretary.

Alas, the famed artist proved far from the perfect roommate. His gift of cherries proved an apt metaphor for their relationship—succulent on the outside, pits within. At his insistence, Françoise became pregnant with Claude and Paloma, but the day she gave birth to their daughter, he refused to allow his chauffeur to drive her to the hospital until he had been dropped off at an important conference. Françoise was also disturbed at being the target of the paparazzi; she felt if one is not a goldfish, it is not pleasant to live in an aquarium. There was also the dreaded ritual of waking up the man of the house. The artist underwent an existential blue period every morning, and it was up to "la Picasotte," as she was known to the neighborhood, to coax him from depression to studio. And while she was happy to serve as his muse, she was reluctant to pose as his model. She explained this was because she never wanted to be relegated to "the Gilot period" in the fashion of the Fernande/Eva/Olga/Marie-Thérèse/Dora Maar periods. She said, "I knew that Picasso's way of killing off one woman after the next was to make their portraits."

A further tribulation of being Madame Picasso was it was akin to being Mrs. Bluebeard, the wife of the violent nobleman from a French folktale who murders his wives who try to avoid the fate of her predecessors. The difference was that Picasso's former flames were on canvas rather than in the closet. His estranged wife, the Russian ballerina Olga Khokhlova, obsessively stalked Françoise; another mistress, Marie-Thérèse Walter, continued to make Picasso the sun around which she orbited; and Dora Maar, though born Jewish, became a nun, explaining, "After Picasso, only God."

A further nail in the coffin of their relationship
was that Picasso began to lose his sexual interest
in Françoise after a decade. With the demands
of looking after two children and her third,
Picasso, she hardly ate. He reproached her,
"You look like a broom. Do you think
brooms appeal to anyone? They don't to
me."

   After the liberation, he began a very
public affair with Geneviève Laporte—the
rude awakening that Françoise's father had
long ago warned her. She had learned the
painful lesson that Picasso's first love was
art, his second love was himself, and his
third was what women could do for him. An
oft-repeated aphorism of the great man was,
"For me there are only two kinds of women,
goddesses and doormats." Françoise was tired of
being either. She recalled of her observation, "He
always saw me from without, not within. When I left him,
it was because I knew him but he still did not know me, and I
thought, after ten years, that's a bit much."

   When she informed Picasso she was leaving, the words served
as a red flag to his ego, and he became an inflamed minotaur. He
stormed, "No one leaves a man like me!" He threatened her that as
his common-law wife, she was entitled to none of his hundreds of
millions of dollars, and the art world would be put on notice: anyone
who befriended her would be his enemy. When a taxi arrived to
usher her from the old world to the new, he uttered "*Merde.*" In
Picasso's eyes, Françoise had committed the ultimate sin; she had
dared to put her needs before his. Picasso, even in his twilight, did

not possess insight into his own emotional bankruptcy. He often compared himself to Charlie Chaplin, saying, "He's a man who, like me, has suffered a great deal at the hands of women."

Picasso's sense of entitlement can be traced to an anecdote he once shared with Françoise: "When I was a child, my mother said to me, 'If you become a soldier, you'll be a general. If you become a monk, you'll end up as the pope.' Instead, I became a painter and wound up as Picasso." The artist's canvases had always served as his visual diary, and after Françoise's departure, he painted *L'Ombre*, a gut-wrenching work that shows his black shadow hovering over her nude body in the bed they once shared.

Pablo's retaliation was, upon the death of Olga, to marry Jacqueline Roque, a young divorcée who worked in a pottery shop and became his last muse. Françoise also entered into matrimony with an artist she had known since her teens, Luc Simon. For their honeymoon, they went to Venice, where she had often begged Picasso to visit. Although the marriage included the dream vacation and daughter Aurelia, it did not last. Luc wrote to his wife's ex, "Françoise may be my wife, but she will always be yours."

After the demise of her marriage, Françoise briefly traded her paintbrush for a pen; no one lives with Pablo Picasso for a decade and does not walk away without a juicy tell-all. In 1964, in an attempt to free herself from the Spaniard's shadow, she published *Life with Picasso*. Despite its affectionate dedication—*To Pablo*—it exposed considerable cubist soiled laundry and sent a stake into the heart of his deified reputation. Although the portrait of the artist as a sexist pig was not wholly unflattering—it highlighted his brilliance as well as his blemishes—he was infuriated. He did not appreciate her references to his Bluebeard persona. He sued, unsuccessfully, and in retaliation cut off all contact with her, as well as Claude and Paloma, a vendetta that lasted to his death at age ninety-one. He felt without him, Françoise would be destroyed, and yet she was the only one of the Picasso muses to survive: Olga became a crazed hysteric, Dora Maar ended her days as a recluse surrounded by dust-encrusted relics of her time with Picasso, and Marie-Thérèse and Jacqueline both committed suicide.

After publication, Françoise felt, after surviving the Nazi Occupation and Picasso, that it was time to trade the old world for the new. She little imagined life in America would lead to another rendezvous with a colossus. In the summer of 1969, in La Jolla, California, Françoise met Dr. Jonas Salk, the famed inventor of the polio vaccine, through mutual friends. Françoise stated it was love at third sight: the first encounter was at a business lunch, the second at a dinner party, the third when Salk invited her on a tour of his oceanfront institute. When she left for her home in Manhattan, Salk followed and then trailed her when she left for Paris. Within a year, they decided to walk down the matrimony aisle, both for the second time. Unlike Picasso who basked in the press, Salk took pains to avoid its glare. Two weeks before their wedding, they went for dinner at New York's 21 Club where they ended up dining at two separate tables as they did not want to alert the journalists of their relationship. When they left for their wedding in France so Françoise's mother could be present, they flew as Mr. and Mrs. Peterson, and did the deed five days earlier than the announced date. Even Françoise's children did not know of the event until it was a *fait accompli*. Upon their return to La Jolla, Françoise settled into Salk's contemporary wood frame home whose windows showcased a spectacular view of the Pacific. Comparing her two titian husbands, Françoise stated, "In Jonas Salk, the man is equal to the artist. Picasso, the man, was not on the same level as Picasso, the artist." Unquestionably the good doctor was easier to live with. In her twenty-five-year marriage to Salk, Françoise found the joy that had once proved unattainable as the wife of Picasso.

Intrigued by the story of the woman who had been the love interest of two of the men profiled on *Time* magazine's most influential men of the twentieth century, Larry King interviewed the possessor of the singular romantic résumé, curious if she possessed more than normal pheromones. When he inquired what it was like to have captured Picasso and Salk, Françoise responded, "I'd like to think they had me. Lions mate with lions, not with mice."

CHAPTER TWENTY-TWO

CAMP BETTY

Mrs. Gerald Ford

T he name Ford conjures the product that rolls off Detroit's assembly lines, the Californian addiction center, and the Omaha-born American president. However, there was a Ford whose bouffant hair and prim exterior belied an interior far from docile. Despite whatever storm she was at the center, she was always Gerald's first lady.

While Germaine Greer spearheaded the women's liberation movement, another who contributed to its fight (though no burning bras were involved) was a free spirit from the start. Elizabeth "Betty" Ann Bloomer was born on April 8, 1918, in Chicago but was raised in Grand Rapids, Michigan. Her two brothers were considerably older; as her mother phrased it, Betty "popped out of a bottle of champagne." As a child, she was so overweight Mrs. Bloomer hung a sign on her back: PLEASE DO NOT FEED THIS CHILD. Her idyllic youth was shattered upon her father's accidental death from carbon monoxide poisoning while repairing his car. As an outlet, she took to dance, and her talent  was such that at age twenty she was offered tuition by idol Martha Graham. Ecstatic, she relocated to Greenwich Village where she mixed with liberal artists who helped form the broad-minded views that were to become her trademark. Although she performed at Carnegie Hall, she was devastated when she failed to secure a permanent placement in the famed troupe.

Within a year, Betty Bloomer married an old school sweetheart, William Warren, who, like her father, was a traveling salesman. When she realized life was better when he traveled, she decided to part ways. However, she stayed to support her husband during his two-year near-fatal medical ordeal. Thrust into the role of breadwinner (she worked on a production line in a frozen-food factory), she honed her passion for women's equality when she experienced gender discrimination in the workplace. After five years, when Warren recovered, liberation followed. Betty eschewed alimony, feeling it unjust to take from a man one no longer loved.

Through a mutual friend, Betty met, as she stated in her memoir, *The Times of My Life*, "probably the most eligible bachelor in Grand Rapids," the one she wanted to dance with for the rest of her days. She said of Gerald Ford's 1948 proposal, "He's a very shy man and he really didn't tell me he loved me. He just told me he'd like to marry me—I took him up on it immediately."

Ford seemed a relief after alcoholic Warren. But Betty was to discover that he too had a secret vice—a monomania of all things political. Ford was concerned his marriage to a divorced ex-dancer would alienate voters; however, love triumphed and the nuptials took place on October 15, 1948, at Grace Episcopal Church. Betty looked ravishing while Gerald walked the aisle in dusty brown shoes that did not match his suit. The ceremony had been scheduled for a Friday so that the groom's plans to go to a Northwestern-Michigan football game the following day would not be interrupted. (He had played center for Michigan.) He made a late appearance—not from cold feet but because he was out campaigning. They spent their two-day honeymoon in Ann Arbor attending Republican Party rallies.

Two weeks after she became Mrs. Ford, Ford was elected to Congress, and they relocated to the capital for a two-year stay that stretched to twenty-eight. Betty settled into the time-honored role of a Washington wife and became the mother of three sons (Michael, John, and Steven) and daughter Susan Elizabeth. As spouse of an up-and-coming politician and mother of four, Betty's life appeared cut from the cloth of a 1950s sitcom, but there were cracks. She had long, lonely periods when her husband was absent working with his congressional district in Michigan, which cast her in the role of single mother. In addition, she felt inferior to the Washington wives who carried a BA after their name while she only carried a MRS before her own. Nevertheless, she threw herself into her role, and while her husband was absent with leave, she spent the early years tripping over bags of marbles, burying pet alligators, visiting the emergency room, and measuring out life in pablum spoons. But by 1965, she could be the bionic woman no longer and began to take comfort in the bottle and with painkillers.

Shakespeare wrote in *Twelfth Night*, "Some are born great, some achieve greatness, and some have greatness thrust upon them." Betty always believed this to be true of her husband, but events in American history were to push her private sentiment onto the world stage. In 1973, when Vice President Spiro Agnew was removed from office after he pled no contest to tax evasion, Nixon filled the vacancy with the appointment of Gerald Ford. The move was as great a shock to Betty as to the rest of the country. She was embarking in uncharted waters but knew she did not want to sail in the same direction as predecessor Judy Agnew, also the mother of four. The ousted Second Lady had stated, "I don't take stands on anything. I stay out of the political end of it. When people ask me what I majored in, I proudly tell them, 'I majored in marriage.'" Betty may very well have felt the same.

Less than a year later, with Nixon's own resignation from the Watergate scandal, Gerald Ford was sworn in as the only chief executive in American history who had not been elected either as vice president or president. During the inaugural address, Betty held the bible on which her husband laid his hand to repeat the presidential oath. Ford said in his first public words he was "indebted to no man and only to one woman." Wearing a simple blue dress, Betty remained silent; her Living Bible decreed, "Put a muzzle on your mouth." It did not take long for her to remove her muzzle.

While Ford's task was clear—to heal a nation torn asunder by Vietnam and Watergate—for his First Lady, the waters were far murkier. Within twenty-four hours, the erstwhile housewife found herself as hostess at a state banquet for King Hussein of Jordan. She said, "I was an ordinary woman who was called on stage at an extraordinary time. I was no different once I became First Lady than I had been before. But, through an accident of history, I had become interesting to people." And interesting she proved.

In the White House, Betty tried out disco steps and shimmied to the bump at dinner dances. On a trip to China with her husband, she enchanted by kicking off her shoes and dancing in her stockinged feet at a Beijing school. She also provided a field day for the press when she uttered the most unladylike comments in First Lady history. On *60 Minutes* in 1975, her bouffant hair perfectly coiffed, she declared that smoking marijuana was like "having a first beer." When questioned how she would react if she discovered her teenaged daughter was having an affair: "Not surprised." Her response to how often the president and she had sex: "As often as possible." Ford's reaction: "Honey, you just lost me twenty million votes." She was also open about the fact the Fords not only shared a bedroom but they even had the section separating the First Lady's and president's compartments on Air Force One torn down. Presidential advisors suggested the president rein in his outspoken spouse, but he declined, commenting she was fully entitled to her own views. Critics, however, were aghast and one wrote, "The First Lady—no lady."

Betty brought a relaxed touch to her stately address. After she had moved in, she inquired why the staff never returned a greeting and was informed Richard and Pat Nixon had preferred they take a stance of silence. Under Gerald and Betty, the president and the butler compared golf scores and the staff were treated like members of their extended family. Betty eschewed formality and insisted she never be call Mrs. Ford—she would only answer to Betty. In another instance of a lighthearted White House, when Ford remarked she was too thin, she borrowed a skeleton from a hospital, dressed it in her hat and coat, and sat it in a bedroom chair.

First Ladies have to choose their battles, and Betty's foremost one was equal rights for women. It is not known whether she employed the strategies of Lysistrata, who organized the women of ancient Greece to withhold sex until they ended the Peloponnesian War, but she was successful in getting her husband to appoint a woman as ambassador to Britain. She also persuaded her husband to bestow on Martha Graham the Medal of Freedom. Still, even pillow talk did not succeed in the appointment of a woman to the Supreme Court nor one as vice presidential running mate, issues for which she was a fierce advocate. Another of her hot-button topics was abortion, on which she stated, "Having babies is a blessing, not a duty." Once a lethal silence had enveloped the subject of breast cancer like a London fog; however, after seven weeks in the White House, she underwent a full mastectomy. She went public with her health issue and there resulted an unprecedented number of mammograms and mastectomies by other American women. Upon her return from the hospital, the White House staff lined up with signs: "We love you, Betty." Perhaps the American public was beginning to as well. Her Midwestern pluck made her an intrepid woman-in-chief.

During Ford's bid for a second term, campaign buttons urged voters to "reelect Betty's husband." The First Lady often gave speeches with smiling grace. She joked that if her husband lost, she would get him back to herself, "so I win either way." When Jimmy Carter proved the victor, Betty blissfully contemplated getting back both life and husband. Before they left the White House, she took a moment to climb on a cabinet table, beautifully set, and dance.

After leaving the White House, Betty became another emblem of courage. Ironically, the famously forthright First Lady had been keeping a secret, even from herself. Over the years, alcohol and pain medicine had taken control. As the dual demons usurped her life, her loved ones staged an intervention and after initial denial—wherein she called them "a bunch of monsters"—she entered the Long Beach Naval Hospital. Alongside sailors and officers, she underwent a grim detoxification.

The Betty Ford Center was a direct result of Mrs. Ford's victory over her addiction. The industrialist-tire heir and recovering alcoholic, Leonard Firestone, organized its funding and Betty served as chairwoman, working tirelessly till age eighty-seven to convince America addiction was not a moral failing but a disease like any other, one that deserved compassion rather than condemnation. She welcomed new patients with the words, "Hello, my name's Betty Ford, and I'm an addict and an alcoholic." Celebrities such as Elizabeth Taylor, Liza Minnelli, Mary Tyler Moore, Mickey Mantle, Robert Mitchum, Tony Curtis, and Johnny Cash as well as 90,000 noncelebrities have adopted its motto of "clean and serene." Betty's favorite quip to Ford was he was only an ex-president but she was an active one. Mrs. Ford was a woman with a voice who once told a critic, "Being ladylike does not require silence."

In her nineties, Mrs. Ford asked her children, "When are you going to let me go be with my boyfriend?" On July 8, 2011, she joined her dancing partner. Thousands mourned her passing, regardless of political affiliation. Because of her indomitable spirit, at the end everyone was a member of Camp Betty.

<<<<<<<<<>>>>>>>>

CHAPTER TWENTY-THREE

THE POLISH RIDER

Mrs. Aldous Huxley

I n the nightscape of *Brave New World*, sex is easy but love is banned. The goal is pleasure without moral repercussions. This alienation mirrored Aldous Huxley's own zip-locked soul; however, just as John the Noble Savage was introduced to love by Lenina Crowne, the British author connected with his Italian soul mate.

The Archera family lived in Turin, Italy, across the street from where Holocaust survivor and writer Levi Primo jumped from his third-floor apartment. It was Laura Archera's first association with literary immortality. She was born on November 2, 1911, daughter of Felice, a stockbroker, and Fede, a homemaker, younger sister of Rossana. Tragedy touched the family with the scarlet fever death of the youngest child, Franco, followed by the passing of Fede four years later. To help his daughter cope with tragedy, Felice suggested she take violin lessons. She proved a prodigy and studied in Berlin, Paris, and Rome and as a teenager gave recitals across Europe, once before Queen Marie José of Italy. When she was twenty, her father gave her a 1705 Guarnerius violin that she played in 1937 at her American debut at Carnegie Hall. In 1940, she was about to board a liner to Turin when her father, whose mother was Jewish, under scrutiny by the fascists, telegraphed her not to return. Laura was permitted to remain in the country as an enemy alien and joined the Los Angeles Philharmonic.

For the next five years, her significant other was Mozart until she met Virginia "Ginny" Pfeiffer, who altered the trajectory of her life. Ginny invited her to live in her Hollywood Hills home, perched below the first *O* of the fabled Hollywood sign. Her older sister Pauline, a Paris-based *Vogue* editor, had been the second Mrs. Hemingway after she had weaned Ernest from his first. Ginny's love made Laura no longer feel an enemy alien; she remarked of these years she had "never been treated so well." To spend more time with Ginny, Laura abandoned the career of a virtuoso whose demands she called "soul-sucking" and began to work as a film editor for MGM. There she latched on to the idea of making a documentary about the Palio, the centuries-old annual horse race held in the Tuscan town of Siena in honor of the Virgin. John Huston told her that the best chance of actualizing her celluloid dream was to convince Aldous Huxley to write a script as he had already successfully produced the screen versions of *Pride and Prejudice*, *Jane Eyre*, and *Alice in Wonderland*. However, nothing came of the latter as Walt Disney had abandoned the project, admitting he could only "understand every third word."

Laura wrote the famed author of *Brave New World*, who was living in the little town of Wrightwood in the California desert. After an agonizing wait, Laura called what she thought was his private phone line, unaware the number belonged to the local post office. When the person who answered asked if it was an emergency, she replied in the affirmative, and as she wrote in her 1968 memoir, *This Timeless Moment*, "It was on the long-distance phone that I heard for the first time that sensuous and beautifully modulated voice." Huxley invited her to visit the next day; although her dream picture never materialized, it was a meeting that would produce the backstory behind *This Timeless Moment*. The memoir, as well as a paean to her husband, offers a set of what she called recipes for getting through life's many difficulties.

These include punching a tetherball, imaging one's own funeral, and dancing in the nude.

Over lunch, Laura shared her vision on the Palio, unaware Huxley and his wife, Maria, who had lived for years in Italy, were knowledgeable about the event. The conversation swirled into innumerable tangents born of the rapport among Belgian Maria, British Huxley, and Italian Laura. Another commonality later became manifest: Maria, like Laura, was "omnifutuent" (Huxley's word for bisexual). For a decade, husband and wife had partaken in an affair with Mary Hutchinson, wife of writer Clive Bell. "Aldous," Maria wrote to Mary, "has just come into my bed & he smelt so strongly of you still that it made one giddy." Laura returned to Los Angeles eager to share with Ginny her meeting with the author whose name carried the mystique of his eminent family: his grandfather Thomas Huxley was known as "Charles Darwin's bulldog," and his great-uncle Matthew Arnold was the famed poet of "Dover Beach."

Ginny had been instrumental in changing Laura's career from music to film, and she did the same when stricken with cancer. After the Mayo Clinic delivered its terminal prognosis that Pfeiffer had a year to live, Laura refused to acknowledge the death sentence and abandoned her film career to plunge into alternative medicine. She started a dietary regime that eschewed eating meat and embraced what later was termed new-age healing. She practiced her methods on Ginny, and when the cancer went into remission, Laura continued in this field, realizing she had discovered her vocation.

In 1955, Maria succumbed to cancer and Huxley, emotionally adrift without his wife of thirty-five years, began inviting Laura to his Los Angeles home for dinner, over which they would discuss everything under the sun. On a January evening in 1956, Huxley gave Laura a smile that she was to refer to as "luminous." It was on that night he asked her, in a proposal that did not rank high on the romantic Richter scale, "Have you ever been tempted by marriage?" Apparently the wordsmith saved his best for his writing, but the request was followed by his smile, of which she wrote, "All the poems in his library could not have described his smile."

If popping the question was mundane, the venue Huxley chose for their 1956 wedding further lowered the bar. He opted for the Drive-in Wedding Chapel in Yuma, Arizona. This may have been his attempt to distance himself from his über British Victorian upbringing. Rather than exercise veto power, the idea appealed to the future Mrs. Huxley's anti-ritualistic streak. Upon arrival at the clapboard shack, Laura changed into her canary-yellow suit, which Ginny and she had literally removed from a store mannequin when the saleslady refused to comply. When she returned, she sat beside Huxley on a sofa that had seen better days. It was then the bearer of the yellow suit had misgivings: she was fiercely independent and was not willing to lose herself in Huxley's giant shadow as Maria had done.

However, it was not of this apprehension she spoke. She merely said she also loved another. To this, Huxley replied, "It would be awful if you didn't." Laura's checkered sexual history never fazed him. Of these escapades, he merely informed her that he once thought of writing her biography, "but the best parts would be unprintable." She never had to worry about Huxley's jealousy; she wrote, "Jealousy has a thousand overt and hidden faces—not one I had ever seen in Aldous." The purple fluorescent light on the ceiling made the assembled party (the ladies' room attendant stood in for the required witness) cast its glow on the dusty artificial flowers. When the minister asked for the ring, Laura panicked until she remembered one in her traveling bag that she had picked up at a five-and-ten store in Europe. She retrieved her luggage and spilt its contents on the floor, rummaging for it.

Afterward, they went to dinner at a nearby diner when two

reporters, perhaps alerted by the wedding witness, descended. The news was on the radio within the hour. Worried he had neglected to inform his son Matthew of his forthcoming nuptial, the groom quickly dashed off a letter. He explained his speedy remarriage was not an affront to Maria's memory, "but tenderness is the best memorial to tenderness." The six-foot-four-inch Huxley said he married the petite Laura for her fragile beauty and kingfisher mind. As he was wont to tell his wife, "You have the motor of a Thunderbird in the body of a Topolino." (Literally "little mouse," the name of the smallest car in Italy.)

The Huxleys purchased an estate on Mulholland Drive, five hundred yards up the hill from the Pfeiffer home. Virginia had become one of California's first single parents when she adopted the eighteen-month-old Paula and infant Juanito. Laura chose to remain childless. When asked the reason, she would reply, "I never thought I was old enough to have one." In lieu of maternal obligations, Laura and Aldous hosted a tradition of Saturday luncheons whose guests included members of the intellectual and avant-garde of the 1950s: Christopher Isherwood, Igor Stravinsky, T. S. Eliot, D. H. Lawrence, Timothy Leary, Ray Bradbury, Allen Ginsberg, Ram

Dass, and Charlie Chaplin among its lengthy list. In later years, the artist George DiCaprio would bring his son Leonardo over to play hide-and-seek in the extensive garden with Ginny's children. Michael and Cynthia Horowitz gave their daughter Winona (Ryder) the middle name of Laura in tribute. Timothy Leary served as the future star's godfather.

When the Huxleys were not engaged with entertaining, careers, and travel, Aldous created another script of *Alice in Wonderland*— paying particular attention to the role of the hookah-smoking caterpillar. He experimented with psychedelic drugs in order to obtain the knowledge that he always sought. His experiments formed the basis of his book *The Doors of Perception*, the title an allusion to the William Blake quotation, "If the doors of perception were cleansed, everything would appear to me as it is, infinite." In a nod to Huxley's role as the vanguard of the psychedelic '60s, Jim Morrison named his group *The Doors*. Huxley's image was included on the cover of The Beatles' *Sgt. Pepper's Lonely Hearts Club Band*. On one occasion, Laura took LSD with him while listening to Bach, wherein they experienced "aesthetic revelations."

In the early 1960s, two back-to-back tragedies knocked on the door whose patio looked out on the world-famous sign. The first occurred when Ginny left for a weekend and Laura and Huxley were at her home feeding her cat Edgarallancat. Laura soon became aware of scorching heat from the canyon and became immobilized when she realized both the Pfeiffer home and her own would imminently be engulfed in flames. She lost precious moments in shock; Hemingway letters and all other contents were consumed in the fire. She roused herself to hurry home where she salvaged her hundreds-year-old violin and a cherished Chinese dancing lady of the Tang Dynasty—the companion piece was destroyed in Ginny's home. The Huxleys were to rebuild a white airy home close to their original; in a nod to "if the walls could talk," the home is currently the residence of actor Channing Tatum.

Two years later, Huxley, in the last stages of cancer, passed away on November 22, 1963, the same day as fellow British writer C. S. Lewis. However, their deaths were overshadowed by the assassination of President Kennedy. Huxley's last request was for Laura to inject him with a final dose of LSD. As she kept her bedside vigil, she took from the wall a Rembrandt reproduction of a man astride his horse, Huxley's wishful alter ego who embodied a life of adventure and daring. Showing it to her dying husband was Laura's message he had lived a life, in its fashion, as daring as *The Polish Rider*.

◇◇◇◇◇◇◇◇◇

CHAPTER TWENTY-FOUR

AND GOD WALKED IN

Mrs. C. S. Lewis

I n a nod to the idea that dreams do not just have to be for sleeping, a lonely Oxford don, C. S. Lewis, achieved autumnal romance with a woman whose early life was bereft of joy, in a story as magical as the one the Pevensie children discovered behind the wardrobe.

Parents who christen their children after values (Hope, Faith, Chastity) often desire their offspring embody these traits, but this did not come to pass with Joy Davidman, born in the Bronx in 1915 to Polish-Ukrainian immigrants. The word used in conjunction with Joy was "prodigy"; at age eight, a bedtime story was H. G. Wells's *The Outline of History* (which caused her to declare herself an atheist), and more lighthearted fare were books of fantasy. Her IQ tests nearly broke the charts. As a sickly teenager who suffered from scarlet fever and anemia, Joy spent her days reading philosophy, history, and literature and completed her master's from Columbia before she was twenty.

Her firecracker academic momentum dissipated during the Depression when studying at Hunter College she witnessed an incident that shattered her belief in the American Dream: a starving orphan jumped to her death from one of the school's buildings. The horror haunted Davidman for years and led to her joining the Communist Party, which she believed was the solution for society's ills. Another form of catharsis to assuage her chronic angst was writing, and she became the recipient (along with Robert Frost) of a $1,000 award for her collection of poems, *Letter to a Comrade*. As word of her talent spread, she was hired by Metro-Goldwyn-Mayer and spent six months writing scripts before, unimpressed with Hollywood, she returned to New York City as an editor for *The New Masses*.

The Communist Party doubled as matchmaker when Joy fell in love with fellow left-wing writer William Lindsay Gresham, who volunteered as a medic during the Spanish Civil War. When he returned, after a stay in a tuberculosis ward and a suicide attempt, they were married in 1942. Gresham had become disillusioned with communism during his experiences in Spain and influenced his wife to leave the party after the births of sons David and Douglas. Joy was content with her role as homemaker, and financial success followed with the publication of Gresham's novel *Nightmare Alley* (dedicated to Joy Davidman) as well as a substantial sum from Twentieth Century Fox for its movie rights (which starred Tyrone Power). The family fully abandoned their earlier communist tendencies by moving to a mansion in the New York countryside. To replace their lost faith in Marxism and her lack of fulfillment with Judaism, they became members of Pleasant Plains Presbyterian Church. She eagerly embraced Christianity, but as with communism, it did not provide Gresham with the elixir for what he wanted or from what he was running. The Southern alcoholic could have stepped from the pages of Faulkner or Tennessee Williams, his depressive demons spawned from his experiences in the war, in the tuberculosis ward, and in hidden recesses of his interior nightmare alley. Deeply troubled, he dabbled in Buddhism, Dianetics, tarot cards, and *I Ching*. Joy was tolerant of these but not so much when he dabbled in extramarital affairs and chronic drinking.

Over the years, the bottle took its toll and the money dried out, which fueled domestic abuse. For diversion, Gresham took to firing rifles into the ceiling. *Nightmare Alley* soon became an apt metaphor for their lives. One afternoon in 1946, Gresham called from Manhattan to say he was having a nervous breakdown and did not know if he would ever return home. When Joy hung up, she felt the world was a hammer, she its anvil. Suddenly, a ray of light appeared at that very moment out of nowhere. "There was a person with me, a person so real that all my previous life was a mere shadow-play. God came in."

With her renewed belief in Jesus and her love of fantasy novels, Joy immersed herself in the works of British writer C. S. "Jack" Lewis with whom she began a two-year correspondence. She was delighted the Oxford don and author of *The Chronicles of Narnia*, who had appeared on the cover of *Time*, took time to correspond. She felt him a kindred spirit when he wrote, "I believe in Christianity as I believe that the sun has risen—not only because I see it, but because by it I see everything else." The letters with the British postage soon were the only rays of light as her marriage continued to spiral into a yawning abyss.

At the breaking point, when her cousin Renée Rodriguez moved into the Gresham home as an escape from her own tempestuous marriage, Joy left her to care for her sons and fled to London and then eventually to Oxford. A lifelong Anglophile, she adored the ancient town awash in a sea of history and felt at home at last. Her first meeting with Lewis occurred at the East Gate Hotel, where he autographed her copy of his book *The Great Divorce*. Lewis was a crusty, middle-aged academic, a devout Anglican more comfortable in discoursing with God than the opposite sex. He had spent his

years following the same comforting pattern, a pipe-smoking bachelor who lived in a world of theology and fantasy.

All that was to change upon his introduction to the brash New
Yorker. After several luncheons with Lewis and his brother Warren,
the latter noted in his diary that a "rapid friendship" had developed between Jack and Joy, whom he described as, "A Christian
convert of Jewish race, quite extraordinarily uninhibited." She spent
Christmas at their home, the Kilns, and her visit exceeded her wildest expectations. However, news from home immediately cast her
back to the shadow-land. Gresham wrote he was involved in an
affair with Renée and wanted a divorce; Joy, afraid to lose her old
world without possessing another, returned to the States. Upon her
arrival, Gresham magnanimously suggested that Joy, Renée, and he
live in a bizarre ménage à trois.

Joy's response was to move lock, stock, poetry books, and sons
to England. However, when Gresham, whose parenting skills
amounted to "out of sight, out of mind," failed to send child support, Joy became destitute. Lewis, a knight clad in tweed, came
to her rescue and found her a flat near the Kilns and graciously
agreed to pay her bills. Joy fell in love, but the feeling was not
reciprocated by the confirmed bachelor. He merely regarded her
as an agreeable intellectual companion, one who shared his love of
God, literature, and whiskey. Warren wrote, "For Jack the attraction
was undoubtedly intellectual. Joy was the only woman whom he
had met who had a brain which matched his own in suppleness, in
width of interest, and in analytical grasp, and above all in humor
and a sense of fun."

The idyll was threatened when the British government, regardless of her feeling England was her spiritual homeland, declined
to renew Joy's visa, owing to her communist past. Lewis was hor-
rified and did not want to lose his platonic soul mate, especially

as her return home would entail the wrath of a brutish husband and possible persecution by the House Un-American Activities Committee. Although it jarred his ethical code, he decided to enter into a civil marriage so she could remain in the country, informing the Inklings, a group of his male literary friends (which included J. R. R. Tolkien) who met weekly at a pub, the Eagle and Child, "the marriage was a matter of pure friendship and expediency." His circle judged Joy as the royal family did Wallis Simpson: a Jewish convert to Christianity, divorcée, and gold-digger New Yorker. Nevertheless, the don felt it his Christian duty to tweak the law, and Joy and Jack married in a civil ceremony in St. Giles, Oxford, in 1956. They became husband and wife in name only—until God walked in, though in a guise far from recognizable. Joy was in her kitchen when she tripped over a telephone wire and fell in agony to the floor, which resulted in breaking her left leg. At the Churchill Hospital, it was determined the injury had stemmed from incurable bone cancer, and a malignant breast tumor was also detected. It took this tragedy to make Lewis realize he was desperately in love. Utterly distraught, he called Father Peter Bide, an Anglican priest, to Joy's bedside to pray for her cure, bestow religious wedding vows, and perform a last rite. On March 21, 1957, in the presence of Warren Lewis, the priest administered the sacrament of marriage and the dying Joy Davidman Gresham became Joy Lewis.

Miraculously, the cancer went into remission, and Joy and her sons moved in with Lewis and Warren at the Kilns. The connection between the two may not have begun with a thunderclap, but it ended with an electrical storm. The couple went on a honeymoon to the Lewises' native Ireland followed by a trip to Greece. Lewis remarked to his friend, "I never expected to have, in my sixties, the happiness that passed me by in my twenties." Joy was instrumental in helping with his writing, and in appreciation and love,

she once again became the recipient of a husband's book dedication, this time in *Till We Have Faces*. The relationship of the couple was destined to last a decade: they had begun corresponding in 1950, and ten years later, the cancer returned, this time inoperable. Joy Lewis passed away on July 13, 1960. Lewis honored her wish that she be cremated and her ashes spread over an Oxford rose garden, thereby becoming one with her spiritual homeland. Lewis raised her sons as if they had been his own: the brothers eventually became estranged from one another, perhaps because Douglas embraced the Christian faith while David turned to Orthodox Judaism.

Upon her death, Lewis was paralyzed with grief and, as in his teens, suffered a crisis of faith. He felt God was the White Witch, casting his Narnia into an endless winter, one sans any Christmas. He penned *A Grief Observed* as an outlet for his anguish, writing, "She was my daughter and my mother, my pupil and my teacher, my subject and my sovereign, and always, holding all these in solution, my trusty comrade, friend, shipmate, fellow-soldier. My mistress, but at the same time all that any man friend (and I have good ones) has ever been to me. Perhaps more." And for those who knew their story, much more. Lewis eventually made peace once again with his God, realizing at least they had been permitted a time free from the shadow-land. Love had served as the magician who had unlocked the wardrobe that allowed a lonely man and woman to enter a magical kingdom.

Three years later, Lewis passed away on November 22, 1963,

his American obituary obscured by the avalanche of coverage of another far more famous Jack, gunned down on the same fateful day in Dallas. Warren chose for his brother's epitaph a quotation that their beloved mother had hung in their childhood home: "Men must endure their going hence." The line from *King Lear* was apropos because like Lear, Lewis was not able to recognize truth till almost the end.

C. S. Lewis was able to discern the face of love, one he had once only understood in his books, when, in a guise far from recognizable, God walked in.

CHAPTER TWENTY-FIVE

A BRIEF HISTORY OF LOVE

Mrs. Stephen Hawking

I n this unique story, a great woman stood behind a man whose brilliant mind was imprisoned in a paralyzed body. Had it not been for her, the world would not know Stephen Hawking, the twentieth-century Isaac Newton.

Jane Wilde was seven years old when she first laid eyes on Stephen Hawking during the time they were students at one of the world's oldest schools—founded in 948 AD, St. Albans in Hertfordshire, England. Although they never spoke, they both suffered the pangs of arriving at school in cars of inferior model to their classmates': Jane in a prewar jalopy and Stephen in a makeshift London taxi. The four Hawking children—including siblings Mary, Edward, and Philippa—took refuge on the floor of their vehicle to escape detection by far-from-accepting peers.

Jane first interacted with the budding physicist at a 1963 New Year's Eve party when he was a Cambridge student. She wore a dark-green synthetic silk outfit and bouffant hair, attempting through external bravado to camouflage extreme shyness. There she glimpsed Hawking, leaning against the wall, dressed in evening geek couture of black velvet jacket and red velvet bow tie, replete with large black glasses. She was overjoyed when a few days later, she received a card inviting her to his twenty-first birthday, which was coincidentally exactly three hundred years after the death of Galileo. While the Italian scientist had to fight against the Roman

Inquisition, the British one was pitted against motor neuron disease (more familiarly known as Lou Gehrig's disease), which carried with it a life expectancy of two years. When Jane discovered his dire prognosis, she nevertheless continued to accept get-togethers: theater at the Old Vic, a May Ball in Cambridge.

The following summer in Spain, although the trip was a long-anticipated dream, Jane was miserable as she missed Hawking and tearfully thought of his blue-gray eyes and dimpled smile. She understood because of his illness a relationship would be precarious, heartbreaking, and fleeting. However, she felt a brief time with him would be preferable to none at all. She further reasoned that, with the threat of nuclear war hovering, all life was tenuous.

When she returned to London and a reunion with Hawking, his physical condition had deteriorated and his usual brilliant discourse was stifled—he was drowning in a tsunami of depression. His bleakness manifested itself in endless hours of listening to Wagnerian opera played at full volume. She recalled in her

memoir, *Traveling to Infinity*, "A quick fling was probably all he could envisage and that was not what I, in my innocence and in the still puritanical climate of the early Sixties, dared contemplate." Hawking, an atheist, respected Jane's devout Christian mores, and they announced their engagement. Dr. Hawking, Stephen's father, bluntly informed her that as his son's life was to be short, as would his "ability to fulfill a marital relationship," she should have children as quickly as possible.

Similarly, Mr. Wilde made his future son-in-law promise he would not interfere with his daughter's pursuit of a degree. A chaplain married Stephen and Jane on July 14, 1965, in the chapel of Trinity Hall. Standing at the altar, manifested by the groom's cane, was what was to be the third party in their relationship—his debilitating affliction.

In his new role as husband, Hawking was distracted from self-pity and busied himself with obtaining a career that necessitated finishing his PhD. He ended up enjoying his thesis to such an extent he refused to call it work, stating, "Someone once said scientists and prostitutes get paid for doing what they enjoy." Jane, for her part, abandoned her aspiration of a career in the Diplomatic Service. Her motto became St. Albans' own: *non nobis nati* (born not for ourselves).

The Hawking marriage began with Andrew Marvell's "Though we can't make time stand still/At least we can make him run." And what made this happen was the 1967 birth of Robert George. Jane fought off the pangs of labor by her memorization of Brahms' double concerto for violin and cello, a birthday recording from her husband. The new parents delighted in their firstborn, but Jane experienced frustration: when she played with her baby, her conscience nagged that she should work on her thesis. When she did so, maternal instinct reproached she attend her infant. A further impediment was that as Hawking's speed of movement slowed, Robert's accelerated. Despite the fullness of her plate, daughter Lucy arrived three years later. A daily walk involved holding newborn in a sling, pushing husband's wheelchair, toddler dashing ahead. Hawking, the object of stares, once more must have felt like taking refuge on the floor of a London taxi. However, the cerebral couple took solace that he was surviving far longer than his dire prognosis had prophesied.

Because Jane kept the Cambridge fires burning, Hawking was free to engage in the pursuit of the cosmos. His eureka moment arrived a few days after his daughter's birth when he discovered that a black hole—a collapsed star—leaks energy and fades to nothing. He declared of his epiphany, "There is nothing like the eureka moment of discovering something nobody knew before. I won't compare it to sex…but it lasts longer." The theory led to his election of the Lucasian Chair of Mathematics at Cambridge University, a position once held by Isaac Newton. The year 1977 proved a watershed one: Hawking's prestigious appointment, birth of son Timothy Stephen, and Jane's meeting with a man that would result in a big bang.

What had begun as a 1960s love affair a decade later had segued into a mere charade of marital bliss. After the birth of their third child, Hawking's theory became a metaphor for Jane: a black hole fading to nothing. She found her role as a wife had dissolved into one of nurse, her function "maternal rather than marital." To add to her feelings of being asexual, as Hawking's work led to ever-stratified stratospheres, his interaction with his family dwindled. Jane was angered that while she was running ragged, he just sat there, head in hands, like Rodin's *The Thinker*. Ironically, the man who strived to "know the mind of God" was oblivious to his wife's pain. She could understand why Einstein's first wife had cited phys-ics as the correspondent in her divorce. In a lec-ture, Hawking had once quipped, "What I'd really like to control is not machines, but people." Jane was quickly beginning to believe he had been literal.

Compounding Jane's sexual and emotional frustration, she felt despondent at her failure to earn a doc-torate in medieval Spanish poetry. Her lack of a PhD was magnified as a result of her zip code: Cambridge wives viewed those without letters after their name as Vatican matrons viewed those who earn a living on unsavory street corners. E. E. Cummings wrote a satirical poem that stated these matrons "live in furnished souls/are unbeautiful and have comfortable minds." Jane recalled, "I was happy to be a wife and mother, but in Cambridge those words were synonymous with stupidity. The intellect reigns supreme there, and as a wife and mother you are simply nobody." She was forced to the painful realization there was a jagged discrepancy between the Hawkings' shining public image and their darkening private face. Jane prayed for salvation but felt the situation so hopeless even God could not provide salvation.

For diversion, Jane began to sing at the local church where she met choirmaster Jonathan Hellyer Jones, a recent widower who had lost his wife to leukemia. She employed him as Lucy's piano teacher, and before long, he was accompanying her to strains of Schubert. In her memoir, Jane revealed although Jones was years younger, she found he possessed such strong spirituality "we truly trod the holy ground which, in Oscar Wilde's words, is present when there is sorrow." Despite an intense attraction—which made Jane no longer feel devoid of gender—neither was willing to succumb to adultery. She said, in Cambridge lingo, if she gave rein to her desires, "The end result might be only the jarring sound of Flaubert's cracked kettle rather than move the stars to pity."

A platonic affair developed with Jones and wifely ministrations with Hawking. Hawking's attention was focused on completing his book *A Brief History of Time: From the Big Bang to Black Holes.* Everything came to a shocking standstill when Jane, on route to Switzerland to join her husband where he had gone to visit CERN—the Geneva citadel of physics—received a call: her husband had contracted pneumonia and was on life-support. When a stricken Jane arrived, the doctors asked if they should end his misery and let him die. Her response was an unmitigated refusal, and they returned to Cambridge where she helped nurse him back to health. The tracheotomy that saved his life had robbed him of the power of speech.

They say nothing keeps a great man down, and Hawking completed his book in 1987, which cast him in the role of scientist superstar. He appeared on the cover of *Time* magazine, and *A Brief History of Time* was purchased by the millions, though understood by few. The book postulated the big questions where did we come from and where are we going? They were the selfsame ones Jane had to confront in regard to her marriage.

Hawking had eschewed nurses, but when his disease reached critical mass, he required round-the-clock care—privacy became a remembrance of things past. To add to the chaos, Hawking was a publicity hound, but movie cameras and groupies became intrusive. The house ceased to be a home, and the situation was aggravated when Hawking, a cult figure, became inflated with ego: Jane constantly chided he was not, indeed, God. To alleviate her black hole of despair, Jane desired to finally change her relationship with Jones to the physical plane—and couched her foray into adultery with a scientific approach. She told Hawking as she was worried he would die soon, she wanted someone who would give her and the children support and marry her when he was gone. She also made it clear it would in no way threaten their marriage, as family was her *raison d'être*. Hawking acquiesced and Jones was installed in his own room. No doubt in Hawking's own there were endless hours of listening to Wagnerian opera played at full volume. There was also no doubt Cummings's Cambridge ladies took a break from intellectual parlance to dabble in Hawking gossip, "while permanent faces coyly bandy scandal of Mrs. N and Professor D."

In 1990, Hawking did something that must have resulted in Jane's scream heard around the cosmos—at the very least, around Cambridge: he left her and moved in with his nurse, Elaine Mason. Jane looked upon his act as the epitome of "Et tu, Brute," abandoning his twenty-six-year marriage for which she had endured a Sisyphean sacrifice: the constant trauma of living for a quarter of a century on the edge of a black hole. However, Professor Hawking, the epitome of rationalism, viewed it as logical: to swap his wife-nurse for a nurse-wife, the latter of whom seemed willing to worship at his feet. Elain may have also had more than a brief interest in Hawking's $20 million fortune.

In 2007, Dr. Hawking took a ride on a specially padded aircraft where he was able to float free, unfettered by his paralyzed muscles and his wheelchair. The flight was provided free of charge in order to allow the world's expert on gravity the opportunity to experience zero gravity. In the same year, Jane's memoir ended with a 2007 postscript of Hawking's magical out-of-body experience. She wrote how his triumphant smile would have moved the stars, saying, "It certainly moved me profoundly and made me reflect what a privilege it was to travel even a short distance with him on the way to infinity." Stephen and Jane Hawking's unique story merits a chapter in the annals of romance—*A Brief History of Love*.

CHAPTER TWENTY-SIX

THE BOOK OF RUTH

Mrs. Bernie Madoff

There is nothing unusual about a girl marrying her high school sweetheart; however, in one woman's case, a walk down the aisle made her first a most enviable and then a most desperate housewife. The union that was to have dizzying highs and paralyzing lows began in a mundane venue: a public high school in Queens, New York, with fellow student Bernie Madoff.

Ruth Alpern was born the second of two daughters into a middle-class Jewish family to an accountant father, Saul, and homemaker mother, Sara. Her parents were extremely proud of their modest yellow clapboard home in Laurelton, not far from what is now the John F. Kennedy Airport, a big step up from their former apartment in Brooklyn. Sisters Joan and Ruth's wish-upon-a-star fantasy was to move to Belle Harbor, an affluent Queens community, home to "the golden girls, the girls with money, whose parents did not have to worry about sending them to college." She attended Far Rockaway High School, whose alumni consisted of five notable names: Dr. Joyce Brothers, three Nobel Prize recipients, and a twentieth-century robber baron. Ruth and her sister dressed in the standard garb of the times: saddle shoes and poodle skirts topped with upswept hair. Because she was an honors student, a cheerleader, and a beauty, Ruth was voted "Josie College," a 1950s yearbook colloquialism that pegged her as preppy, bright, and going places.

In her freshman year, she started dating a junior who lived four

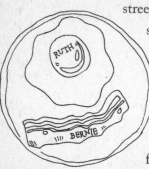

streets away. Bernard Madoff and Ruth became so inseparable classmates referred to them as eggs and bacon. When the couple wed at the Laurelton Jewish Center on November 28, 1959, no one was surprised. Mike Beck, a classmate, remarked of the marriage that Madoff had traded up. With her flaxen hair, fair skin, and green eyes, Ruth was his Jewish *shiksa* goddess, so much so a local shopkeeper asked why she wore a necklace with a Star of David. Bernie, as he preferred to be called, was not sure what career path to follow; he only knew he wanted it to lead to the wealth that had eluded his father.

The Madoffs purchased a ranch house in Roslyn, New York, and their tight bond strengthened with the birth of Mark in 1964 and Andrew in 1966. Madoff founded the Wall Street firm Bernard L. Madoff Investment Securities LLC in 1960 with a startup investment of $5,000 earned from his jobs as lifeguard and sprinkler installer. His business grew with the assistance of his father-in-law, who convinced relatives and friends to invest in the fledgling company. The profits from his business proved so astronomical that the woman who had once only dreamt of moving to the right side of the tracks in Queens now began to collect high-end real estate as others did charms for a bracelet: beach house in Montauk, penthouse in Manhattan, apartment in France, mansion in Palm Beach. Other fringe benefits as Mrs. Midas were a 10.5-carat diamond and a thirty-five-foot yacht christened *Bull*. However, Ruth was not

one to sit on her designer laurels: during this time, she earned a master's of science at New York University and co-edited *Great Chefs of America Cook Kosher*. It sold poorly and garnered a review of a "cooked book."

In her *tsoris*-free life, Ruth's sons made their parents proud: Mark graduated from the University of Michigan and Andrew from the prestigious Wharton Business School. Mothers of daughters from the graduating class of 1958 Far Rockaway High endlessly lamented why their daughters didn't hook Madoff.

With the sun never setting on a bad day at Bernard L. Madoff Investment Securities, Ruth easily slipped into the luxurious life of Manhattan's elite: every six weeks she colored her hair at the Pierre Michel Salon where she would sip a glass of Poland Spring water while Giselle, a colorist cited in *Vogue* and *Allure*, applied foils to attain the shade of soft baby blond. In her quest to sip from the fountain of youth, one of the duties of a manager in their London branch was to keep her supplied with Boots No. 7 Protect & Perfect Beauty Serum. Her one-hundred-pound frame was maintained by boycotting carbohydrates, and when she had consumed her allotted protein, she poured copious amounts of salt on her meal to prevent furtive bites. Her charmed life was a Manhattan fairy tale—until her handsome prince transformed into a dark knight.

On December 11, 2008, Bernard Madoff had a family meeting wherein he tearfully confessed he had been running a $65 billion Ponzi scheme and had played his last card. Ruth allegedly asked, "What's a Ponzi scheme?" His sons, the embodiment of the first syllable of their surname, immediately called the FBI, and at 7:00 a.m. the next morning, Madoff was under arrest. Ruth claimed when she heard the news she had no idea her husband had cheated thousands of people, including relatives, friends, charities, and senior citizens (one was Holocaust survivor Elie Wiesel) of life

savings. In his relentless quest for investors, Madoff was an equal opportunity predator.

The question remains if Ruth really was a member of the clueless wives club. However, even had she suspected the truth during the gilded era, she would have been confronted with a Carmela Soprano-esque choice: to push for him to come clean, which would mean the end of the road for her and her family, or to stay silent. Ruth posted his $10 million bond, which stipulated he had to live under house arrest. Madoff came home and sat day after day in front of the television as tears poured down.

Devastated, Ruth went through the next four months like a robot, still not able to hate the man who had been the orbit of her life since she had been a teenager. She had always played the role of his albeit loved, Stepford wife, and she knew no other. She had decorated his fastidious homes, socialized with his friends, and tolerated his obsessions: he insisted all his boxer shorts were custom-made with buttons up the side because he hated elastic. A further kidney punch to the soul was when Mark and Andrew forced her into a *Sophie's Choice* situation: she would have to abandon her husband or lose all contact with them and her grandchildren. The former Ruth Alpern—whose wish-upon-a-star dream had been for wealth—became the embodiment of St. Teresa of Avila's pronouncement: "There are more tears shed over answered prayers than over unanswered prayers."

On Christmas Eve, pilloried in the court of public opinion, alienated from her sons, on the threshold of losing fortune and husband, Ruth was at the end of her proverbial rope. She told Madoff she wanted to kill herself and he immediately agreed to die with her. The Romeo and Juliet of corporate greed lay down on their heaven-knows-what thread-count sheets and swallowed handfuls of Ambien. Fifteen hours later, they awoke feeling groggy and decided to soldier on. When news broke of the aborted double suicide attempt, the public response was that their act was a mere sympathy ploy. One victim stated that people who are smart enough to con millions of colleagues out of billions are smart enough to know how many sleeping pills to take to get the job done.

There was no empathy for the fallen Caesar or his wife. When she explained she had been kept in the dark about her husband's work and the family finances, like most women raised in the '50s, the response was similar to the name of the Madoff yacht: *Bull (%$#&)*. Too humiliated to face the frenzy of victims outside the courthouse, which Madoff entered wearing a bulletproof vest, Ruth did not attend her husband's trial. A journalist wrote the only injustice of Madoff's 150-year-prison sentence was he wouldn't live to serve every last miserable day of it. When the verdict was read, the onlookers cheered; for once the judge did not silence the crowd with his gavel.

Ruth, the modern Icarus, had flown too near the sun, and her fall from grace was as dizzying as her rise. While her husband had been condemned to death by incarceration, she now had to live in an equally horrible prison, one without bars. Like Fitzgerald's Gatsby, her list of enchanted objects began to diminish. In the aftermath of the scandal, she became one of the most reviled women in America, with millions viewing her as Ruth-less. It didn't help Camp Ruth when, in Tammy Wynette fashion, she decided to stand by her man. Rather than distance herself from Madoff and claim she had been as much his victim as anyone else, she continued to love her childhood sweetheart, whose name had become synonymous with "greedy dirt-bag." What further enraged the victims, many destitute, was her deal with prosecutors to keep $2.5 million in exchange for surrendering a potential claim to $80 million in assets, including her four stately pleasure domes. The sum is a princely one but was once an amount she would not have thought twice about putting on her American Express.

Fighting for survival, in phoenix style, Ruth attempted to rebuild her shattered life from the ashes, but this proved daunting. After her primary residence had been repossessed, she attempted to find another. However, whenever she tried to rent a modest home, the notorious-by-association Mrs. Madoff was told by numerous New York City co-op boards and landlords to look elsewhere.

Eventually she located to Boca Raton and moved in with her sister Joan Roman, age seventy-four, practically the only one who had not abandoned her. This was surprising as Joan had lost her life savings in Madoff's Ponzi scheme and was reduced to shuttling people to the airport to make ends meet. As Florida was as rife as New York with victims, Ruth attempted to dress incognito. The soft baby-blond highlights were dyed red, her blue eyes obscured under large tortoiseshell frames, and her surname replaced by her maiden one. In a *mea culpa*, Ruth embarked on a vigorous round of volunteer work, spending her days working for Meals on Wheels and renting books from the local library. Some felt her acts of contrition did not suffice and she should be rightfully washing the feet of lepers in Calcutta. Ruth also made side trips in her 1996 Infiniti clunker to North Carolina to see her husband, inmate Number 61727-054. She said of these heart-wrenching encounters, "It was like having a husband who had died but you could still visit."

If Ruth had not had her fair share of sorrows, yet another horrifying one awaited. She was in Boca Raton when she received a phone call that her first-born, Mark, had hung himself with his dog's leash in his six-million-dollar Soho loft while his young son slept in the adjoining room. She let out a series of screams. In the Old Testament, the relationship between Naomi and her daughter-in-law Ruth was forged in steel; not so with the modern mother and daughter-in-law Stephanie. When the sixty-nine-year-old Ruth flew to New York, she was barred from the funeral service. Although the death was the cruelest of all of fate's blows, Ruth still did not abandon her husband. It was yet another incident that would forever sever the marital bond that the couple had treasured.

In 2009 Sheryl Weinstein, a former executive of Hadassah (a Jewish charity that Madoff swindled), published a kiss-and-tell book in which she explained she and Madoff had done far more than kiss: *Madoff's Other Secret: Love, Money, Bernie, and Me.* When Ruth confronted Madoff, he denied to death, but as Sheryl had revealed things only the wife of a monogamous man would know (boxer shorts with buttons), Ruth finally decided it was time for the eggs—Ruth, to be sans the bacon—Bernie.

Either in a nod to karmic justice or the vagaries of fate, Ruth was dealt another kidney punch to her soul in 2014 when her younger son, Andrew, died from cancer. Through the vagaries of marriage and motherhood, Mrs. Madoff rode a carousel that caused her to trade in her American Express card and made her a card-carrying member of the cruelest of all clubs—to have once been happy—and have little hope for it again. It is impossible to know if she was culpable; the truth lies hidden in the Book of Ruth.

CHAPTER TWENTY-SEVEN

MAZA SHELAZA

Mrs. Jim Henson

I t's not easy being green." Kermit's remark has universal resonance as most find life's journey an epic uphill climb. What
made the green easier for Muppet-master Jim Henson was the
love of his fellow puppeteer.

Jane Nebel had the unique position of being the mother of a
brood of different colors—yellow, blue, and green—prior to marriage.
The birth of her fuzzy foamed offspring was one even her father, a
writer for the column *Your Personal Astrology*, could not have fath-
omed. She was born to parents Winifred and Adalbert on June 16 in
Queens, New York City, where she joined brother Brereton and sister
Margareta. As a teenager, Jane moved to Salisbury, Maryland, and
was admitted to the state university in 1951. She decided to major in
fine art, which offered a course in puppetry.

There she met eighteen-year-old Jim Henson, who had opted
for the program that exempted him from science requirements, free-
ing him to take more art classes. A secondary reason was the male-
female ratio: six guys to five hundred girls. He appreciated the odds
as he was self-conscious over his severe acne. His mother, Betty,
refused to allow him to take medication as it went against their
Christian Science faith. In the future, he would grow his trademark
beard to hide his deeply pockmarked face. Fortunately, Betty also
had a lighthearted side. She would tell Henson to say "when" as she
poured a glass of milk and, if he didn't, would keep pouring till the

glass overflowed. Henson referred to his childhood, saying, "I was a Mississippi Tom Sawyer." Jim's talent in puppetry surpassed the teacher's, and in no time he had taken over the class. His transition from amateur to professional arrived when he was hired to work on a variety show for a local television program, and his wizardry was reviewed in the *Washington Post*. Impressed with his talent, he was given a prime time evening slot. The Muppets were launched on their journey to icons.

Word of Henson's puppet mastery resulted in the NBC television offer to produce puppet segments under the name *Sam and Friends*. Jim packed some of his creations, which he had christened Muppets (a blend of the words "marionette" and "puppet"), and asked the talented Jane to accompany him as fellow performer and designer. Among the show's cast of furry foam characters was Yorick, a purple skull-like creature for whom Jane provided voice, and Henson's favorite, Kermit, a future icon who sprung from humble origins. He was created from his mother's discarded felt coat with eyes fashioned from a bisected Ping-Pong ball.

Jim and Jane operated the characters, working together in a cramped space to make them real—a furry rendition of God breathing life into Adam. Jane well understood: "There is something about putting life in the inanimate doll. There's a bit of divinity in it that all puppeteers understand." In 1956, they performed on Steve Allen's *Tonight Show* where Kermit lip-synched the song "I've Grown Accustomed to Her Face" from the Broadway hit *My Fair Lady*.

Life imitated puppet art as Jim and Jane had also grown accustomed to one another, and in 1959, after a sojourn in Europe, where he discovered puppetry to be a time-honored tradition, Henson asked for Jane's hand. His mother insisted the prospective groom shave off his new beard for the wedding. Henson put the shearings in an envelope and mailed them to Jane with a note, "From Samson to Delilah." The ceremony took place on May 28, 1959, at Jane's family home in Salisbury; the minister was Henson's Uncle Jinx. The following spring, the Hensons welcomed their first child, Lisa Marie. A family photograph shows the new father wagging Kermit in front of the baby, an early indication Lisa would be sharing her life with a unique sibling. Over the next ten years, she would be joined by ones of flesh as well: Cheryl, Brian, John, and Heather. Jane said of her five children, "I don't know that I was a very good mother, but they taught me all I know." With her growing brood, she transitioned to the role of full-time homemaker, yet she was still considered to be a major behind-the-scenes force.

Along with their growing offspring came phenomenal successes. In 1969, the Muppets became residents of *Sesame Street*, and millions of children were transfixed by Kermit, Oscar the Grouch, the Cookie Monster, and BFFs Bert and Ernie. Seven years later, *The Muppet Show* introduced über diva Miss Piggy, obsessed with finding the perfect frock and pursuing love interest Kermit. She became the most famous martial arts practitioner since Bruce Lee—in the throes of passion, she would smother Kermit with kisses, and when angry, give him a karate chop followed by an enraged "Hiya!" After a courtship as lengthy as their contemporaries Barbie and Ken, Kermit and Miss Piggy wed, though, as she revealed, Kermit is "in a wee bit of denial about the exact nature of our marital status."

Cemented as the ultimate puppeteer in history by the Muppet movies and massive merchandising, Jim Henson became a power-house in the entertainment world, heady fare for the self-described

Mississippi Tom Sawyer. However, he never adopted the antics of the prima donna Miss Piggy. When he was displeased, he would merely mutter "hmm"; when pleased, he would say "lovely." And, in these cup-runneth-over years, there was much that was lovely—the girl from Queens became one herself, as owner of homes in New York, Orlando, London, and Malibu, decorated with costly antiques juxtaposed with all things Muppet. The heart of their estates was the family homestead that held, in addition to the five children, eight cats, two dogs, six rabbits, and a ferret. It was a scene from a Norman Rockwell portrait, albeit populated with Muppets and the extreme wealth they had bequeathed. Still, Jane hungered for the hungry days; she later recalled, "But we had fun back when it was just the two of us."

Kermit's philosophy was "Keep it simple," but from this his creator diverged. While his alter ego had a dissected Ping-Pong ball for eyes, Henson developed a wandering one. He began to discreetly date younger women, and as a multi-millionaire who had created the television world his girlfriends had grown up watching, there was no impediment to forays into adultery. Henson did not want to hurt his wife and was reluctant to say "when" to his marriage, but he was also unwilling to continue with a double life.

After he returned from a year in London, he did not want to move back to his house in suburban Bedford, New York—did not want to return to Jane. Pathologically nonconfrontational, he told his wife that he had purchased an apartment on the nineteenth floor of the Sherry-Netherland hotel in Manhattan. Jane misunderstood and thought he was merely saying he wanted a place to stay in the city when he had to work late nights. Over an omelet breakfast the next morning, she asked how he wanted her to decorate. When he replied he would do it himself this time, reality finally sunk in. Devastated, the feisty Jane, à la Miss Piggy, could well have replied with a karate chop to the offending part of Jim's anatomy followed by a "Hi-ya!"

The legal separation resulted in Jane not only losing Henson but the company she had helped create more than two decades earlier. The break-up of "Bert and Ernie" left their five children with the Cookie Monster's own hue. When Hamlet held in his hand the skull of the court jester, he opined, "Alas, poor Yorick! I knew him, Horatio." Jane, who had been the muppet Yorick's voice, could not utter the same sentiment toward Jim, the husband she thought she had understood.

Henson's encounters had not consisted of emotional adultery until he became romantically involved with employee Mary Ann Cleary, whom he pronounced "lovely." Smitten, Henson and his lover celebrated his fiftieth birthday with a yacht cruise in Sardinia and later a romantic Paris and London interlude. Mary Ann introduced him to his first nude beach in Palm Beach. However, eventually she began to chafe over the fact he never went public with their relationship, and her promotion in the company may have been Henson's method of compensation. The truce was shattered when Henson brought the star of *Splash*, actress Daryl Hannah, to one of his opulent masked balls where they were costumed as Beauty and the Beast—the latter costume finally something mistress and wife could agree upon. Gossips speculated there might be a mermaid Muppet in the future, but nothing came of their shared evening. Infuriated, Mary Ann broke it off but they later reconciled, continuing an off-again on-again relationship of two years' duration. It eventually ended when Henson refused to consider remarriage; Jane was the only possible Mrs. Henson. Although legally no longer a couple, neither was ever ready to cut their emotional umbilical cord. Jane said of the breakup of the father and mother of the Muppets, "He had just sort of grown on to another stage. It seemed like we were always kind of married,

but not really. Still together, in a different way."

The year 1990 was tense as Henson was in the throes of selling his production company to Disney in a $150 million-dollar deal. It was during this time he also fell ill, a foreign condition to a man who had always enjoyed lifelong health. He had joked about growing old and turning an island into an Old Puppeteer's Home. Jane, who had been informed by daughter Cheryl he was ill, came to visit, bringing along a pot of chicken soup. She was alarmed at his appearance, but Henson reassured her and asked her to stay.

During the night they spent together, there was no talk of the ocean of hurt between them, no fingers pointed in blame. In his hour of need, Jane was comforted it was she her husband wanted. It was admission enough that despite his tongue-in-cheek note to her before their marriage, she had proved not his Delilah but rather his source of strength. Even though he was coughing blood, he refused to go to the doctor. Jane attributed this to his abandoned though still hovering Christian Science background and his lifelong insistence of not being a bother. Henson was suffering from pneumonia brought on by a rare strep infection. In the hours after finally being admitted to the hospital, his body began to shut down and he suffered a severe cardiac arrest. Eventually his heart stopped beating.

The headquarters of Jim Henson Productions in Manhattan epitomized the grief felt at the loss of the Grand Puppeteer. There were framed letters of sympathy that spanned the spectrum from President Bush to a child who had written, "God must have needed

Muppets in heaven." The Walt Disney Company had sent an over-sized condolence card that encapsulated bereavement: it showed Mickey Mouse with his arm around the shoulders of a downcast Kermit, his head in his hands. No condolence words were needed. Jane visited and sat under a painting in which Kermit the Frog was outfitted as Gainsborough's *The Blue Boy*. She spoke of her gentle genius, as she always would, in the present tense.

Henson's funeral service was held in Manhattan's Cathedral of St. John and, per his request, no one wore black. One of the many heartrending moments was when Big Bird sang a moving rendition of Kermit's "It's Not Easy Being Green." Jane became the keeper of Henson's flame and in 2010 donated the original Kermit and nine of his buddies, including his adoring Miss Piggy, to the Smithsonian. When asked for her reaction seeing the Henson collection on display, she replied, "I don't think of it as historical. It's my life."

When Jane passed away in 2013 after a long bout with cancer, tributes poured in from around the world, the most touching from her daughter Cheryl. In the Henson family lexicon, she said, "We called her the great Maza Shelaza of the Muppets." Roughly translated, she added, that meant the mother of all the muppets.

CHAPTER TWENTY-EIGHT

WHAT'S IN A NAME?

Mrs. Malcolm X

nitially because of delicious food, a woman embarked on a drama-filled path that rivaled an ancient Greek tragedy. Although it involved unimaginable heartache, she later remarked of her marriage to Malcolm X, "It was hectic, beautiful, and unforgettable—the greatest thing in my life."

Betty Dean Sanders was the illegitimate offspring of twenty-one-year-old Shelman Sandlin, who went MIA before her 1934 birth, and the teenaged Ollie Mae Sanders. The young mother failed to give her daughter a birth certificate or anything remotely resembling stability, and when Betty was nine years old, she moved in with her foster parents Lorenzo and Helen Malloy in Detroit. Although they provided Betty with a nurturing environment, they never prepared her for the hostile one that existed in her 1940s racially charged city. They adopted the stance of the proverbial three monkeys, though hearing, seeing, and speaking no evil did not have the desired effect on their foster daughter. Betty later recalled, "Race relations were not discussed and it was hoped that by denying the existence of race problems, the problems would go away. Anyone who openly discussed race relations was quickly viewed as a 'trouble maker.'"

The riot that occurred during her childhood when the Sojourner Truth Housing Project was desegregated comprised what she would term the "psychological background for my formative years." Nevertheless, her sheltered home kept bigotry at bay; her life consisted of attendance at the local Methodist church, movies, and social activities. She described her metronome teenage years, "Pick a week out of my life. If you understood that week, you understood my life." However, it was Betty's fate to live (as the Chinese curse states) in interesting times.

After graduation, Betty left Detroit to pursue a teaching degree from the black Tuskegee Institute in Alabama, Lorenzo's alma mater. In the confines of campus, she could avoid prejudice, but in Montgomery, she was caught in its tsunami. The whites spoke of the "uppity Niggers at the Institute" while fellow students referred to their oppressors as having necks of red. When she complained to the Malloys, their mantra remained, "If you're just quiet, it will go away." When it did not, she relocated to Brooklyn where she changed her career path to nursing. Discrimination proved to be a moveable feast when she discovered African American nurses were given worse assignments than their Caucasian counterparts. Betty felt she had merely exchanged Jim Crow laws for a more genteel prejudice.

Betty was invited to a Friday night dinner party at the Nation of Islam Temple in Harlem, an evening whose echo would follow her all the days of her life. She later recalled of the cuisine, "The food was delicious. I'd never tasted food like that." Her friend told her about the charismatic minister who was not present that evening: "Just wait until you hear my minister talk. He's very disciplined, he's good-looking, and all the sisters want him." As a devout Methodist, Betty had no interest in a meeting; however, as the food was sumptuous, she agreed to return.

While the food was what drew her in, it was on that second night Betty met the man who irrevocably altered her destiny. She recalled the first time she saw him: "He was tall, he was thin, and the way he was galloping, it looked as though he was going someplace much more important than the podium. He got to the podium—and I sat up straight." She began to attend all of Malcolm X's lectures, which led her friends and family to question whether her interest lay in the religion or in its minister. Two years later, to the Malloys' horror, she was a convert to the Nation of Islam. In accordance with the precept of the temple, just as Malcolm Little had become Malcolm X, Betty Dean Sanders became Betty X, a nod to its teachings that blacks had their identities stolen by slave-owners.

Malcolm X and Betty X did not have a conventional courtship, as one-on-one fraternizing between the sexes went against the teachings of their temple. Instead, the couple stepped out with group dates consisting of dozens of others. This countered the staggering amount of babies born out of wedlock in the African American milieu, something that Betty, who had been one herself, understood.

One afternoon, Betty received a call from Malcolm in Detroit, who said he was getting gas, when he popped the question, "Look, do you want to get married?" Although the proposal fell short of the on-the-knee-bearing-a-ring variety, Betty was a woman in love and she accepted. Their wedding took place a week later on January 14, 1958, in Lansing, Michigan, the same day she received her license as a nurse. Malcolm approved of her career as it fit the nurtur-ing image of Muslim womanhood. Betty well  understood that by marrying the man, she was also agreeing to live with a demanding mistress of sorts, Malcolm's fanatic dedication to his cause. Her role was further daunting as her husband harbored views of females as "tricky, deceitful, untrustworthy flesh."

At the onset, their union followed the Nation of Islam's strictures concerning husband and wife; Malcolm set the rules and Betty obeyed. The dynamics shifted when Malcolm told her what he expected of his wife and Betty countered with what she expected of her husband. Because of his wife, Malcolm changed his perspective on gender, saying, "When you teach a man, you teach a community; when you teach a woman, you raise a nation." Betty's sweetness and support helped the angry man find the gentleness that he had lost in Harlem and in prison. Her love broke down his romantic barriers and he called her by pet names such as Brown Sugar and Apple Brown Betty.

Unfortunately, as a minister, there were long periods of separation when Malcolm traveled the country on his mission "to awaken the brainwashed black man and to tell the devilish white man the truth about himself." His philosophy was summed up when he pronounced the only thing he liked integrated was his coffee and his quotation, "We didn't land on Plymouth Rock. Plymouth Rock landed on us." He was so often on the road Betty always kept a packed suitcase so he could quickly exchange one for another. The enforced separation was made harder for Betty when she was forced to raise her four daughters mainly on her own: Attallah, named after Attila the Hun; Qubilah, named after Kublai Khan; Ilyasah, named after Elijah Muhammad; and Gamilah Lumumba named after Patrice Lumumba, the Congolese independence leader. Their christenings showed they were to be future freedom fighters. Attallah would later relate when her parents were together, they were "silly and giggly and whimpery. They'd go off on long walks alone, and even

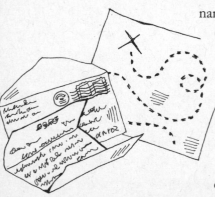

when he was traveling, he'd leave her treasure maps with love letters at the end. I know now how extraordinary their love affair was."

The turning point of their lives occurred after the assassination of President John F. Kennedy, when Malcolm X declared of the cataclysmic event, "The chickens have come home to roost." The radical remark meant as the history of America had been riddled with violence, it was fitting its president likewise had met a violent end. The Nation of Islam had issued a directive that its ministers not speak about the killing and thus was further angered at the extremity of Malcolm's denunciation. Louis Farrakhan, one of the Nation's top leaders, disciplined him through demotion. Malcolm's response was his refusal to be muzzled, and in 1964, he founded his rival movement: the Muslim Mosque. The Nation, who owned their home, evicted them and cut off his salary, which left the family destitute. Seeking enlightenment, Malcolm embarked on his hajj (pilgrimage to Mecca), where he returned with a new philosophy and a new name: the couple became El-Hajj Malik El-Shabazz and Betty Shabazz, renouncing the *X* that tied them to the temple from which they had become self-excommunicated. While her husband was in the Middle East seeking wisdom, Betty, alone with four children and pregnant with twins, was the recipient of constant threats from their former ministry. One anonymous phone call: "Just give Malcolm this message. Just tell him that he's as good as dead." Upon his return, the Shabazz home was fire-bombed on Valentine's Day.

Malcolm did not often invite his wife to hear him speak, preferring to keep his private and public life separate, but on February 21, 1965, his family came to the Audubon Ballroom in Manhattan to hear him lecture to an audience of 400. Almost as soon as he reached the microphone, he was shot in the chest with a sawed-off shotgun, quickly followed by a front-row firing squad that riddled his body with an additional sixteen bullets. Betty pushed her four daughters to the floor, where she shielded the hysterical children with her pregnant body, screaming, "They're killing my husband!" When the shooting stopped, she rushed to Malcolm and performed CPR. Police officers and his followers escorted him to Columbia Presbyterian Hospital where he was pronounced dead.

The distraught widow found the strength to endure with her own pilgrimage to Mecca and the remembrance of the words of Malcolm: "Don't look back and don't cry. Remember, Lot's wife turned into a pillar of salt." Seven months later, Betty gave birth to twins Malikah and Malaak. Despite her circumstances, dire under any perspective (homeless after the firebomb, mother of six young daughters, penniless, and widowed through assassination), she refused to don the mantle of self-pity. What helped bring her strength was the friendship and support of two other women made widows of the civil rights movement: Coretta Scott King and Myrlie Evers-Williams. Betty had always viewed her life as not existing pre-Malcolm, and now she had to live it after the man who had been the pillar of her world. She determined to prevail. He would have expected no less.

Financially the family was supported by Alex Haley, the coauthor of *The Autobiography of Malcolm X*, who donated royalties to help. Further assistance came from Juanita Poitier (wife of actor Sidney Poitier), and Betty was able to purchase a home in Mount Vernon, New York, from Congress member Bella Abzug. In 1975, she became Dr. Shabazz when she earned her doctorate in education at the University of Massachusetts at Amherst, which brought on raucous cheers from her six daughters. Tragically, misfortune was to dog her footsteps once more.

Betty had always pointed the finger of blame for her husband's assassination at Louis Farrakhan, and her hatred was absorbed by Qubilah, her troubled second daughter. Embittered over her father's murder she was charged with negotiating with hit man Michael Fitzpatrick (a former schoolmate who was working as an FBI informant) to murder Farrakhan. Following Qubilah's arraignment, Betty furiously defended her daughter and denied that she had raised any of her children to seek revenge. The charges were eventually dropped, but Qubilah had to agree to undergo treatment for alcoholism and psychiatric care. Her son Malcolm, conceived by a father she met while studying at the Sorbonne, went to live with his grandmother. The angst-ridden adolescent set fire to Betty's apartment, where she suffered burns over 80 percent of her body. His troubled life ended with his murder in 2013 in Tijuana, Mexico. Thus he continued the legacy of family violence. Betty managed to cling to life for three weeks, supported by pints of blood donated by hundreds of volunteers.

In tribute to Betty's passing, the U.S. flag flew at half-mast and more than 2,000 mourners attended the memorial service, among whom were Coretta Scott King, Myrlie Evers-Williams, Maya Angelou, Muhammad Ali, Ed Koch, and Rudy Giuliani. The public viewing was at the Unity Funeral Home in Harlem, the same site where Malcolm X's viewing had taken place thirty years earlier. The funeral service was held at the Islamic Cultural Center in New York City. Inside the mosque, the mourners shed their shoes and knelt beside the coffin while chanting the Islamic prayer for the dead. When the mosque emptied, Betty's daughters stood side by side, feet bare and heads covered with shawls in Islamic fashion. Betty was interred in Ferncliff Cemetery in Hartsdale, New York, Plot No. 50, her coffin resting on top of her husband's. They share a single headstone whereupon is engraved "Hajj-Malik El Shabazz, Malcolm X 1925–1965, Betty 1936–1997."

Juliet on her Verona balcony had asked "What's in a name?" and realized it was of no relevance what one was called. However, that was not the case with Betty, whose evolving names serve as her encapsulated biography: Betty Dean Sanders, foster child; Sister Betty X, member of the Nation of Islam; Betty Shabazz, Sunni Muslim; and Dr. Shabazz, post-doctorate. What began with delicious food led to a life of unimaginable peaks and valleys, one never regretted as it entailed a treasure map with love letters at the end.

CHAPTER TWENTY-NINE

THE STOLEN HOURS

Mrs. Samuel Beckett

I n *Waiting for Godot*, two hapless tramps struggle to find meaning in a landscape of existential emptiness. They embody "the dangling conversation," to pretend to be connected to another, to drown out loneliness waiting in the wings. Their only hope is the enigmatic Godot, who remains a steadfast no-show. But the author, Samuel Beckett, was rescued from such soul-sucking alienation by succor from across the sea.

When twin baby girls were born to the Jacobs, Jewish immigrants from Belgium and Holland, in London on November 24, 1924, friends commented on their identical features. They shared prodigious intellects as well; both became fluent in French and worked as translators but otherwise tread far divergent roads.

In an unusual situation for a mid-century girl from a low-income home, Barbara was admitted to Cambridge, financed through a state scholarship. It was at university she also took a husband, John Bray, an Australian RAF pilot who had been a prisoner of war. The couple embarked for Egypt where she taught for three years as a lecturer in English language and literature at the University of Alexandria and at a college in Cairo. When John (by then estranged from his wife) was killed in an accident in Cyprus, the thirty-four-year-old widow was left alone with daughters Julia and Francesca. Rather than "trouble deaf heaven with bootless cries," she supported her family with a position in the BBC Third Program. Working under Donald McWinnie (with whom she embarked on an affair), she championed postwar writers such as Jean-Paul Sartre, Harold Pinter, and the man who would electrify her life.

The Nobel Prize-winning writer of *Waiting for Godot* first laid eyes on Barbara when she assisted him on the production of *All That Fall*—which is what she immediately did. She was entranced by his voice, which she described as sounding like the sea. In her memoir, she recounted, "I fell in love with Beckett's work even before I met him personally and had the 'real,' once-and-for-all *coup de foudre*." She added their meeting was "the great epiphany of my life. It took all of thirty seconds to fall in love." She thought Beckett, a towering genius eighteen years her senior, would forget the scriptwriter upon his return to France. He had become a British expatriate, as he explained, "I preferred France in war to Ireland at peace." However, after his departure, she received daily letters with Parisian postmarks. Bray remained awestruck—and was thunderstruck—when Beckett altered their relationship from an epistolary one when he phoned out of the blue and invited her for dinner. After this initial date, it became apparent they were soul and mind mates. They were to discover they were body mates as well.

In 1961, after three years of an intense long-distance relationship, Barbara decided to surprise Samuel and relocate to Paris. Loved ones thought she was acting like the name of the avant-garde theater—absurd. They advised against quitting a secure position, leaving country and family, uprooting her daughters, for a man who did not dangle a ring. Moreover, there was the matter of the Beckett bleakness, manifest both off and on stage. Beckett's friend had once mentioned of a balmy afternoon it was "the sort of day that makes you glad to be alive," to which Beckett demurred, "Oh, I don't think I'd go quite so far as that." Despite well-meaning admonitions, Barbara felt Beckett her Godot, and she was not willing to wait for him any longer. Even women who have always been guided by intellect sometimes become ruled by emotion. It was her ardent wish by joining him that she would transform from Barbara Bray to Barbara Beckett.

In *All That Fall*, a Mr. Slocum asks, "May I offer you a lift, Mrs. Rooney? Are you going in my direction?" to which the female character replies, "I am, Mr. Slocum, we all are." Life imitated art as any number of women were seduced by Beckett, notwithstanding his appearance: he sported thick round spectacles, bristly hair, and gaunt physique. The American writer Susan Sontag—no slouch herself in the bleakness arena—referred to him as the sexiest man she had ever met. When he had first moved to Paris, he had worked with James Joyce, whose daughter Lucia was the portrait of the daughter as a lost cause. She sang of Samuel with whom she had become romantically involved, "You're the Cream in My Coffee." When his interest waned and he explained her draw had been her father, Lucia dissolved into depression. After she had been institutionalized, throughout her life she would ask where and with whom her Samuel had been seen.

Another of his smitten suitors had been art collector Peggy Guggenheim, who received an education in modernism when she spent a night and day in bed with Beckett, interrupted only by her demand he depart for champagne. The American heiress was in turn dropped for Suzanne Déchevaux-Dumesnil, whom he had met in an unforgettable fashion. In 1938, a crazed panhandler randomly stabbed Beckett in the chest, narrowly missing his heart. Suzanne, a bystander, had jumped off her bicycle and accompanied the stranger to the hospital, where she remained at his side. After he had recovered, he visited his assailant in prison and asked him the reason for the assault. The answer: *"Je ne sais pas, Monsieur,"* (I do not know, sir). This episode reinforced Beckett's view of the senselessness of existence. It had another effect: he began a relationship with Suzanne. She also stayed by his side when he joined the French Resistance and slept with him in various haystacks as they fled from the Nazis.

When Barbara (unaware of his relationship with Miss Déchevaux-Dumesnil) and her daughters arrived in Paris, she informed Beckett she had moved because she could not bear the separation of the Channel and indicated she would like to make their union official. His response came a few months later, on March 23, 1961, at which time she received a black-and-white picture postcard of Shakespeare Cliff, Dover. It was devoid of text; it contained just the closing words *Pensées affectueuses* (affectionate thoughts). The missive and the endearment may have given Barbara hope; however, it turned out to be just fool's hope, the type experienced by Beckett's two tramps. On March 24, in a civil ceremony, he ended up marrying Suzanne in Folkestone, England. Although Barbara was his spiritual and sexual soul mate, something his wife was not, he did not feel justified in abandoning his twenty-year relationship with Suzanne, especially after all they had been through—what with the haystacks and all. For most women, the situation would have proved the Beckett title *Endgame*. Indeed,

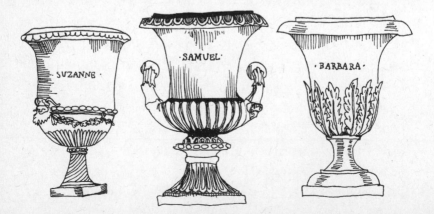

having uprooted her life only to have her lover marry another might have led to yet another knife attack. Afterward, rather than provide the explanation "*Je ne sais pas*," she could have replied, "Let me the count the ways…" Instead, Barbara's response was akin to Beckett's philosophy of why he was an Irish expatriate: she preferred Beckett married to life without him.

Juggling a full-time wife and mistress was not any easier for the great man than it would be for lesser ones. This became apparent in *Play* (1963), featuring a man, his wife, and his mistress trapped together for eternity in funeral urns as they vindictively obsess about the other members of the ménage à trois. The situation was also not without consequences for Julia and Francesca, Barbara's daughters, who had to grow up in the emotionally laden minefield of a mother in love with another woman's husband. Back in England, Barbara's twin sister Olive, who had become, along with husband André Classe, a lecturer at the University of Glasgow, must have read symbolism in the title of Beckett's short story collection, *More Pricks than Kicks*.

Barbara settled into a historic home (in close proximity to her lover's) on the rue Séguier, situated near the back wall of Picasso's atelier; the flight of stairs that led to her door dated from the time of Napoleon. It was here Beckett would drop in at unusual hours, to talk or play the piano. As with his letters, she kept all the music he used, largely classical pieces. However, her *Happy Days* (the title of another Beckett play) and nights were in Beckett's country retreat in Ussy-sur-Marne, where he escaped the unwelcome spotlight of fame.

He had purchased his house pre-*Godot* wealth, with money from his mother's will. Perhaps his rocky relationships with women can be traced to mother issues. Of his own, he stated, "I am what her savage loving has made me." Beckett had been his mother's favorite child, and he had remained as emotionally tethered to her as Lucky was to Pozzo in *Godot*. Suzanne had become bored with country life, which left Barbara free, for a time, to share in the overnight intimacies of a wife. In a series of poignant photographs, she captured Beckett in his garden, mowing the lawn, lighting bonfires.

She also had the privilege of sharing another type of intimacy, as eyewitness to the great man writing pages that would become masterpieces. However, as Beckett biographers concur, Barbara did not merely observe. This came to light in 1997 when Trinity College, Dublin, paid her £250,000 for 713 letters, together with manuscripts sent to her over the course of their thirty-year relationship. These show Barbara was his sounding board and literary adviser and reveal his difficulties and thoughts while working. He wrote sometimes twice a day, even if they were planning to meet, welcoming suggestions, seeking help with translations, asking for encouragement. She was the only person with whom he regularly shared his work in progress and one of the very few with whom he discussed his writing. Barbara was also the one who could make the somber man less serious; she recounted how the two shared laughter. In gratitude, he assisted her financially, helping particularly with the education of her daughters.

Suzanne's loyalty and Barbara's devotion did not preclude other romantic extracurricular activities. In the late 1960s, when Beckett went to Germany to direct *Endgame*, he embarked on an affair with a young Israeli, Mira Averech. Meanwhile, Suzanne flew in to watch the rehearsals and Barbara arrived to see the play. Somehow Beckett managed to avoid Caesar's fate as he climbed the steps of the forum.

While Barbara's happiest days were spent in Beckett's country

home, her saddest were when he traveled and all she had were letters, which contained the name of his travel companion, his wife.
On one of these trips, the Becketts were in their Tunisian hotel
room where Suzanne, after hanging up the phone, turned to her
husband with the words, "*Quelle catastrophe!*" The call from Sweden
had informed her that Beckett had won the Nobel Prize. Rather
than celebrate, they merely worried about the intensified spotlight
of fame. Beckett's fear of the resultant media scrutiny was that
his clandestine relationship with Barbara would be exposed. He
remained fiercely loyal to his wife, to whom he attributed finding an
initial publisher, saying, "I owe everything to Suzanne. She was the
one who went to see the publishers while I used to sit in a café 'twid-
dling my fingers' or whatever it is one twiddles." Who he "twiddled"
and shared his parallel life was Barbara,
who remained steadfast until Beckett
passed away in 1983, interred in
Montparnasse Cemetery. She was
devastated at the loss of the man
who had been her life's North Star
and felt the same sentiment as the
last line in Beckett's novel *The Unnamable*:
"You must go on. I can't go on. I'll go on." Although Barbara paid
a steep price for loving a man she could never have, at least she had
meaning in that landscape of existential emptiness, one kept at bay
by the stolen hours.

CHAPTER THIRTY

ONE HUNDRED TIMES MORE

Mrs. Nelson Mandela

Moses and Mandela famously had to endure long walks to freedom through the wilderness—the Desert of Sinai and the desert of apartheid. But what is less known is that as they each gave their rallying cry, "Let my people go!" they were both supported by women in the wings: the biblical prophet helped by his wife, Zipporah, the contemporary leader by his own helpmeet, part Mother Teresa, part Lucrezia Borgia.

The one who was to stand behind the future emancipator of her country knew oppression from the start. Winifred "Winnie" Madikizela was born September 26, 1936, in the village of Bizana. Perhaps her fate was ordained when she was given the first name Nomzamo, meaning "she who will go through trials and tribulations." She started life with a rusty spoon, rather than silver: her parents were devastated with her birth, a sixth daughter when they desperately had hoped for a son. Not only did she face sexism, she also had to endure the South African government-sanctioned racism.

Winifred did not own shoes until she entered school. A gifted student, she ended up in Johannesburg and, as a witness to the horrors inflicted on the black majority by the white minority, refused a scholarship to America, saying, "I'm needed here." Against formidable odds, she became the first black female social worker in Soweto, a black township bordering Johannesburg. It was there the girl from an impoverished village met the man who was to make her life assume the dimensions of a Shakespearean drama.

Based on contemporary pictures and YouTube snippets—which depict Mandela as frail and Winnie as matronly—it is easy to forget the couple were once extremely good-looking, a South African township equivalent of Elizabeth Taylor and Richard Burton. She was twenty-two and standing at a bus stop when Mandela, an attorney in his late thirties, drove by. He was thunderstruck at her regal beauty but resisted the urge to stop his car.

In a nod to serendipity, a short time later they were introduced by a mutual friend. Winnie was taken aback at the attention from the successful attorney who was a rising hero among black South Africans. He invited her to an Indian restaurant where she experienced curry for the first time—and a passionate kiss. Winnie was understandably flattered by the man renowned as the Black Pimpernel, so named as a daring freedom fighter committed to rescuing his people. In later years, he stated he had no idea whether such a thing as love at first sight existed, but he admitted after their first date he wanted her as his wife. At the time, he was in a decade-long marriage to Evelyn, a devout Jehovah's Witness, mother of his three children. His first wife did not stand a chance.

In Winnie's 1984 memoir *Part of My Soul Went with Him*, she recounted Mandela's own brand of proposal. "One day Nelson just pulled up on the side of the road and said, 'You know, there is a woman who is a dressmaker. You must go and see her. She is going to make your wedding gown. How many bridesmaids would you like to have?'" She replied, "What time?" Winnie was ecstatic; Evelyn less so, who had learned of her divorce through a newspaper. On the day of their June 14, 1958, wedding, the bride's father cautioned his daughter, whom he had tried to dissuade from the marriage: "If your man is a wizard, then you must become a witch."

Mandela had received the name Nelson from a British school-teacher; his tribal one, Rolihlahla, meant "one who brings trouble on himself." (In given names, Winnie and Nelson were indeed a perfect match.) Rather than live a comfortable life as an attorney, Mandela joined the African National Congress (ANC), an organization devoted to replacing the racist regime of South Africa with a multiracial democracy. He was gone so often, often taking refuge in hidden houses, his wife stated, "Life with him was life without him." He understood her great sacrifices and wrote, "The wife of a freedom fighter is often like a widow. Winnie gave me cause for hope. My love for her gave me added strength for the struggle that lay ahead."

When passive resistance failed to bring about reform, in a nod to desperate times call for desperate measures, the ANC embarked on extremist acts. Shortly after their marriage, Mandela was forced underground after he had launched a series of bombings on power plants and rail lines. He was captured and stood trial in a Pretoria courtroom. Winnie attended, clad head to foot in a beaded headdress and ankle-length skirt. Mandela entered the dock wearing a lion skin, the traditional garb of a native chief. He raised a clenched fist and cried *"Amandla!"* "Power!" and everyone in the gallery, including the media, rose as one. The authorities were far from impressed with the Mandelas' display of African nationalism. Mandela received a life sentence of imprisonment in Robben Island, a craggy windblown Alcatraz. His wife mourned that part of her soul went with him.

On average, usually every two years, Winnie could visit her husband for thirty minutes. They were not allowed to touch, merely stand with palms pressed against a glass partition. In his memoir, *Long Walk to Freedom*, Mandela included words from a letter: "My dearest Winnie, your beautiful photo still stands about two feet

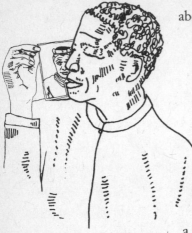

above my left shoulder as I write this note. I dust it carefully every morning, for to do so gives me the pleasant feeling that I'm caressing you as in the old days. I even touch your nose with mine to recapture the electric current that used to flush through my blood whenever I did so."

She quickly discovered the truth, that it is not easy being the wife of a martyr. A wife-turned-semi-widow, Winnie was left to raise two infant daughters, Zenani and Zindzi, hampered by the infamy of the name Mandela. His imprisonment had made him a martyr to his black South Africans, a dangerous demagogue to its whites. Had she chosen to retreat into obscurity, she may have been able to survive with a modicum of peace, but then again she would not have been true to her name of Nomzamo.

Instead, Mandela's imprisonment was his wife's call to arms, and she became the face of the ANC, proudly clad in its colors of black, green, and yellow. She also became the target of the government that she was dedicated to annihilate. Retaliation was swift, but her defiance of arrests, banning orders (government-enforced restrictions against potential enemies of state that, among others things, prevented their traveling without state approval), and daily police harassment served to keep the Mandela name in the international press at a time when her husband had been effectively silenced. If it had not been for her intrepid acts, the world would not have seen the modern-day Gandhi that Nelson Mandela was to become.

Intent on destroying the galvanizing force, in 1969, Winnie was apprehended under the Suppression of Terrorism Act and dragged from her house to the accompaniment of her children's screams. She endured seventeen months in solitary confinement as Prisoner 1323/69, during which time she was subjugated to torture. She ate off a sanitary bucket that was returned to her unrinsed from the night before. Her blanket was covered with urine, vomit, and bugs. She contemplated suicide but desisted, remembering her husband and her children.

Upon release, she remained unbroken and resurrected her struggle to liberate her beloved country. In appreciation, her grateful people and husband praised her as "Mama Wethu," "Mother of the Nation." But behind the public façade was a lonely woman, and the First Lady of South Africa's liberation movement took a young lover.

In the vein of Henry II's quote about thorn-in-his-side Thomas Becket, "Will no one rid me of this turbulent priest?" the South African president's next tactic was banishment. Mrs. Mandela was removed to the fly-blown Afrikaans town of Brandfort, deep in sheep country where the black population lived impoverished in dilapidated homes of corrugated tin. It was an exile designed to silence her voice; she did not speak the local African dialect, and the white townspeople were ultra-conservative Afrikaners. Once again, their tactics backfired. Winnie thumbed her nose at the authorities by ignoring WHITES ONLY signs in shops and cafes and wearing the forbidden ANC colors. In exile in Brandfort, she still managed to galvanize the native population, and a procession of influential people, such as Richard Attenborough and Ted Kennedy, came to call, trailed by a host of journalists.

Tragically, it was also in Brandfort Winnie begun to unravel. She started to drink heavily, so much so that her half-her-age lover had to turn a hose on her before the arrival of the Kennedy entourage.

By the mid-eighties, the South African government realized their tactics against Mrs. Mandela were only making her a martyr, and in deference to the imprisoned Mandela's wish, they allowed Winnie to return from exile. It turned out to be a fateful request. His wife continued to be the great man's blind spot. Although so prescient of politics, he failed to see what she had become—an embittered woman who had strayed from the high road he had learned to walk. Although the ANC declared she was out of control, Mandela, in jail and in declining health, refused to believe ill of his wife. This was a time of anarchy in the townships, and in the ensuing lawlessness, Winnie, the archetypal victim, became victimizer. She assembled a thuggish neighborhood mafia, the Mandela United Football Club, whose agenda was far from any innocuous sport. It became the instrument of her brand of neighborhood justice. She made incendiary remarks: "We have no guns—we have only stones, boxes of matches, and petrol. Together, hand in hand, with our boxes of matches and our necklaces we shall liberate this country." *Necklacing* meant an agonizing death by placing an oil-soaked burning tire around a perceived traitor's neck. Of her metamorphosis, Winnie stated, "I am the product of the masses of my country and the product of my enemy."

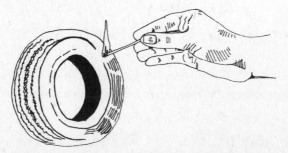

The most heinous act attributed to her orders was the abduction of a fourteen-year-old boy, Stompie Moeketsi, whose throat was slit on the grounds he was an informant. Her spree as vigilante endorsed the brand of black-on-black violence that played into the hands of the hated regime. Like her name, her father's words came to pass—"you must become a witch."

In 1990, in a photograph that left an indelible mark on the world, Mandela walked out of prison, a man freed by his very captors, the apartheid government. Winnie was there at the prison door for this long-awaited moment. The Mandelas, who had not touched in twenty-seven years, made their walk to freedom holding each other's hand, their fists raised in solidarity. If the script of their lives were in the hands of Disney, they would have spent their remaining years basking in their long-denied love, in a country that no longer wept. Unfortunately the ensuing scenario was more akin to pages from the Grimm brothers.

The marriage, which had been kept alive in brief visits and lengthy letters, soon felt the strain of reality. Three decades before, they had been on the same page, but they were now on different ones. After all, Mandela had left a man and had returned a mythical hero. In the years at Robben, he had learned the Lovelace lesson, "Stone walls do not a prison make." He had adopted the peaceful resistance stance of his civil rights predecessor thirty years prior and halfway across the world, Martin Luther King Jr. Winnie's views were more akin to the violent protesting of Malcolm X. Although he publically supported Winnie in her trial for her role in Stompie Moeketsi's kidnapping and murder, as she had in his, privately he condemned her actions.

Another crushing blow for the man who had been nourished by the photograph of his wife was his discovery of her adultery. History might forgive her for taking some comfort for herself during that dark time, in the light of all she had endured for her husband. It was likely hard enough playing the role of Mother of the Nation without also playing Mother Teresa.

But Mandela did not apply his national approach to peaceful reconciliation to his errant, long-suffering wife. In 1996, their acrimonious divorce played out in public as Mandela took the stand in the Supreme Court of Johannesburg and went on record saying, "I was the loneliest man during the period I stayed with her. Ever since I came back from prison, not once has the defendant ever entered our bedroom while I was awake. If the entire universe persuaded me to reconcile I would not. I am determined to get rid of this marriage." He never stopped loving Winnie but could no longer continue their marital charade. Later he gave a softened view of the breakdown of his relationship, saying, "I part from my wife with no recrimination. I embrace her with all the love and affection I have nursed for her inside and outside prison from the moment I first met her."

Although the South African love story between the leader and the country's First Lady dissolved, Winnie, just like she did at his trial a half century before, was a constant presence during Mandela's final illness. Witnesses to his passing understood that despite their unfortunate split, they remained the love of each other's lives. Like his beloved people, Mandela was never truly willing to cut the apron springs of the Mother of the Nation.

Winnie remains a sphinx, shrouded in secrecy: did she really try to be an avenging angel for her people or did she become intoxicated with personal power? Perhaps the best insight into her soul came when she was once asked if she would do it all again. She nodded and said, "One hundred times more."

CHAPTER THIRTY-ONE

MRS. BLUE EYES

Mrs. Frank Sinatra

When one conjures the image of Francis Albert Sinatra, it is of a Jersey crooner with the velvet voice, the bruised romantic with shady mob ties. The biography of the first modern pop superstar is the stuff of legend, with his second wife Ava Gardner and third, Mia Farrow. However, his fourth wife, like Sinatra's trademark lyric, lived and loved her way.

Barbara Ann Blakeley was raised the daughter of a kosher butcher in whistle-stop town Bosworth, Missouri, in 1926. The family relocated to Wichita, Kansas, and in the spirit of Dorothy and Toto, she was destined to trade her gray Midwest home for an emerald Oz. She first heard "The Voice" (as Sinatra's velvety vocals were called) at fifteen in a drive-in movie where, she recalled, the tenderness in his song melted her tomboy heart.

In her late teens, the family moved to California where Barbara won the Miss Long Beach Beauty Pageant and married a part-time bartender, gambler, and singer, Robert Oliver. He claimed he sounded like Sinatra and hoped he would make money from the connection. Apparently audiences did not share his view, and the couple was soon drowning in debt.

The birth of son Bob did not prove a strong enough adhesive to keep the marriage together, and Barbara became involved with another singer, Joe Graydon, whose repertoire consisted of Sinatra hits (sense a theme here?). When he accepted a position as a DJ

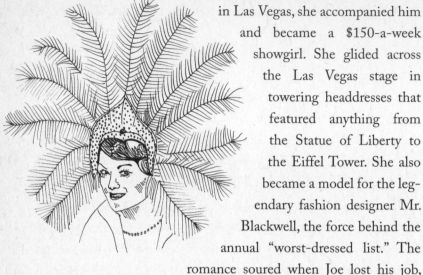

in Las Vegas, she accompanied him and became a $150-a-week showgirl. She glided across the Las Vegas stage in towering headdresses that featured anything from the Statue of Liberty to the Eiffel Tower. She also became a model for the legendary fashion designer Mr. Blackwell, the force behind the annual "worst-dressed list." The romance soured when Joe lost his job, and Barbara became a regular at the Riviera hotel/casino, a watering hole for possessors of deep pockets. Barbara used the casino in the hope to hit her personal jackpot: a high roller who would keep her rolling in the green. It was there she first met inveterate gambler Frank Sinatra, seated at the bar with his Rat Pack buddies. They invited the blond bombshell to join them, and though tempted by the opportunity to meet her idol, she declined. She did not care to be around the inebriated, nor did she care to be a footnote in the sexual swordsman's romantic résumé.

A middle-aged man attended the casino every night to watch Barbara; Zeppo Marx had retired from show business to indulge in golf, gambling, and women. He was the least funny but wealthiest of his famous brothers. In 1958, he invited Barbara to his home in Palm Springs, where her love for the designer desert won over her lack of interest in the man. Soon, Mrs. Barbara Marx enjoyed the proximity of the stars, especially Frank Sinatra, who lived next door with Mia Farrow in the mansion called the Compound.

Post divorce from Farrow, Sinatra dated a never-ending stream of the world's most desirable women, many of whom Barbara met when she and Marx were his guests. One evening there was a game of charades, and Barbara was on his opposing team where, as time-keeper, she held a large brass clock. When Barbara announced the time was up before Sinatra's team had solved their charade, Sinatra smashed the clock against the wall to Barbara's horror. Fortunately, there was a comedian in the room, Pat Henry, who diffused the situation with the quip, "I just guessed the charade: 'As Time Goes By.'"

The relationship between Barbara and Sinatra shifted from clocks flying to sparks flying one enchanted evening. When the crooner made a pass at her, she explained her infidelity by claiming Sinatra was such a force of nature she "didn't have a choice." Marx did not concur. Upon discovering his neighbor and his wife had simultaneously broken the seventh and tenth commandments, he filed for divorce. Although he was worth millions, Barbara received only $180,000 and a four-year-old Jaguar.

The Sinatra-Marx affair continued; one of her draws was that Sinatra liked a woman who could hold her liquor, and Barbara never disappointed in that aspect. He also hated women who smoked (though he loved his unfiltered Camels), and she quit cold turkey. The sacrifices one makes for love.

One evening, shortly after they had first become intimate, she stepped into a car thinking she was on the way to dinner. She was correct, but in order to get to the restaurant, they had to board Frank's G2 Gulfstream jet, headed for Athens. He laughed and explained, "I fancied Greek food tonight." There was also take-out culinary treats for, as Frank called her, "Barbara baby." Pizza flown in from New York, crab claws from Florida, and cheesecake from Chicago. The Emerald City, compliments of her blue-eyed magician, had landed her in the lap of luxury.

Despite the jet-setting life style in the company of the A-list,

Barbara lived in a constant state of uncertainty, fearful one younger, more beautiful, waited in the wings. On one of Sinatra's world tours, they stayed in Jerusalem and visited the Wailing Wall. In the shadow of King Solomon's ancient temple, Barbara penned a prayer and slipped it in the crack of the wall. It was a heartfelt plea to God for continued happiness with Sinatra and, in a plaintive PS, that he ask for her hand in marriage. To help alleviate her anxiety, her lover showered her with expensive gifts of a Palm Springs home, a new Jaguar, and jewelry, but he failed to offer what she most coveted: marriage.

A night to remember occurred when the man known for his mob affiliation showed his Italian romantic side when he filled a hotel room with flowers and gave her a mammoth pear-shaped diamond, instructing her to take it to Jeweler's Row and choose its setting. In a nod to "hope springs eternal," she designated it as a ring and shipped the finished product to Sinatra. When he re-presented it to her, she coyly told him to choose which finger it would adorn. When he picked the left-hand digit, it produced a gasp heard around Palm Springs.

The life of Sinatra's fiancée became a fairy tale far from one predicted for a kosher butcher's daughter; as Barbara wrote, "He turned every day into Christmas." Now, instead of wearing the Eiffel Tower as a headdress, she visited it in the company of the man dubbed the entertainer of the century. She hobnobbed with the world's who's who: Prince Rainier and Princess Grace, Gregory Peck, Cary Grant, Liza Minnelli, and the Rat Pack. Another couple they socialized with was Liz Taylor and Richard Burton; Ms. Taylor received her famous sixty-nine-carat diamond as a *mea culpa* when Burton unfavorably compared his wife's legs to Barbara's.

The wedding for which Barbara had expended infinite prayers was July 11, 1976. Its venue was Sunnylands, the 25,000-square-foot

Rancho Mirage California estate of mogul Walter Annenberg. In the spirit of Henry IV's "Paris is well worth a mass," she converted to Roman Catholicism to secure her long-awaited prize. This still did not win over her future mother-in-law, Natalina, to take to the Jewish, twice-divorced single mother. Instead, the Italian mother confronted her son: "Aren't there enough whores around?" Additional members on the anti-Barbara front were Sinatra's three children from his first wife, especially his daughter Nancy. Her one hit had been "These Boots Are Made for Walking," and she knew exactly where she wanted her boots to land—as footprints on her new stepmother. On the morning of the long-awaited day, romantic Sinatra had his attorney deliver a prenup—if Barbara did not sign, the blessed event dangled in front of her would, like the name of the Annenberg estate, remain a mirage. Confident of her compliance, Sinatra had invited glittering guests who included Governor Ronald and Nancy Reagan, Kirk and Anne Douglas, Gregory and Veronica Peck, and Sammy Davis Jr. Barbara signed. The ceremony was officiated by Judge James H. Walsworth and when he asked the bride, "Do you take this man for richer or poorer," the groom quipped, "Richer, richer!"

Mrs. Frank Sinatra IV became the official chatelaine of the Compound as well as various other stately pleasure domes. Her spouse had a great eye for precious stones, and a king's ransom of gems would be hidden in random places—pillows, purses—for her to stumble upon. One emerald bauble, originally made for Madam Cartier, was dubbed "the Holy S_____!" for obvious reasons to anyone who laid eyes on it. Another gift came in plain view, her birthday present: a blue Rolls-Royce Corniche. If the gods had not upended the

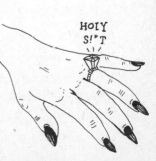

cornucopia enough on Barbara's ever perfectly coiffed head, she had a respectful husband in the house as well. Sinatra was no slob; for him, slumming was lounging around the mansion in silk pajamas as he was a Type A neat-freak. In a nod to a Sinatra lyric, it was a very good year.

That said, as she relayed in her memoir *Lady Blue Eyes*, the sun around which she revolved possessed a dark side, which erupted after Sinatra spent time with his ever-present companion: Jack Daniels. He insisted his drink only hold four ice cubes. If it did not, he would snap at a bartender, "What am I, an ice-skater?" After too much imbibing, Dr. Jekyll would turn into Mr. Hyde—the street tough from Hoboken, New Jersey—which was Barbara's cue to take refuge in her bedroom with the door locked. This explains the sign over their home's service entrance: "Never mind the dog. Beware of the owner." Sinatra also never lost his lust for the ladies; however, Barbara stoically adopted the Jesus admonition, "turn the other way." When asked about Ava Gardner for whom Sinatra had carried a lifelong torch, Barbara responded, "A very wise French lady once said to me, 'You don't worry about old flames—just new ones.'" Mrs. Sinatra obviously earned every diamond. "My Way" was not just Frank's signature song but the way he conducted his marriage.

Given his proclivity for the ladies, she was not shocked when random strangers would approach claiming to be the mother or the grandmother of his child. She, for her part, remained true to her marital vows. This may be because while in a movie, Sinatra was *The Man with the Golden Arm*, he may have possessed another golden part of his anatomy. Barbara stated, "He had a sexual energy all his own. Even Elvis Presley, whom I'd met in Vegas, never had it quite like that." Sinatra's famous libido made headlines in 2014 after a *Vanity Fair* interview where Mia Farrow claimed her son Ronan may possibly be the biological son of the famous crooner rather than director Woody Allen. The DNA of public opinion weighed in, saying Ronan shared the famous lady-slaying blue eyes and was more Frank than Woody. Ronan tweeted his take, "Listen, we're all 'possibly' Frank Sinatra's son." Barbara, who was married to Sinatra when Ronan was conceived, dismissed the whole affair as "a bunch of junk." At least Rosemary's baby knew his true paternity. Another of her spouse's Achilles heels was his temper. When he was out on a bender, his drinking buddies reached out to her for backup; Barbara was the one to bring her errant husband home. Another famous display of temper occurred in an Italian restaurant when he noticed his pasta was soggy. While other similarly dissatisfied patrons would send the offending dish back, Frank hurled his plate against the wall. Before storming out, he examined the mess of splattered tomato sauce and, dipping his finger in it, signed the mess "Picasso." The owner of the eatery put a frame around the unorthodox work of art.

In her memoir, Barbara explained she was the best one to keep Mr. Hyde at bay and wrote that during her twenty-two-year marriage, she proved his companion, consultant, psychiatrist, and lover. In one of their over-the-top residences is a photograph with the inscription: "Love is…us." Dean Martin had once made the observation, "It's Frank's world. We just live in it"—a sentiment his spouse well understood. Barbara was the wife with whom he truly coexisted, the only one who did not come with an expiration date. Most of all, she was his ever faithful "paesano" friend; she once remarked having Sinatra on your side was akin to having a whole army.

One of Sinatra's pronouncements was, "You gotta love livin', baby, because dyin' is a pain in the ass." In 1998, he had a heart attack and Barbara rushed to the hospital. She tried to reassure him as to his recovery by reminding him how many times he had defied illness. He then uttered his final words, "I can't," and the famous blue eyes closed forever. Condolences poured in from around the world, though none was forthcoming from stepdaughter Nancy, who complained his children had not been summoned to the hospital so the newspapers could report he died in his wife's arms. Nancy added with vitriol, "Karma is too good for her." Barbara's contentious relationship with her husband's children had always been an enormous elephant in the Sinatras' lavish rooms.

Sinatra was a megastar who belonged to the world, so his widow decided his funeral would not be the small ceremony that she claimed she would have preferred. Sinatra was dressed in his finest suit, and family and friends slipped mementoes into his coffin: a flask of Jack Daniels, unfiltered Camel cigarettes, and Zippo lighters. Private grief was public mourning as well: at his passing, the Empire State Building was bathed in blue for the departed Ol' Blue Eyes; the neon-drenched Las Vegas strip dimmed its lights in honor of its adopted son.

In *Lady Blue Eyes*, Barbara recounts that when she visits his grave, she is photographed by hordes of reporters and fans. She writes, "I sometimes wonder what they think of me, this woman in her eighties keeping vigil for her dead husband. Few knew where I came from or how I got there. They know nothing of my life before Frank, or how rich it became once I met him. If they only knew the places I've been, the things I've seen, the people I've met on my journey. That was some candy jar!" For most people, a candy jar is filled with various hued jelly beans; however, for Barbara, it was filled with a "Holy S___!" ring, the company of the rich and famous, and jet-setting around the world. But its true sweetness came because it was shared with the man who made her Mrs. Blue Eyes.

CHAPTER THIRTY-TWO

AFTER THE FALL

Mrs. Arthur Miller

F amous playwright Arthur Miller went through life asked what it was like being married to Marilyn Monroe. It was an all-too-obvious euphemism for the real question: what was it like to have sex with the goddess who went to bed wearing only Chanel No. 5? Miller took the answer to his grave but was never loathe to wax eloquent on his last wife after Marilyn: "This marriage makes the past seem worthwhile."

A photograph in a 1957 issue of *Life* magazine shows a car on Times Square with a llama's head protruding from a window. Even in expect-the-unexpected Manhattan, the image was unforgettable—as was the woman who had captured the shot. Ingeborg "Inge" Morath was born in 1923 in Graz, Austria, to liberal Protestant parents. They had converted from Roman Catholicism before marriage to have an escape route if conjugal bliss proved elusive. Her future wanderlust was fostered by the Moraths' constant moves due to Dr. Edgar Morath's academic postings. They ended up in Berlin—as the Chinese curse states "in interesting times"—at the outbreak of World War II.

It was here Inge had her first encounter with the avant-garde through the *Entartete Kunst* (Degenerate Art) exhibition organized by the National Socialist Party. Its purpose was to inflame the public against this type of art; it ignited a passion in Inge who stated, "I found a number of these paintings exciting and fell in love with Franz Marc's *Blue Horse*." As it was heresy to show approbation, she kept her private thoughts private. After high school, she passed the final exams and was compelled to complete six months of service for the *Reichsarbeitsdienst* (Reich Labor Service) before she could enroll in Berlin University.

Life under the Third Reich was far from comfortable for the anti-Nazi Moraths, and the teenaged Inge ran afoul of the authorities. She refused to join the National Socialist *Studentenschaft* (Student Organization), which resulted in expulsion. In retaliation she was compelled to labor in an airplane parts factory at Tempelhof that became a repeated Allied target. After the plant had been subjected to a particularly heavy bombardment, she ran through the rubble holding a bouquet of lilacs above her head as a talisman against death raining from the sky of Berlin. She later recalled walking through the countryside and witnessing the devastation of war: "Everyone was dead or half-dead. I walked by dead horses, by women with dead babies in their arms."

With her teenage years branded by Nazi repression, Inge turned for self-expression through the lens of a camera and took as her mantra Goethe's quotation, "We are born seeing, but we are required to look." It was this capacity for observation that informed her oeuvre, as she said, "When you take a picture you trust your eye and cannot help but bare your soul."

At the conclusion of the War, Inge moved to London and obtained a position under art director Simon Guttman at the magazine *Picture Post*, where she met her future husband, journalist Lionel Birch. To her grave disappointment, instead of apprenticing as a photographer, she was given secretarial chores or tasks at the *Post* such as heating Guttman's shaving water. Starved for professional fulfillment, she began freelancing and sold her works under the pseudonym "Egni Tharom," her name spelled backward. Disillusioned with job and marriage, she left both and moved to France to work with the Magnum Agency, the first woman admitted to the intensely macho club. Photography became her main source of self-expression because she was ashamed to speak German after the war, viewing the language as a millstone of guilt.

It was in Paris that Inge saw a performance of *The Crucible*, her first experience with the American playwright who would impact her life. But it was not until she made her first trip to the United States in 1956 that she understood firsthand the significance of the play's anti-McCarthy message. Coming through customs, she was detained for carrying in her baggage a book that, though about movie stars and called *Stardust in Hollywood*, had been published by the Left Bookshop in London. With characteristic *chutzpah*, she pointed out she could not possibly have survived the Third Reich had she been a communist. She further added it would be more pertinent to ask those with Austrian passports if they had been Nazi sympathizers. When she left the airport, she encountered a woman handing out leaflets ordering people to report any suspicious un-American activities. After a few months at Magnum, Inge became an assistant to Henri Cartier-Bresson, who told her that photography was, "The courage to walk up and hold your breath and take your picture."

So great was her talent she began receiving assignments from around the world. One of these included a trip to Iran where she wore a *chador* that disguised her ever-present Leica. During Ramadan, she sneaked inside a grand mosque to photograph the men prostrate on the floor. One worshipper sat up and alerted the others, who began pelting her with stones. Fortunately there were not too many of the makeshift weapons lying around and she was able to flee without injury. In Spain to photograph the running of the bulls, she won the rare position of entering a famous matador's dressing room. It was considered bad luck for a woman to see the fighter before the bull had the opportunity, but she convinced him that by snapping pictures she was not looking at him with female eyes. Her work eventually grew to include the iconic people of her era, such as Alexander Solzhenitsyn, Eleanor Roosevelt, and Andy Warhol, as well as places such as Boris Pasternak's home and Mao Zedong's bedroom.

In 1960, Magnum sent Inge to Reno, Nevada, to shoot stills of *The Misfits*, the film Arthur Miller had written for his wife Marilyn Monroe, whose psyche was crumbling along with their marriage. There she captured one of her most famous shots—the screen siren in a black cocktail dress, lost in thought and kicking up leaves in the Nevada desert. The picture captured anguish crouching behind celebrity.

The playwright first encountered the woman behind the camera when she and director John Huston were in the Maples Bar, deep in reminiscence of an earlier film. Miller later spoke of his first glimpse of Inge, who was to complement and complete him: "She was a slender, noble-looking young woman with bobbed hair and a European accent, who seemed both shy and strong at the time." However, Miller was too preoccupied to say more than hello as *The Misfits* was experiencing more off-the-set drama than on. Marilyn was spiraling out of control, and Huston was often so intoxicated he fell asleep while directing. Inge, for her part, only viewed the famed writer with professional interest. She had determined after her divorce that her only significant other would be her Leica camera.

Several months later, Inge and Miller ran into each other in New York and he asked her for dinner. Despite their differences in religion, nationality, and backgrounds, Inge knew she had found her flesh-and-blood *Blue Horse*. She recalled of that first date, "I thought he'd be terribly stern and serious. He's really very funny." The playwright, whose titles veer far from lightheartedness (*Death of a Salesman*, *The Misfits*, *The Crucible*), did have a sense of humor as evidenced in his classic anecdote that Billy Wilder found hilarious. When Miller and Marilyn had first become engaged, he took her to New York to meet his mother, Gussie. Mrs. Miller lived in a tiny apartment with walls so thin that when Marilyn went to the bathroom she worried everyone might hear her and turned on the faucet full blast. The next day, he called his mother to ask what she thought of her future daughter-in-law, to which Gussie responded, "She's sweet. But she pisses like a horse!" He also found out what Inge and Huston had been recalling at the Maples Bar. In 1950, when the director was in Mexico filming *The Unforgiven* and Inge was taking its photographic stills, the actor and former war hero Audie Murphy's boat had capsized and he was in danger of drowning. Inge quickly stripped to her underwear and towed Murphy back to shore while he was holding on to her bra strap. In gratitude, he gave her his watch that he had carried throughout the war.

Miller, who had recently undergone an excruciating divorce from Marilyn, claimed his "reasoned resolve" was to never again walk down the matrimonial aisle. His play *After the Fall* was a thinly veiled confessional of the anguish he had endured with America's sex symbol, even if she was the hourglass sheathed in silk. It was readily understood why writer Truman Capote had pronounced of the Miller-Monroe marriage: "Death of a Playwright." Miller had likened her to a smashed vase: "It is a beautiful thing when it is intact, but the broken pieces are murderous and they can cut you." However, his feelings for Inge, the diametric opposite of Marilyn, made for a change of heart. He explained, "Maybe all one can do is hope to end up with the right regrets." A month after ending his marriage to Marilyn, Miller wed Inge. Miller later said the forty years he spent with her proved the best of his life. In tribute, he dedicated his autobiography, *Timebends*, "For my wife, Ingeborg Morath." Love allowed the angst-ridden writer to finally escape his crucible.

Miller had named his 1940 play *The Man Who Had All the Luck*, and it was a phrase widely, if mistakenly, used to describe its writer's fraught marriage to Marilyn Monroe. However, Miller considered himself the titan of luck as the husband of Inge. The couple made their primary residence a ten-bedroom estate in Roxbury, Connecticut (which he had purchased and renovated while married to Marilyn), whose privacy they ensured by planting an army of trees. Under the influence of his wanderlust wife, the inner voyaging Miller became a world traveler, and they collaborated on books of their journeys in which she provided the photographs and he the text. However, their greatest collaboration was daughter Rebecca, born in 1962; four hours before going into labor, the feckless mother to-be was on the top of a tall crane taking photographs in the Brooklyn Navy Yard.

Unfortunately the tall trees surrounding their property and the bouquet of lilacs did not serve as protection against heartbreak. In 1966, Inge delivered her second child, Daniel, who was born with Down syndrome. Inge wanted to keep him, but Miller arranged for the "mongoloid," as he referred to him, to be institutionalized. Though his mother visited on Sundays, his father rarely did. The infant was excised from the playwright's life as if a character too discordant to the overall plot. *Timebends* had no mention of son Daniel Miller. This chimed a jarring note from the author who had written in *Death of a Salesman*, "Attention must be paid." Despite this heartbreak, Rebecca was an endless source of joy and her parents were pleased with her marriage to actor Daniel Day-Lewis, whom she had met during the production of *The Crucible* and with whom she had sons Ronan and Cashel.

From the 1980s onward, Inge stayed for longer periods at her Roxbury home, where she made little alteration other than to convert the heart-shaped swimming pool (shades of Marilyn) back into a natural lake where she swam daily. A vegetarian, when not behind a camera, she often enjoyed being in front of a stove where the kitchen was aromatic with the fragrance of baking bread and Austrian cakes and pastries. This was a far cry from Marilyn's stab at domesticity when she attempted to dry pasta with her hair dryer.

In 2002, diagnosed with lymphatic cancer, Inge decided to return to the country of her birth and documented the occasion in her final work *Last Journey*. Of his wife's photography, Miller was always her most ardent fan, saying, "She made poetry out of people and their places over half a century." She passed away later that year at age seventy-eight in New York Hospital. Inge's greatest gift to Miller was an emotional resurrection *After the Fall*.

CHAPTER THIRTY-THREE

FOR REMEMBRANCE

Mrs. Timothy Leary

D r. Timothy Leary pronounced the paradoxical catchphrase, "If you can remember the sixties, you weren't really there." Leary was not only there, he was its vanguard, and beside him, his psychedelic pioneer and muse. She was his soul mate who left her Midwest home hoping for adventure, which she received in spades—a result of her love affair with an amalgam of the King of Hearts and the Joker.

Rosemary ("Ro") Sarah Woodruff was born in St. Louis, Missouri, on April 26, 1935, to a middle-class conservative family. As a child, she mythologized everything, longing for the ordinary to be replaced by the extraordinary. When placed in a baptismal pool at age seven, rather than the hoped-for religious experience, all she received was a cold. The only form of magic she experienced in childhood was as the daughter of an amateur magician. Her father picked pennies from her ears and dealt cards that appeared in her hair. She later wrote, "His hand had to be watched carefully; it created invisibility."

She escaped when she dropped out of high school at seventeen and married an air force officer. She fled from the military base and husband after six months and migrated to New York City. A marriage to a jazz musician also dissolved, and she supported herself with modeling. (To give a sense of her beauty, only Tina Louise—the actress of *Gilligan's Island* fame—beat her out for a bikini cover on *Esquire* magazine.) She also experimented with peyote, a drug derived from cactus mainly found in Mexico, and finally had her religious experience meeting the Pied Piper of pharmaceuticals.

On May 1, 1965, Rosemary took a fateful trip to a sprawling mansion, Millbrook Estate in Duchess County, owned by the Mellon-fortune heirs, where the original nutty professor, Dr. Timothy Francis Leary, had retreated post dismissal from his university for trying to turn on all of Harvard to drugs. By the time Ro met Leary, he had completed his startling metamorphosis from Ivy League academic to counterculture evangelist. At Millbrook, he was the high priest of hallucinogenic hedonism where guests eagerly enacted his mantra that became the rallying cry of a generation: "Turn on, tune in, drop out." The word was out that at Leary's lair, the panties dropped as fast as the acid, the god Krishna received a heavy dose of chants, and The Beatles were on the record player twenty-four-seven.

When Leary first saw the thirty-year-old Rosemary in his kitchen, he was immediately drawn by the magnet of her beauty. He recalled in his autobiography, *Flashbacks*, "A cloud of pheromones floating from her body awakened my off-duty pheromones. My knees wobbled." On a subsequent visit, after taking LSD, Leary and Rosemary spent their first night together in the meditation room. The following morning, they outlined a pair of interlocked triangles on the chimney, the Maha Yantra, the ancient Oriental symbol for sexual union. The doctor interpreted this as whatever sexual problems he had experienced in his former relationship would be resolved with Rosemary. While others may have been (pardon the pun) leery of involvement, Rosemary simply stated of the charmer cum laude, "I fell in love with him, and he with me."

Although Rosemary was familiar with the Leary myth of the infamous hippy guru who had become the spokesman for the turned-on flower people, she soon uncovered his romantic history. His first wife Marianne had committed suicide on the eve of her husband's thirty-fifth birthday; his second wife Mary departed before following suit. He was introduced to his third, *Vogue* cover-girl Nena von Schlebrügge, through Salvador Dalí, who left him on their Himalayan honeymoon. She nevertheless retained a soft spot for her ex, and Leary became godfather to her daughter Uma Thurman.

Rosemary felt she had found the soul mate with whom she would have a baby and, in the future, a home with a white picket fence. She moved into Millbrook and tried to become the perfect mate to Leary and mother to his children, Susan and Jack. Chemistry was not the problem but rather constant arrest. The first time was in Laredo, Texas, where Susan was hiding the family's marijuana in her underpants. The next brush with the law was when Leary's nemesis and future Watergate burglar, G. Gordon Liddy, in his job as Duchess County assistant district attorney, raided Millbrook. The third was when the police busted the quintessential hippie couple for marijuana possession in Laguna, California.

Although subpoenas, attorneys, and court dates do not rank high on the aphrodisiac ladder, Rosemary and Leary decided to marry on November 11, 1967, on a mountaintop of the Joshua Tree Monument in a California National Park. The service was performed by Samu, a famous Plains Indian medicine man, who was so stoned on peyote he had trouble conducting the ceremony. Similarly, the groom was in the grip of

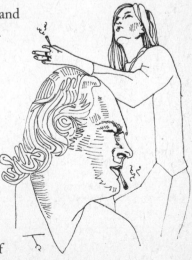

mescaline, a drug known for its hallucinogenic properties, and could not stop retching. As the undertaking was not the bride's dream nuptials, they had a do-over, retying the knot at their new home in Berkeley, this time by an East Indian fakir—though with the same anti-ambience results. Hoping a third time would prove the proverbial charm, a final marriage was enacted at Millbrook. In a wedding photograph that appeared on the front page of the *New York Post*, Leary is seated with a garland of white flowers around his neck, barefoot, while the bride's features are adorned with red-and-white tribal markings.

The following year, Leary received a phone call from another counterculture couple, John Lennon and Yoko Ono, inviting them to Montreal for their "bed-in." After Lennon had played a few songs on his guitar while Rosemary kept beat by banging on Tommy Smothers's guitar, the Beatle crooned, "John and Yoko, Timmy Leary, Rosemary, Bobby Dylan, Norman Mailer, Allen Ginsberg, Hare Krishna. All we are saying is give peace a chance." An iconic photograph of the event showed the two infamous couples in bed, Leary's head resting on his wife's shoulder. Leary asked Lennon for assistance in his campaign for governor of California, known by its mantra "Luv for Guv." When he said his slogan was "Come Together, Join the Party," John took his guitar and improvised what would be the classic "Come Together."

It was after the bed-in that Rosemary most truly entered the rabbit hole of life with Leary. In 1970, a judge sentenced her to prison for six months for the Laguna marijuana bust while Leary, whom President Nixon had now branded "the most dangerous man in America," was faced with a sentence of up to twenty-eight years. Characteristically, Leary compared himself to Christ harassed by Pilate and Herod. Before the bailiffs led him away, he embraced his wife. Freed on bail, Rosemary described her incarcerated spouse as the hero chained to the rock.

In a surreal collaboration of minds that could only have occurred in that stand-alone era, Rosemary worked with the Black Panthers, the Weather Underground, and the Brotherhood of Eternal Love to spring Leary from the California Men's Colony at San Luis Obispo. She later quipped that this should have qualified her for a "Stand by Your Man" award. Leary shimmied along a telephone cable over the prison fence and was picked up by a Weatherman operative. Rosemary, the Midwestern girl seemingly born for obscurity, was now an infamous fugitive from the law for violating her own parole and facilitating the prison break of a felon. However, the die was cast; she was a woman in love. Donning disguises, Leary shaved his head and dressed in foreign garb—conservative attire. Rosemary transformed her appearance from a dark-haired hippie chick to a blond bouffant hairdo, push-up bra, and heels. With forged passports, the couple fled overseas.

The Learys' destination was Algiers, where they, along with Anita Hoffman (wife of Abbie), became the house guests of exiled Eldridge Cleaver. The Black Panthers enjoyed diplomatic immunity and initially provided a safe house in their compound. Alas, there was a conflict between the two male visionaries. Leary's penchant for smoking hashish smuggled to him by his old buddies in the Brotherhood alienated his host, especially as Algeria, an Islamic country, was not keen on drugs. Eldridge also began to harass his guests, who became his prisoners. It was time for the magician's daughter to disappear once more.

It was in Switzerland where Rosemary had an overdue epiphany: life with Leary was never going to lead to a home with a white picket fence. Leary had taken up with an international arms dealer, Michel Hauchard, who had agreed to protect him in exchange for thirty percent of the royalties from books the good doctor had agreed to pen. Irritated with the lack of progress, he had Leary arrested in the belief he would be less distracted in confinement. Thanks to his wife's exertions, Leary was released after a month.

It was finally clear that by Leary, she was not going to be a mother, that his delight in greeting camera crews superseded all other desires. With tears and angst, Rosemary negotiated their separation, which she said was merely a necessary time-out. When she returned, it was to discover he had taken up with another woman who was wearing her clothes. She stormed she was no longer responsible for his debts—karmic or financial—and left to face life on the lam without the man who had molded her into the role of fugitive. Bereft at the loss of Rosemary, Leary turned to heroin. He was ultimately arrested in Kabul and incarcerated in Folsom Prison. In the next cell, Charles Manson, the crazed groupie cult leader who had terrorized Los Angeles, told him, "I've been wanting to talk to you for a long time, man."

Mrs. Leary remained underground for twenty-three years, living in Afghanistan, Sicily, and Central and South America. As a fugitive, Rosemary learned from a newspaper that a Los Angeles judge had dissolved their marriage, granting Leary a divorce petition he had filed without her knowledge. In 1976 Governor Jerry Brown had approved Leary's release in the belief Nixon's most dangerous man in the country no longer posed a threat. After secretly returning to the United States, she used the name Sarah Woodruff and worked a variety of jobs in Cape Cod and California. When a judge cleared her of her charges, the magician's daughter stepped from the shadows and lectured at the University of California at Santa Cruz for a course on the era her flawed, tragic hero had defined. She reconciled with Leary after fifteen years devoid of contact when his deeply disturbed daughter, Susan, hung herself in custody after shooting her sleeping boyfriend at close range.

Despite the tumultuous times, Rosemary seemed to have had no regrets. She reminisced, "I'd like to do this whole thing all over again on a sunny day with some wine." Before her death at her home in Aptos, California, from congestive heart failure at age sixty-six, Mrs. Leary gave her fifth and final annual farewell party for the late Dr. Leary. She passed out seventy-five plastic bags with portions of his cremated remains, some of which had been rocketed into space in fulfillment of his final wish. Mingled in the ashes was body glitter so his remains could sparkle when airborne. The words of Ophelia to Hamlet could well serve as her own: "There's rosemary, that's for remembrance."

CHAPTER THIRTY-FOUR

THE MERRY PRANKSTER

Mrs. Jerry Garcia

T he Summer of Love. Those four words conjure a 1960s moment frozen in an American snow globe: mythical months in San Francisco when visions of peace, love, and harmony hung in the air, interspersed with quantities of sex, drugs, and rock 'n' roll. It also represented a love story, one between the guitarist-troubadour Captain Trips and his Mountain Girl.

The original hippie girl, born in 1946, Carolyn Elizabeth Adams was raised in an intellectual family, in the city referenced in the movie *Sex and the City* when Carrie, in Mexico, explains Charlotte had "Poughkeepsied in her pants." Her maternal grandfather was a missionary in India where her mother was raised; on her father's side, she was descended from Samuel Adams, a physician during the Revolutionary War. Her parents, Ruth, a botanist, and Alfred, an entomologist, valued knowledge over materialism, and she grew up the tomboy, nature-loving sister of two academically gifted brothers. Although the Adams parents were progressive, they still gave their sons more latitude, and Carolyn's wish-upon-a-star was independence.

Although her home life was happy, the same could not be said of school, where she was the outsider, a beatnik in the making. True to her inner drummer, she eschewed the fashions of the time and refused to tease her hair to unnatural heights or wear makeup. Her personal style was black turtlenecked sweaters, and in lieu of friends, she had poetry. Her P.E. teacher, not impressed with her streak of rebellion, always had it in for the nonconformist, and she was expelled six weeks before graduation. (She received a diploma via the U.S. Postal Service.) At loose ends, she was only too happy to climb aboard her brother's Volkswagen bus when he offered her a ride as he headed for Palo Alto for graduate work at Stanford. Carolyn ended up at Stanford, but not as a student. She had a night job at the university's lab, analyzing the precursor to LSD, and was fired for dipping into the experimental psychedelic chemicals. Once again, she was at loose ends—the only difference was the coast.

She was at a Palo Alto café, immersed in a book, when Beat icon Neal Cassady (on a run for bennies, slang for the drug Benzedrine) noticed the pretty seventeen-year-old. His radar signaled she was a fellow blithe spirit, and he invited her for a ride. She agreed to go with the stranger when she realized he was the Dean Moriarty of Jack Kerouac's book *On the Road*. They ended up at the log cabin La Honda home of Ken Kesey at five in the morning, riding high (literally) on the success of Kesey's recent novel *One Flew Over the Cuckoo's Nest*. Cassady, because of Carolyn's free spirit, introduced her as a mountain girl to the Merry Pranksters, a motley crew who orbited around Kesey. She immediately felt she had met the people who spoke her language. The connection was mutual. During an acid trip, they invited MG (as they called her) to join their inner circle, which inextricably bound her to an iconic epoch in American pop culture.

In 1964, Mountain Girl was on the Pranksters' Day-Glo-painted 1939 International Harvester school bus named *Further* on the way to the New York World's Fair. The trip had the dual purpose of liberating the country from the conservatism of the '50s and to promote Kesey's new novel *Sometimes a Great Notion*—a reference to a song where the great notion was "to jump in a river and drown." This was to be no ordinary road trip, accompanied by enough drugs that on a windless day, one could get high just strolling past the bus. The odyssey, immortalized in Tom Wolfe's *The Electric Kool-Aid Acid Test*, would become the mythologized starting point of the psychedelic '60s.

In 1965, Kesey, in trouble in conjunction with a marijuana bust, faked his suicide and split for Mexico, hidden in a car trunk. Carolyn, pregnant with his baby, joined him and gave birth to daughter Solano (Sunshine). They did not get married because of the real Mrs. Kesey, with whom he had three young children. The eighteen-year-old Carolyn, perhaps in an atavistic nod to her conservative Poughkeepsie mores, to avoid the stigma of unwed mother, married fellow Merry Prankster George Walker. However, shortly thereafter, Kesey and Walker became past tense in the heart of Mountain Girl.

In 1966, the Pranksters were conducting an acid test at San Francisco State when Carolyn met guitarist Jerry Garcia of the rock band the Grateful Dead. Garcia had come up with the name that refers to a folk ballad in which a kind person helps a ghost find peace. There was an instant connection, and he played all night for the girl, who was accompanied by baby Sunshine, nestled in a basket. From that moment on, Mountain Girl and Captain Trips (so named for an obvious reason) were inseparable.

TO MY CAROLYN-MOUNTAIN GIRL.

The couple moved into the nerve center of the counterculture, 710

Ashbury, Garcia's commune in the Haight; however, their house-mates never saw them as they rarely left their bedroom. Garcia had the fortune—or misfortune—that when he fell, he fell hard. But it was more than chemistry and the flush of her first true love that tethered Mountain Girl to the legend with whom she had daughters Annabelle and Theresa. Carolyn recognized his genius and obtained a divorce from Walker. She settled into the role of homemaker, though far from the one portrayed by Mrs. Cunningham of *Happy Days*.

For a while, she was fulfilled raising her three children and living with her man in the epicenter of San Francisco's burgeoning hippy scene. However, in 1974, their blissful partnership became a little less so. Garcia never met a temptation he could resist, whether it was drugs, food, or women, and he began taking more and more space. Mountain Girl knew there were any number of Deadheads (Grateful Dead groupies) who slept with him, but she never felt threatened.

This changed, however, when Garcia inexplicably went MIA. Carolyn questioned his bandmates, but they denied knowledge of his whereabouts. She became the clichéd wife who is "the last to know." He had moved in with Deborah Koons, a twenty-year-old University of North Carolina filmmaker. She had become acquainted with Garcia when she hopped on the Dead's bus after seeing her first Grateful Dead concert in 1973 at the Nassau Coliseum and sat next to him on the return trip to Manhattan. The news produced less than perfect harmony. Carolyn attempted to fight back by storming into the San Rafael film studio where Deborah worked and handing her a one-way ticket to New York, which Deborah promptly cashed in. Garcia, torn between the two women, continued to live with Deborah though he came in and out of Carolyn's life. In an attempt at reconciliation, Carolyn accompanied the Dead when they went to Egypt to play at the pyramids.

Upon return, she had reached her saturation point: her Summer of Love had morphed into her Winter of Discontent. She could not cope with his new love interest and his drug use, his every move a media frenzy. It might have been the milieu for Mountain Girl, but not for Mountain Mama who had to look out for the interests of her three girls. It was time for her to fly west and escape the cuckoo's nest.

Carolyn relocated to Oregon where Kesey, his wife, and children, along with the Pranksters, had settled. However, Garcia, when his relationship with Deborah ended, sought forgiveness and his white flag was a proposal. Carolyn Adams Walker caved and became Mrs. Garcia in 1981, between sets at the Dead's traditional New Year's show in the Oakland Auditorium. The ceremony was performed by a Jewish friend who was also a Tibetan monk and administered the rites in full Tibetan regalia. Garcia promised they would get a house together and he would stay true to his marital vows.

When this failed to pan out and Carolyn found herself on the same drug-fueled merry-go-round, she returned to Oregon to a simple house with a lot of land. Although bereft of her husband, she had achieved her youthful wish upon a star. She kept her distance from the man who had made a secondary career of capturing and breaking her heart.

The Garcias' separation lasted until a 1986 phone call informed her Jerry was in Marin General Hospital in a diabetic coma. She immediately rushed to his side, willing him to survive. When he did, his brush with mortality made them realize the old flame had never been extinguished, and Carolyn and children moved in with Garcia in San Raphael, where she finally caught a glimpse of the family life she had always craved. Six months later, he had some dental work, and the siren song of painkillers returned him to the lap of addiction. It closed the coffin on their cohabitation.

In 1993, Garcia, who had reconnected with Deborah when he had run into her at a health food store, asked Carolyn for a divorce so he could wed his current love interest. The epilogue to their tumultuous marriage was a one-paragraph separation agreement, stipulating Garcia would grant his wife a five-million-dollar settlement, payable in monthly installments of $20,883. Eighteen months later, Garcia passed away from a heart attack at a drug rehabilitation center. President Bill Clinton mourned his passing on MTV as a "genius," and San Francisco authorities hoisted a tie-dyed flag over city hall. His death resulted in the reincarnation of the Summer of Love, and the Deadheads converged in Haight-Ashbury's Ben & Jerry's ice-cream parlor, the chain that for over a decade has featured a flavor dubbed Cherry Garcia. Unfortunately, the mass wake was accompanied by acrimony between the two Mrs. Jerry Garcias.

The first skirmish was by the widow, who barred Carolyn from the shipboard service where Garcia's ashes were scattered in the Pacific. This was followed by Carolyn, who launched a lawsuit as Deborah had cut off her monthly payment, claiming the homespun divorce agreement was invalid as Garcia signed it when high. Carolyn's heartfelt wish was Deborah would abide by Kesey's great notion. To counter the allegation, Carolyn took the stand and, with voice breaking, read a  letter from Garcia addressed to "Sweet Light" and signed "your devoted ugly Jer," which read: "Your incredible eyes that dance and twinkle and flash and flirt and laugh and stun and also warm and soothe and speak of deepest love." The Marin County court drama aired Garcia's tie-dyed dirty laundry in public: the plaintiff was the love-bead-wearing Carolyn, and the defendant the pearl-wearing Deborah. The trial descended into a "Jerry loved me best" soap opera. Jerry would have been grateful he was dead and thus spared the feeding frenzy his demise engendered. What was lost by the warring wives was the spirit of the Grateful Dead's name: the ballad in which a kind soul helps a ghost to find peace.

In the field of Ken Kesey's Oregon home, the iconic bus Further lies abandoned, the Day-Glo paint peeling off in leprosy-like layers. Daisies have sprung up between its floorboards, and it is no longer possible to gain entry due to the tangle of weeds and a tree that obscure the door. The bus is a symbol for the baby-boomer generation, forever lost to the past that had shaped their futures. It is also a metaphor for the motley crew who undertook a ride without brakes, pushing the envelope, which resulted in the Woodstock Nation. Last but not least, it is also a sad paean to yesteryear when the Haight-Ashbury court was presided over by Captain Trips and his Mountain Girl, his forever Merry Prankster.

CHAPTER THIRTY-FIVE

SET THE NIGHT ON FIRE

Mrs. Jim Morrison

Cemeteries do not rank high in the hierarchy of romance with the exception of Père Lachaise in Paris, where several immortal couples lie together for eternity: Abelard and Héloïse, Gertrude Stein and Alice B. Toklas, Simone de Beauvoir and Jean-Paul Sartre. Another tomb with echoes to love is Père Lachaise's most visited grave—of rock royalty Jim Morrison. A photograph taken over it features a ghostly apparition, a white figure with arms outstretched—the prince of music bemoaning separation from his cosmic mate.

Perhaps the reason why The Doors' front man was trying to break on through to the other side was because he was reaching for his titian-haired muse. Pamela Susan Courson was born December 22, 1946, in a town whose name became her passion, Weed, California. Its sole literary association is that Weed was where Lennie had to flee to escape lynching in Steinbeck's *Of Mice and Men*. Pamela was the younger sister of Judith and daughter of Columbus "Corky," a junior high school principal, and homemaker wife, Pearl "Penny." The family fit in well with the conservative Orange County mentality and morality of the 1950s, where residents declared they were "to the right of Buckley." Their slogan was in reference to William F. Buckley Jr., whose political agenda was to make conservatism predominate, an ideology he espoused in his column, "On the Right." The exception was Pamela, a rebel against many causes. Her first act of defiance was her refusal to wear the Brownie uniform of her troop, which she considered ugly; the troop's leader declared her a bad seed. In high school, she dyed her hair black and dressed as a beatnik, which immediately set her apart from the other girls with their Aqua Net bouffant hair and poodle skirts. In her senior year, she followed Lennie's lead and escaped—to Los Angeles, where she met her dark angel and became a footnote in rock history.

Pamela enrolled in art college and dressed her rail-thin body in hippie garb; her scale never registered more than two digits as a result of anorexia. In the evening, she frequented Sunset Strip, a major artery for the counterculture, where emerging groups such as Led Zeppelin played. Although Whisky-a-Go-Go was the hot spot, she ended up at the London Fog where an unknown band, The Doors, was performing. (Its singer had named the band after a line in a William Blake poem, which Aldous Huxley also borrowed for *The Doors of Perception*.) Behind the scenes, Morrison preferred to be considered a poet and took to heart Blake's quotation, "The road of excess leads to the palace of wisdom."

Jim Morrison was so sexy that Pamela, like legions of other ladies, fell for the tousled-haired singer with the Botticelli face and six-pack abs. Morrison was equally mesmerized with Pamela's fiery hair and white skin whose fragility cried out for protection. Another point of attraction was her frayed jeans with a heart embroidered on the butt. While Morrison was intellectually into the doors of perception, sexually he was a "backdoor man," and he took this as an open sesame. Although Morrison felt he was genetically indisposed to fidelity (his one-night drunken debauches with other women were legion), he gave it his best shot with Pamela, whom he dubbed his cosmic soul mate.

After The Doors snagged a record deal with Elektra Records, Morrison and Pamela, always looking for the untried, tried their hand at domesticity. They moved into a 1922 house in Laurel Canyon; although it was mere minutes from the Strip, the rural retreat seemed light-years away. The neighborhood was comprised of legends in the making: Three Dog Night, the Byrds, Crosby, Stills, and Nash, and the Mamas and the Papas. A feeling of community flowed in the neighborhood whose residents shared song lyrics and marijuana-laced brownies. In tribute to Pamela, who called herself Mrs. Morrison and wore a wedding band, Morrison immortalized his home in his song "Love Street." The scenic spot brought out Pamela's nesting instincts and she cooked while Morrison penned poetry. They would sit on their balcony with their beloved golden retriever Sage and watch the endless stream of hippies. When he toured, he took every opportunity to call her and share his latest poetic entries, immune to teasing from the other Doors. For her steadfast faith in his writing, he dedicated his book of poetry, *The Lords and the New Creatures*, "To Pamela Susan."

The couple was content in their cocoon, but it carried a short shelf life. Morrison's wandering eye lit the fuse and domestic tranquility was shattered when groupie Pamela Miller was lured into the Morrison home by the strains of his lyrics emanating from within. When she entered, she saw the shirtless singer in tight leather pants and proceeded to demonstrate her suppleness by performing a back-bend that sent her purple velvet mini-dress flying over her head. Believing this was overly neighborly, the red-haired lady of the house threw her out. Soon the quiet was punctuated

THAT CHICK HAS ONE HELL OF AN ARM.

by the sounds of smashing vinyl against the wall. Morrison merely ducked the flying records and smirked, "That chick has one hell of an arm." Another form of retaliation included tossing his books out the window. Pamela once stealthily wrote "Faggot" on the back of a vest he wore to a performance.

She also took to taking her own lovers. Morrison bought her a Porsche, and when she got involved with someone else, Pamela and her fling took off for New York and left the car at the airport with drugs in the trunk. Never grounded with practicalities, she did not return for the vehicle for two months, and when it was towed, she found the police at her door.

Pamela proved Morrison's match for crazy antics: in flirtation with death. She drove without headlights on Mulholland Drive's windy road. His specialty was hanging from hotel balconies. What augmented their insanity was their ever-increasing addiction to drugs and alcohol. Morrison downed three bottles of liquor a day while Pamela turned to heroin, a habit she did her utmost to camouflage. Ray Manzarek, ex-Door bandmate, stated, "Pamela was Jim's other half. The two of them were a perfect combination; I never knew another person who could so complement his bizarreness."

With The Doors, ever-escalating success, especially after their hit single "Light My Fire," their excess grew exponentially. While Morrison was increasingly engaged with the demands of fame and frenzied groupies, Pamela felt at loose ends. To placate her, he gave her full rein of their finances to pursue her dream of opening a fashion boutique. The Santa Monica Boulevard shop, which they initially wanted to name Fucking Great, was changed to Themis, after the Greek goddess of justice. Pamela gleefully traveled the globe, buying exotic items of clothing, and decorated the ceiling with innumerable peacock feathers, tie-dyed curtains for the fitting rooms, accompanied by incense burners to offset the scent of marijuana. One of its designers said Themis was "incredibly exclusive," both because of its exorbitant prices and the fact it was rarely open. However, when Pamela did manage to show up, so did the wealthy, one of whom was Sharon Tate—later the pregnant victim of Charles Manson—who purchased a black and white outfit. Morrison sank approximately $300,000 into the losing venture, a fact that did not bother him as it made Pamela happy.

But fame caused Morrison to spiral further out of control. When Ed Sullivan told him to delete the drug reference in "Light My Fire" during his appearance on the host's show, the uncompromising artist sang, "Girl, we couldn't get much higher" over international airwaves. When the show's producer told The Doors they would never work *The Ed Sullivan Show* again, Morrison replied, "Hey, man. We just did *The Ed Sullivan Show*."

Morrison, who always lowered the bar on behavior, met his 1969 Waterloo in his birth-state of Florida. He appeared at a Miami concert and launched into a drunken and profanity-laced anti-authority rant. He was accompanied by a lamb that he claimed he would not have sex with as it was too young and grabbed a policeman's cap and threw it into the audience, shouting, "Love your neighbor—till it hurts." However, the real legal bone of contention, so to speak, was he was accused of "taking it out." What with the screaming fans and the haze of marijuana fumes, the truth was blurred. The keyboard player, Ray Manzarek, claimed Jim only pretended to expose himself and there was no debut appearance of Jim's "magnificent member." Florida didn't agree, donning the robes of Themis and sentencing him to six months in prison and a $500 fine.

Frantic at the threat of jail time, Morrison decided to escape to

Paris. The city appealed to his romantic imagination as he felt he was following in the footsteps of the famous expatriate writers such as Fitzgerald, Hemingway, and Stein. The only remnant of the old world he took to his new one was Pamela. They envisioned living in a converted church, a spiritual cocoon, in which he could write and love in peace—a place to detox from the insanity. However, in Steinbeck fashion, "The best laid plans of mice and men do often go awry." And indeed they did for these cosmic soul mates.

In Paris, Morrison and Pamela stayed in L'Hôtel on the Left Bank, where Oscar Wilde had met his demise. On the night of July 3, 1971, they went to a late-night showing of the Robert Mitchum film *Pursued* and then came home and went straight to bed. Upon awakening, Pamela discovered Morrison's lifeless body in the bathtub. The cause of death was a heart attack, presumably brought on by an overindulgence in Pamela's stash of heroin.

Pamela dissolved into full-blown grief; Morrison had been the sun around which her world revolved. She gave his occupation as poet on the death certificate and purchased a double plot in Père Lachaise Cemetery. In a state of shock, she returned to the States where she found some comfort, if only material. In his will, he had left everything to her; he had tried to protect her in life and tried to do the same in death.

Pamela's mental stability had always been as frail as her waiflike body, and after Morrison's death, she became increasing reclusive. One afternoon, she walked into Themis and poured perfume over all the clothing. Afterward, she drove a truck headlong into the storefront, shattering its windows and damaging the front of the building.

In April 1974, Pamela was twenty-seven, the same age Morrison had managed to survive to before he "broke on through to the other side." Unable to continue life without her soul mate, she most likely embraced death by injecting an overdose of heroin. Ray Manzarek said of her demise, "Pamela and Jim are going to go down in the history books as great lovers. It's *Romeo and Juliet*; it's Héloïse and Abelard. It's Jim and Pam." Her parents listed her burial site as Père Lachaise, but due to legal issues, she was interred in Fairhaven Memorial Park in Santa Anna, California, under a marker bearing the name Pamela Susan Morrison. At her funeral, guests were asked not to wear black, and Manzarek played a haunting rendition of "Love Street." Although Jim's Père Lachaise grave is France's most visited and Pamela's is long forgotten, in this Southern California spot lies the muse behind the man of the Dionysian '60s who "set the night on fire."

CHAPTER THIRTY-SIX

LITTLE FROG

Mrs. Lech Walesa

At the eye of Solidarity's storm in Poland was Lech Walesa, the leader of a rebellion that struck a shattering blow to the sickle and hammer. However, it was his First Lady in freedom's fight who created a peephole into their domestic Iron Curtain.

On occasion, the spotlight of fame descends on the most unlikely: Miroslawa Danuta Golos started life in 1949 in Poland, the second of nine children, in a farmhouse without electricity. Her education ended at fourteen, and five years later, she left her village because she "needed something different." Miroslawa loved flowers and was thrilled when she obtained a position in a florist shop near the Lenin Shipyard. The nineteen-year-old had no idea the "something different" was about to enter her life and turn it into an unimaginable roller coaster.

On an autumn afternoon, Lech Walesa, an electrician from the shipyard, walked into her florist shop to get change. The rest was history—world history, in fact. She did not think much of him then or when he came back the next day and handed her a gift of a package of gum. She would have preferred a flower, and it would not have taken much of an effort considering the nature of her shop. For his part, Walesa was taken with the petite brunette whose smile revealed dimples. He invited her to the movies every night for a month; since they were both living in boardinghouses, it was the only place that afforded privacy. A month later, they were married on November 8, 1969.

Soon after that, Danuta (Lech preferred her middle name) bore babies in rapid succession. Despite the cramped condition of their squalid Soviet-issued apartment with their large brood, Danuta was delighted with her role as homemaker.

The Walesas' first serious roadblock occurred in 1970 when Lech's involvement in trade unions led to his dismissal at the Lenin Shipyard. Danuta had first heard of the strike from the news, which reported there was blood on the streets of Gdansk. Walesa comforted her with the promise everything would be all right. His words rang hollow as the next day, the Civic Militia came for him. Before he was arrested, he handed her his watch and wedding band to sell when she ran out of money. He was in custody only a few days, but upon his release found himself unemployable because of his reputation as an agitator.

Ever resourceful, he came up with a plan. His family would go to the supermarket, and when it came time for him to pay, he was simply going to hand over his ID card and say, "Tell the police I will be waiting for them at home. My children need to eat." It never went into effect. The following morning, a Communist Party official arrived, explaining he was delivering funds from the government-controlled trade union. Lech understood it was not just the Greeks to be aware of when they were bearing gifts—the Party was acting magnanimous to prevent the publicity that Walesa's stunt would have generated. He had further anticipated this gesture as he knew their apartment was bugged. From this plan of resistance, the Soviets understood Walesa was a resourceful opponent, his union understood he was a powerful leader, and Danuta understood he was not a conventional husband.

When the sun rises, most people assume the day will be like any other; however, by sunset, the fabric of one's life can forever unravel. This proved the case with the Walesa family on August 14, 1980, of which date Danuta states: "In August everything was smashed. Our nest was torn apart." Danuta, who views that summer afternoon as Caesar's wife did the Ides of March, sent Walesa to register the birth of their sixth child, Anna, at the city hall in Gdansk. He was on his way when he heard rumors of unrest at his former place of employment. The tension had been instigated when the management of the Lenin Shipyard had fired Anna Walentynowicz, a crane driver who had proved a thorn in her employer's side by demanding a memorial for protesting workers shot by the militia. In solidarity, groups of workers had put up posters of complaints and anger escalated when the managers quickly took them down. The standoff continued until a thirty-six-year-old short, stocky electrician scaled the shipyard wall and stood on a crate. Through the force of his rhetoric, he became their leader. Hours later, Danuta discovered baby Anna still did not have her birth certificate and her husband had spearheaded a movement, Solidarity, a name emblazoned in the world's headlines. The Lenin Shipyard protest became as iconic an event as when the Bastille fell, the Bolsheviks stormed the Winter Palace, Charles I beheaded, and the American Declaration of Independence proclaimed.

The Polish people, who had endured the back-to-back horror of Nazi and Soviet occupation, viewed Solidarity as their salvation; however, Danuta saw its other side. She recalled of those days following the insurrection when her small apartment became the movement's Mecca, "We had crowds of labor union members, advisers, politicians, journalists, and lunatics pouring into our apartment from dawn until late at night. Complete chaos instead of a normal home." In addition, she was left to care for the children, clean, and cook for everyone, including the constant stream of visitors. She described her role in those days, saying, "I was a mother, a teacher, a cook, a cleaning lady, a nurse. I had no time to do anything else." At one point, the dimples disappeared. Her home was overflowing with the usual crowds, and in their presence, she started yelling at her husband. Everyone immediately left, including the recipient of her wrath. A few hours later, he returned and offered a peace offering by suggesting they put a sign on the front door: "Typhoid fever. No admission to strangers."

The USSR put pressure on its party members in Poland to silence the head of Solidarity, and in 1982, Walesa was arrested. The only one allowed to visit was his spouse, pregnant with their eighth baby, who was subjected to strip searches. Walesa was behind bars for ten months, and Danuta was devastated he missed the St. Brigida Church's baptism of their last child.

If the bugging device in the Walesa apartment were equipped with a camera, in 1983, it would have recorded a large oil painting of Polish-born Pope John Paul II, red and white Solidarity banners, pictures of Jerzy Popieluszko, a murdered pro-union priest, and most importantly, a photograph on a bookcase that revealed a smiling Danuta. It was snapped while she was on a telephone call with Norway, upon hearing the news her husband had won the Nobel Peace Prize, the first Pole thus honored. In 1958, Russian author Boris Pasternak had been unable to accept his Nobel Prize for Literature in fear if he left the Soviet Union, he would be denied reentry and would never see his family or adored mistress again. Harboring similar trepidation, Walesa responded, without conjugal consultation, that Danuta would accept the prize on his behalf.

On December 10, in the flower-bedecked Old Hall of University of Oslo, Danuta Walesa finally showed she was more than a self-described "kitchen manager." The speech her husband prepared for her cited the words of the Polish Literature Laureate Henryk Sienkiewicz, author of *Quo Vadis* (*Where Are You Going?*): "In 1905, when Poland did not appear on a map of Europe, Henryk Sienkiewicz said when recieving the Nobel Prize for literature: 'She was pronounced dead—yet here is a proof that She lives on; She was declared incapable to think and to work—and here is proof to the contrary; She was pronounced defeated—and here is proof that she is victorious.' Today nobody claims that Poland is dead. But the words have acquired a new meaning." His words were filled with double entendre—they also referred to Danuta. King Olav of Norway stepped forward to congratulate her, and then one of the violinists in the orchestra began playing the Polish song "*Sto Lat,*" "One Hundred Years." In St. Brigida's Church, her beaming husband listened to her words on Radio Free Europe and said, "Bravo, Danuta," then added, "I've fallen in love with her all over again." From her experience, she received a transfusion of confidence. Unfortunately, on her return home, she was strip-searched by communist authorities. She said of the humiliating ordeal, "I didn't feel anything beyond numbness and delirium. Feelings come later."

The world hailed it as a blow against tyranny when Lech Walesa, in 1990, became Poland's first democratically elected president. However, as no man is a hero to his valet, he was not one to the First Lady, who was incensed he had accepted the position without informing her. To add fuel to the simmering fire, Walesa, perhaps feeling the presidency carried executive privilege to do

what he pleased, called another woman the term of endearment he had formerly reserved for his wife: "little frog." (The nerve!) No doubt Walesa spent the night on his couch under the eyes of the Pope. However, in public, Danuta praised her man and his mission, lamenting the lack of recognition for his contributions to the downfall of communism. As she noted sadly, when people think of the demise of the sickle and hammer, it is not "the flower-decorated Gate 2 of the Gdansk Shipyard in 1980 but the crumbling of the Berlin Wall in 1989 that has become the symbol of the freedom and unity of Europe."

In Walesa's acceptance speech for the presidency, he wrote, "My place is among those with whom I have grown and to whom I belong—the workers of Gdansk." Danuta had long felt her husband's allegiance to them had supplanted the one with his family, and in 2011, she decided to air her private grievances in public with her tell-all book *Dreams and Secrets*. On its cover, she

channeled her latent Princess Diana, outfitted in a stylish white hat with black ribbon, brim adorned with white flowers. She had finally discovered the answer to her own *Quo Vadis*. It was dedicated to her children: Bogdan, Slawomir, Przemyslaw, Jaroslaw, Magdalena, Anna, Maria Wiktoria, and Brygida. Her litany of complaints was lengthy— the tome ran 550 pages—and provided a feeding frenzy for the Polish public. She wrote, "When Solidarity was born...the father and the husband was gone...With that bloody politics, he was less and less involved at home, with the children, with me." She explained her husband was aware she was writing her memoir but "never quite believed that

I would actually do it." She said her book turned her "from a drab housewife into a lady of the house." She added, "*Dreams and Secrets* is only available in Polish, but it's my dream that it one day be translated into English."

The publication shattered their image as the picture-perfect couple. In its conclusion, Danuta states there is no plan to divorce though her husband and she have separate lives. She determined if they lived "*Sto Lat*," they were going to be lived on her terms. Walesa admitted to ignoring his family but explained it was out of necessity rather than for a lack of love. He said being the leader of ten million workers and a family man with eight children was a lot to juggle, but he always juggled the best he was able. He added he has not yet read the book but plans to buy his wife some flowers. Better late than never?

One of the unintended results of a movement that shook the world was that an uneducated country girl learned autonomy; another was that her husband, though a hero of millions, had not proved one to Danuta. Mrs. Walesa, at an interview at Carnegie Mellon University, stated through her translator, "I am master of myself." She transformed herself from an anvil to a pillar of strength, one who refuses to be her husband's—or anyone else's—little frog.

CHAPTER THIRTY-SEVEN

HEART

Mrs. Larry Flynt

N ame's Leasure, rhymes with pleasure," was the manner of introduction of Althea Leasure, fourth wife and first love of pornography baron Larry Flynt. Although many view their love story as a chronicle of depravity, it was nevertheless an against-all-odds romance.

In *Anna Karenina*, Tolstoy wrote, "Happy families are all alike; every unhappy family is unhappy in its own way." This proved the case with Althea, born in 1953 in Marietta, Ohio, who endured a waking-nightmare childhood. At age eight, along with her siblings, she was placed in a Catholic orphanage in Xenia; she ran away at fifteen, claiming the girls there (likely including herself) were subject to sexual abuse. She became an emancipated minor and barely survived but for a $10,000 stipend from her father's insurance policy, which evaporated into splurges for clothes and heroin.

In 1971, in a variation of Rick's lament, "Of all the gin joints in all the towns in all the world, she walks into mine," Jimmy Flynt, who worked at his brother Larry's seedy club, Hustler, on Gay Street in downtown Columbus, hired the attractive brunette as a stripper and exotic dancer. He fired her a month later, as at seventeen, she was underage and had launched a series of expletives at a customer who voiced his displeasure at being chewed out by the girl.

The following day, Larry Flynt rehired Althea, as he had seen her dancing and was captivated with the girl eleven years his junior.

He sensed a kindred spirit: they shared humble origins, X-rated speech, and insatiable libidos. Their proudest boast was they were always ready to mount anything—animal, vegetable, or mineral. When he approached her with the proposition he wanted a rendez-vous at the Howard Johnson Motel, she explained, "You're not the only person who has slept with every woman in this club." Rather than be turned off, Flynt was smitten and the two became joined at the hip (as well as other parts).

Flynt launched the *Hustler Newsletter* to promote his club, which marked his foray into publishing. When the Cincinnati printer looked at the newsletter, he thought it equivalent to the first two syllables of Cincinnati and suggested the raunchy pictures be accompanied by text, in *Playboy* fashion. Althea and Flynt were unyielding; they felt visuals were far more titillating than words. Their newsletter blossomed into *Hustler* magazine and an enterprise destined to put both the go-go dancer and Flynt at the center of a pornographic empire.

Five years later, Althea proposed to her beau in a post-orgy hot tub, and despite three failed marriages, Flynt accepted. They quickly reassured each other (in a far cry from *Love Story*'s "Love means never having to say you're sorry") that love didn't mean monogamy. On the eve of their August 1976 nuptial, they made a celebratory visit to New York's most exclusive brothel where they treated themselves with its most desirable women.

Flynt filled positions in his new magazine with a Kentucky redneck entourage, and at its helm was the love of his life. She had a hand in every aspect of the lowbrow blue book, and on one occasion, far more than her hand. *Hustler*'s first centerfold featured Althea wearing only stockings and a flower-girl white hat. One of her *Hustler* cartoons featured Dorothy in a foursome with the Tin Man, the Cowardly Lion, the Scarecrow, and Toto. Althea explained her antithesis of tasteful layout, saying, "I'm the one who always wants to do it kinkier and kinkier." However, it was the coup of a naked Jacqueline Kennedy Onassis picture, surreptitiously snapped on a Greek island, that caused America to take note of this skin magazine and helped make the priest and high priestess's coffers runneth over.

Throughout their meteoric rise, the couple enjoyed countless partners but emotional intimacy was exclusive. Flynt was not permitted to kiss any other—that would be cheating. In a violation where his wife caught him breaking her one carnal sin with a *Hustler* model, he said she "damned near broke my ribs, punching and kicking." Althea, for her part, gave up other partners, both male and female. She described Flynt as her father figure, lover, best friend, and mentor. He nicknamed her "Heart" and indulged her every whim.

The Flynts' surreal world was a subjectively enviable one: Flynt, son of a Kentucky moonshiner, was a multi-millionaire with a ten-story office building overlooking the Hollywood sign and a twenty-room Bel Air mansion formerly owned by Sonny Bono, lavishly renovated for the duke and duchess of raunch. He possessed power, renown, and a wife who loved Larry for Larry. However, he still felt a void, and in 1977, through President Carter's evangelical sister, Ruth Carter Stapleton, became a born-again Christian. Althea first got wind of his religious aspirations when expletives were replaced by the word "epiphany." Her immediate response was anxiety over how the conversion would impact their tabloid child: "God may have walked into your life but $20 million a year just walked out." While Flynt was in pursuit of Jesus, Althea was left with the reins of running *Hustler*. She became one of the country's highest paid female executives, with an annual salary of $1.6 million, and likened herself to Katherine Graham, another wife who had followed her husband into the boardroom. Unlike Mrs. Graham in her designer power suits, however, Althea wore leather dog collars and swigged from a bottle of Jack Daniels. The following year, Althea's role as executive and Flynt's pursuit of the moral high road came to a screeching halt.

Along Flynt's rise from fifth-generation Kentucky hillbilly to pinnacle of porn, he made legions of enemies and spent many a day in courts fighting obscenity charges. In the film *The People vs. Larry Flynt*, his character defends his magazine, saying, "For those who think the vagina is obscene, don't complain to me—complain to the manufacturer." His philosophy was that sex is natural, and that "the church has had its hand on our crotch for two thousand years." He felt it his mission to loosen that grip.

In 1978, during a trial in Georgia, Flynt was shot at close range by a sniper, leaving him paralyzed from the waist down. He was losing the battle for his life when the doctors suggested it would be more humane to let him die. Althea, forced into the same position as Mrs. Hawking (though the juxtaposition of the two women makes one's mind reel), screamed, "I want Larry to live. I don't care if all I have is his head in a fishbowl!"

The Flynts' merry-go-round lifestyle, astride surreal sexual horses, had the plug pulled. Beside himself in physical and emotional agony, he retreated to his Bel Air estate, a ghostlike paraplegic, confined to a 14-karat gold-plated wheelchair, a gift from Althea. His legs and feet were dead, along with his legendary libido. He stated, "My manhood's been stripped from me in the prime of my life. I'm all mind now. That's all I got left." However, he was also left with Althea, who was true to her marriage vow "for better or worse."

With the unknown assailant still at large, the Flynts' agony was compounded with paranoia, and they installed a five-hundred-pound protective steel door in the entrance of their bedroom, which came to resemble a Gothic chamber of horrors. Flynt likened his physical agony to standing up to his thighs in a vat of boiling water with no reprieve. His days and nights consisted of screaming in agony. Althea, the helpless Greek chorus to her husband's anguish, refused to sleep in another room. The shooting was a macabre echo of the devastating day when she was eight and her father, fueled on a jealousy-induced homicidal rage, had shot her mother, her mother's best friend, and her grandfather before he had turned the gun on himself.

As an antidote to the pain, Flynt took to self-medicating, and his medicine cabinet became an arsenal of drugs, both legal and otherwise: morphine, cocaine, Quaaludes, marijuana, and whatever his wife could get her hands on. In solidarity, Althea joined him drug for drug, and the couple were reduced to a narcotic fog. The once-bursting-with-energy Flynt became a nodding zombie and Althea became an emaciated wraith; her cocaine habit alone cost $20,000 a week. Her only consolation was Flynt was once more an avowed atheist, believing a benevolent God would not have visited him with such Job-like sufferings after embracing the Lord.

When Flynt converted from born-again to porn-again, *Hustler* pushed the envelope to even further depths. Eventually, a doctor found a method to cut off sensory receptors to his spine and the pain subsided. However, he was still hooked on a dizzying array of opiates. He insisted on going cold turkey, which led to a month of crippling depression so severe he contemplated suicide. He stated,

"I swear I wouldn't be here if Althea hadn't practically beat on me, screamed at me to hold on, that we were over the worst and practically home free."

Althea remained a committed Florence Nightingale and continued her vow to be monogamous. She explained, "I'm not a saint or an angel. But Larry is my man, and half of him is good enough for me... He's already got some feeling down there. If anyone can become potent again, he can. And if he can't, that's okay too." Flynt marveled at her fidelity, which persisted though he felt he had been reduced to a useless shell and could no longer perform. He admitted he would not be as steadfast when he stated if she were the one upstairs paralyzed; he would be downstairs screwing the maid. Althea said of the sexual double standard that she enjoyed making her husband happy and knew he would not be if he were monogamous.

She also proved loyal on a financial plane. When *Hustler* underwent a drop in circulation and money crunch as a result of Flynt's evangelical episode and attempted assassination, Althea sold the chinchilla-lined red Rolls-Royce she had won after a bet she could make better sloppy joes than any of his previous wives. With such an incentive, even the most domestically challenged could concoct one hell of a sloppy joe. She also sold the pink company jet purchased from Elvis Presley's estate.

In a role reversal, it became Flynt's turn to be the devoted companion when his spouse was reduced to "a useless shell." Althea's continuous weight loss was diagnosed as AIDS-related; when the press announced she had caught it from her heroin habit, Flynt defended his wife by swearing she had always used clean needles. He insisted she had contracted the disease from a blood transfusion during a hysterectomy, which left him bereft they would never have a child. In desperation, they enrolled in a bid to deep-freeze her

body till a cure had been found. On a June evening in 1987, she left their bed for a bath and when the water never stopped running, Flynt, confined to his bed, screamed for his nurse, Kikumi Okino, who discovered Althea's ravaged, lifeless body.

Althea Leasure Flynt was interred on a grassy hilltop in Flynt's family cemetery. Bob Harrington, the evangelist who had married the couple eleven years before, eulogized Althea as "a daring career woman." Sitting by the graveside in his gold-plated wheelchair, Flynt tossed a single white rose onto her casket and sobbed, "Althea, I'm going to be so lonely without you." Then he watched as his wife was interred in the Kentucky bluegrass, as the dirt covered his Heart.

◇◇◇◇◇◇◇◇◇◇

CHAPTER THIRTY-EIGHT

THE DRAGON'S ROAR

Mrs. Stieg Larsson

The girl with the dragon tattoo is as iconic as the boy wizard with the glasses, and the Swedish author has become as famous as the British. However, while J. K. Rowling basks in her billion dollar fortune, Stieg Larsson's life—and that of his muse—took a more novel-worthy twist.

In 2005, Sweden, which bequeathed the world ABBA, Ann-Margret, and IKEA, became the purveyor of the bestselling Millennium Trilogy: *The Girl with the Dragon Tattoo*, *The Girl Who Played with Fire*, and *The Girl Who Kicked the Hornet's Nest*. Tragically, the author never saw the meteoric rise of his antiheroine, the tattooed, bisexual, cyberpunk Lisbeth Salander. However, this was not the case with his wife Eva Gabrielsson, as the sexy sleuth consumed her life, much as Sherlock Holmes did Sir Arthur Conan Doyle.

Any good Norse saga features a bitter family feud, death, and an element of the supernatural, and the epilogue to the love affair between Stieg and Eva is a composite of this lethal elixir. The couple met at age eighteen at an anti-Vietnam rally in Umea, Sweden, where he grew up. She had been born sixty miles north of there, the daughter of a local journalist. She recalls he immediately caught her eye as he was different from the other self-righteous protestors and rebels searching for a cause. Over endless cups of java, the teens bonded over a shared passion for politics and all matters humanitarian. A year later, they became a couple, something their friends realized would occur before they did.

At age nineteen, they moved to a one-bedroom apartment, just large enough to hang their hats, which was plenty—they did not own much else. As the years went by, they did not undergo the customary transition from bohemian to bourgeois: they remained lifelong activists committed to women's rights. Larsson developed his feminism at age fifteen when he was at a campground where three of his friends gang-raped a girl their age. Although he had not participated, he had not intervened, and later asked the victim, Lisbeth, for forgiveness. It was not forthcoming, and decades later, he sought absolution in his fictional heroine. Posthumously he would owe another woman a *mea culpa*, once again for the sin of omission.

Eva became an architect and Larsson founded *Expo*, a magazine opposed to the Far Right who were violently against the minorities they felt were guilty of defiling their Nordic homeland. As editor, his job demanded long hours with limited remuneration. In addition, it made Larsson a victim of white supremacy threats: one afternoon a gang of skinheads with baseball bats gathered outside his office; however, he foiled their intent by exiting via a rear door. Bullets arrived in the office postbox, and anonymous phone calls threatened his life, calling him a "Jew f____." Fearful of implicating Eva in his potential martyrdom, only her name appeared on their apartment door.

Living under the cloud of neo-Nazi threats, the couple

decided not to legalize their relationship as Swedish law published the addresses of those registering for a marriage license. Instead she remained his *sambo* (Swedish for live-in companion), and the omnipresent danger was also their deciding factor to remain childless. As past and present hippies, it did not bother them to forego a legal union; moreover, not possessing any assets other than their modest Stockholm apartment, Stieg was unconcerned Eva was not legally Mrs. Larsson. In a nod to the fact that their commitment was not limited to a civil ceremony, in 1983 they had two gold wedding bands engraved "Stieg" and "Eva."

In August 2004, the couple was on a vacation in a rental cottage in an archipelago to celebrate; a Swedish publisher had just accepted Larsson's trilogy of crime novels. He planned to scale back his work at *Expo* to devote himself to writing, something made possible by his books' $80,000 advance. As distance from the politically charged magazine would result in his dropping from the neo-Nazi radar, he asked Eva to finally tie the knot. She joked as they already had the rings and had lived together for thirty-two years, it was time. They decided later that year to throw a joint birthday party, and once the festivities were under way, they would inform their guests it was doubling as a wedding reception.

For Eva, this golden time was fraught with angst as she feared the veracity of the presentiment "whom the gods wish to punish they first make happy." She felt something horrible would happen to her and had visions of falling under a train. To help ward off the evil eye, she phoned Larsson from every railway station, every possible opportunity. Unfortunately, phone calls, a twenty-first-century amulet, were of no avail. The horror happened, and it led, in domino fashion, to more horror.

In November 2004 (in an eerie coincidence the anniversary of *Kristallnacht*), Eva was in Falun when she received a call from one of her fiancé's colleagues at *Expo* informing her that he was in the hospital. Fifty-year-old Larsson, a heavy smoker whose only consumption of green was as an ingredient in a hamburger, had suffered a massive heart attack after walking up several floors to his office due to a malfunctioning elevator. His last words were, "I'm fifty, for Christ's sake!" Eva was plunged into a morass of shock and depression, describing herself as a wounded animal. She sought solace in therapy but said all of the therapists had been assigned to treat the Swedish victims of the Asian tsunami. Her sister was able to offer some modicum of comfort when she told Eva at least Larsson did not die at the hand of an assassin, which freed her from having to hate someone for the rest of her life. As it turned out, Eva was left with those to hate.

The widow had been in mourning for nine months when *Män Som Hatar Kvinnor* (*Men Who Hate Women*), better known by its English title, *The Girl with the Dragon Tattoo*, debuted. Eva, who had first read it on pages from her home's printer, started seeing it in special stands in bookstores along with her husband's photograph. She stated, "I was shocked. I trained myself to recognize the colors and the graphics of the books so I could run away and not see them. It reminded me he was gone." Little did she imagine the tattooed lady was to generate hundreds of millions of dollars in revenue. She was also to place Eva at the eye of a literary storm.

Sweden, despite its liberal image, does not recognize common-law marriage, which meant the woman who was with Larsson when he wrote the books, who was his first reader, and with whom he did his research, was deprived of any fruits of their phenomenal success.

The only way blood would not have usurped love would have been if Larsson had left a will, something he omitted to do. This was because between battling the Far Right and writing thousands of pages of his trilogy, he was too preoccupied. In addition, he felt it superfluous as his debts outweighed his assets. Eva contents that though she does not have a legal right to her partner's estate she nevertheless has a moral entitlement.

ALL YOU HAVE ARE BORROWED FEATHERS.

The estate therefore reverted to his father, Erland, and brother, Joakim, who received everything: the rights to his books, the fortune, even half of the apartment that Larsson and Eva owned. The *sambo* was a widow emotionally, but legally she had the status of a concubine. Of course her common-law in-laws could have relinquished their rights to the widow, but they declined. The unexpected riches were too good to pass up. The woman wronged said of her rapacious former relatives, "I also think there might be envy in it. Stieg did something with his life. So this is a way, as we say in Sweden, of getting some 'borrowed feathers.' You borrow someone else's reputation and prestige you could not have got on your own." She pointed out her husband did not intend for his relatives to profit from his writing. In his last email to his father, Larsson only promised him a "signed copy." Eva became the biblical Esau, her birthright stolen by a "mess of pottage." The resulting acrimony became endless grist for the Swedish tabloids.

Lisbeth Salander was a victim who turned into a victimizer, a furious woman-warrior who retaliated with the same brutality she was forced to endure, and it was the same with Eva. Reeling from the fact that she lost first her lover and then her legacy, she penned a memoir called *"There Are Things I Want You to Know" about Stieg Larsson and Me*, a title based on a quotation from a letter Larsson wrote Eva before he left for Africa where he went to aid Eritrean female guerrillas. The book is infused with Biblical revenge. Eva stated, "For Stieg and me, we weren't only familiar with the New Testament and with Jesus who asks one to turn the other cheek; what nourished us was the Old Testament, harsh and violent." The memoir made it apparent why she needed to assert her role in the trilogy: "I had to stay in Stieg's shadow all these years, which was necessary, but it's odd to suddenly come out and not just talk about him, but also to have to prove our life together existed." In her view, "Larsson's work was his life, and his life was also her life, and now all of it has been hijacked." She ended by looking down at her hands. On her fingers she wears both engraved wedding bands.

The only arrow remaining in Eva's quiver is a laptop containing the unfinished fourth volume of the Millennium series, which is in her possession and which the Larssons very much want in theirs. Its whereabouts qualify as the contemporary literary world's equivalent of the Ark. It was tentatively titled *God's Vengeance*, and its plot centers on Lisbeth who, in the process of slaying her dragons, removes the tattoos that marked their power. The Larssons proposed that if Eva relinquished the manuscript, they would give her Stieg's share of her apartment; she viewed the petty offer as extortion. They upped the ante to $2.6 million but she insisted what was more important than cash was artistic control of her husband's books. Negotiations broke down as the animosity escalated.

The woman who got nothing not only resorted to Biblical wrath, but also attempted to exorcise her grief and fury by performing a pagan ritual, replete with a goat's head on a spike, wherein she recited a poem to the Norse gods, cursing those who crossed her man in life and in death. In another she spoke to a crow she claimed was sent by the god Odin as a reincarnation of her longtime love. It sounds like something Lisbeth would pull. Camp Eva viewed this as the pain of a grieving widow; Camp Larsson suggested she was "deranged and demented." The court of public opinion weighs heavily in her favor. After all, unlike the old man in Larsson's first novel who received flowers every year on his birthday, there will be no one to do the same for the woman who lost her life's companion.

As of this writing, no one can foretell how the final epilogue of the Scandinavian saga will play out. However, one thing is a certainty: Larsson would be infinitely grieved to know that the men who hate are his father and brother, and their victim the woman he loved. If he did visit as the crow, no doubt from his throat would have emitted a strangled dragon's roar.

CHAPTER THIRTY-NINE

THE STING

Mrs. Gordon Sumner (Mrs. Sting)

B ehind every great man of rock royalty is a queue of groupies. But there is only one woman with whom Sting cares to walk, "when the west wind blows, among the fields of gold."

One of the world's most successful musicians, Gordon Matthew Thomas Sumner was a performer in Newcastle when his black-and-yellow-striped sweater led to the nickname Sting. The woman who was to become his life's queen bee, Trudie Styler, was born on January 6, 1954, in Worcestershire, England, in a cramped council estate (the British term for public housing). In reference to the lack of space, she later said, "It must have driven my dad mad when us three girls all got our periods at the same time." Her father, Harry, worked in a lampshade factory and her mother, Pauline, as a school dinner lady (cafeteria worker), which did not leave much disposable income to raise daughters Heather, Trudie, and Sabrina.

The childhood incident that was to shape Trudie's life occurred at age two. Her mother was bathing her other daughters when the toddler wandered outside and an unlicensed sixteen-year-old driver of a bread van hit her and dragged her several yards. Most of the injuries were to the child's face, and with the prognosis of lifelong scars, Pauline sued and won £2,000. Because of her disfigurement, Trudie was teased at school and her only friend was Vivien Barrett, who had a strawberry birthmark across her face. The other kids branded them Scarface and Beetroot. Trudie later said that the bullying left her with a reservoir of rage and a seriously fragile self-image: "Until I was about eighteen, I didn't think I was appealing in any way."

In the bare bones existence of the Styler household, there was no television, and the sisters—in the age-old role of make-believe—put on plays behind the sofa. In spite of Trudie's scars and severe dyslexia, she performed in a grammar school play and, thrilled with the attention, determined to become an actress. She also sought the spotlight off stage and was known in her neighborhood as a trauma/drama queen.

Dorothy's pronouncement in *The Wizard of Oz*, "There's no place like home," did not apply to the Stylers. Trudie was self-conscious about her humble home and felt inferior to her middle-class peers. Furthermore, her parents' marriage was unhappy and Pauline took refuge by compulsive eating and at her heaviest weighed seventeen stone (238 pounds). Escape arrived for Trudie at age seventeen; armed with the money from her accident, she underwent plastic surgery and with newfound confidence decided to leave for London to seek her fortune as an actress. Her plans met with her sisters' envy, her mother's approbation, and her father's disapproval: he equated "actress" with "strumpet." Harry was at a loss to understand how the plays performed behind the sofa could ever transform into a proper job. He wanted her to get a respectable position in the local brush factory.

Trudie departed to the Mecca of Stratford-upon-Avon and to supplement her depleting accident fund worked for an actor's family as an au pair. She recalled of her first job, "I was terrible— they got me so many alarm clocks to force me to get out of bed, it was like a fire alarm going off in the house every morning." She was thrilled when she received a scholarship to Bristol Old Vic Theatre

School and eventually studied at the Royal Shakespeare Company. She did become an actress when she appeared in the television soap opera *Poldark*, playing a gypsy girl who fell in love with a preacher. The role turned her into the golden girl on her street and won her father's approval.

It was at this time Trudie first saw Sting, who had just formed the band The Police, as he walked along the street. His stomach a perfect six-pack, his cheekbones sculpted, his hair green, Trudie admitted she fancied it all. Unfortunately, he was already married to fellow actress Frances Tomelty, and they were the parents of a baby named Joe. The family lived in a basement flat two doors from Trudie's own below-ground-level flat.

Three years later, Trudie played the role of a witch and Frances starred as Lady Macbeth in a West End production. Although the show was a disaster, it led to Trudie's romantic involvement with another man with distinctive cheekbones, its leading actor and director, Peter O'Toole. When the passionate relationship foundered, Trudie was devastated and turned to Frances, who had become her closest friend, for comfort. It was then Trudie broke the first commandment of BFFs: she started sleeping with Sting. Matters became complicated when Frances gave birth to daughter Fuchsia Katherine in 1982 and the following year Trudie became pregnant with Sting's child as well.

Sting's *mea culpa* can be expressed in a lyric from "Fields of Gold": "I never made promises lightly/ And there have been some that I've broken." Maybe because the affair coincided with the breakup of The Police or maybe because it was

a man's world, but the press pilloried only Trudie. Her words as the witch were taken as prophetic: "By the pricking of my thumbs/ Something wicked this way comes."

Trudie, unsurprisingly on the defensive, summed up the affair to remember, saying, "Neither of us are proud of a situation that happened—it just happened." Despite this explanation, now that Sting had become an international superstar, she was perceived as a jet-setting, gold-digger home-wrecker, and her acting roles disappeared. Just as she was no longer able to turn for succor to Frances, her sisters likewise closed ranks against her. In 1981, Pauline was diagnosed with Alzheimer's and most of the care fell on Heather and Sabrina as Trudie was flying around the world with her rock royalty lover. What further antagonized her sisters as their mother lay dying, she spoke endlessly of her absent favorite daughter. It was a scenario conducive to the gnashing of teeth.

With the doors of acting shut, Trudie turned her hand to domesticity and gave birth to four children: Brigitte Michael, Jake, Eliot Paulina, and Giacomo Luke. Trudie shared that their offspring, rather than desexualizing their relationship, actually enhanced it and she explained Sting "loved me in a pregnant state, who loves all women in a pregnant state—he thinks they're goddesses—and found it a real sensual turn-on." To legitimize their ten-year relationship, in 1992, Sting took his second plunge into matrimony and they tied the knot in a ceremony that could well vie for the category "over the top." The bride's dress was a white and gold-embroidered £20,000 masterpiece by her friend Gianni Versace, and she sat astride a white horse led by the groom. It is debatable over which threshold she was carried as the Sumners own several: an Upper West Side apartment overlooking Central Park, where Billy Joel strummed his guitar; a Malibu mansion perched above the Pacific, where Barbara Streisand once held rein; a town house in Highgate, where Yehudi Menuhin played his violin; and a lake house, a Jacobean mansion where Madonna honeymooned. The homes, run with Martha Stewart precision, presumably are stocked with everything—though likely with an absence of alarm clocks. Trudie deflects questions as to the extent of Sting's wealth, saying, "I'm not discussing that! You'll be asking me what kinds of panties I wear next." Trudie, like in Seinfeld's *Rochelle, Rochelle*, could also sing, "Well, you made a long journey from Milan to Minsk," the difference being Trudie's journey was from council house to country estate.

Alfred Nobel became the richest man in nineteenth-century Europe through his invention of dynamite, but he did not want explosives as his legacy. By creating the prize that bore his name, he rewrote his epitaph to posterity. Perhaps in similar fashion, to distance herself from stealing Sting from wife and children or deflecting accusations she was behind the breakup of The Police, Trudie turned to charitable causes. However, Styler-bashing remained a British tabloid pastime. When Sting and Trudie went on a mission to save the rainforest, the tabloids wrote they viewed it from the window of their private jet. Similarly, after she agreed to be a guest editor of the *Big Issue*, a publication that champions and is sold by the indigent, the gesture backfired; an *Observer* journalist remarked that a magazine for the homeless should not be edited by someone with several homes. However, what perhaps made Trudie bid cheerio to her native land was when the couple was compelled to pay damages for having unfairly dismissed their pregnant chef after it was deemed they had terminated her based on impending motherhood. An unapologetic Trudie declared, "Rock stars' wives have never been given an easy time. They weren't nice about Linda McCartney until she died."

Tired of the bloodsport, unrepentant Trudie packed her couture creations and cultural crown jewel husband and departed for America. Sting acquiesced; he explained, "Our relationship is successful because I make all the big decisions and she makes all the small ones. Luckily, in thirty-two years together, we've never had to make any big decisions."

Perhaps freed from the stiff upper lip of the Isles, Trudie and Sting talked openly about their boudoir antics, claiming to have practiced five-hour sessions of tantric sex. When she appeared on the *Howard Stern Show*, she discussed having frequented sex clubs, slept with women, and engaged in partner swaps. She told the shock jock (though she herself is no slouch in that department), "It's rock 'n' roll. Isn't that what we're supposed to do?" Continuing in the too-much-information mode, in *Harper's Bazaar* she posed with a shirtless Sting, and the photo shoot was such an ode to PDA—the two touched tongues for starters—that it prompted the *New York Post* headline, "Put on the Red Light." Trudie, glad the American press was on a different track than the British, wrote, "It's been well-documented that we were a bit wild. But now, at our age, we're suddenly expected to be pillars of society, acting like the local vicar and his wife. We're not the Right Reverend Mr. and Mrs. Sting." To add weight to that comment, Sting told a French magazine, "All I think about is my wife's orgasms."

In their Jacobean lakeside manor is a black-and-white photograph of a boy and a girl surrounded by a handwritten poem

Sting wrote for Trudie on their wedding anniversary, which starts, "Sometimes I'm filled with a terrible anxiety that our paths will never cross..." Even after three decades together, they still dote upon one another with the mooning look of love-struck teens.

Trudie Styler, as the queen of several castles, has so many blessings she needs a calculator to count them, the main one being she still walks in fields—and everything else—of gold with the man she loves. And for others, like the sun in the jealous sky, therein lies the sting.

CHAPTER FORTY

HOW DEEP WAS THEIR LOVE?

Mrs. Robin Gibb

The ethereal cadence of the Bee Gees serves as a time machine, transporting baby boomers to the theaters of yesteryear. The songs "I've Gotta Get a Message to You," "How Can You Mend a Broken Heart," and "How Deep is Your Love" melted millions of hearts, including one destined as the soul mate of a Gibb brother.

There were any number of adjectives that could be affixed to Robin Hugh Gibb, whose eccentricities shadowed him from his earliest years. As a young boy in Manchester, while his siblings resorted to the customary pranks of knocking tops off milk bottles for the joy of vandalism or shoplifting from the local Woolworths, he set fires, earning the moniker "the arsonist." Gibb and his brothers Barry and Maurice defied the odds when the working-class trio (Robin stated his family didn't have "a pot to piss in") burst onto London's music scene and quickly took it by storm.

In Northern Ireland, one of their fans was Edwina (nicknamed Dwina) Murphy, born in 1953 in County Tyrone to a conservative Catholic family. One night in 1967, at age fourteen, while watching the Bee Gees sing on Lulu's TV show, her sister Thelma asked if she could marry any of the brothers which one she would choose. While most girls would have readily answered Barry, the group's tall lead singer with lion-mane hair, at that moment, Robin did a little jump as if his twin, Maurice, had pinched his derriere. Dwina appreciated this gesture as she thought it illustrated

a good sense of humor, hence her response, "I'd marry that one!"

In the early 1970s, although close with her parents, Edwin and Sadie, and siblings Raymond and Thelma, the free-spirited Dwina left her Kilskeery village to give free rein to her different drummer soul. In London she studied art at Hornsey College of Art (now Middlesex Polytechnic), and one of her canvases was her hair, dyed the colors of the rainbow in a pattern of concentric rings. After graduation she ran a beanbag factory, and by the middle of the decade had established herself as a fixture on the capital's alternative scene. Although her preference was for women, she took up with a man called David with whom she became an adherent of the Kabala, and their flat became a meeting place for magical ceremonies.

Her next relationship was with Andrew, who grew magic mushrooms and believed he was the Antichrist. They built a dome inside their residence where the New Age couple inhaled pure oxygen. However, it was her next relationship that must have made her conservative Catholic mother contemplate sipping tea laced with arsenic. Dwina became the common-law wife of David Waterfield, a notorious porn baron. In 1975, he stood trial in the Old Bailey for importing hundreds of indecent films and magazines into Britain, smuggled in the back of a bacon lorry, which netted a profit of £6,000 a week. The jury viewed one of his movies, *Snow White and the Seven Lovers*, and the verdict was a three-year sentence. Dwina stood by her man, claiming their porn business was about free choice for women and people not doing what society dictates.

Dwina, like the title of Orwell's book, was down and out in London when she met up with her cousin Ken, employed as a bodyguard and chauffeur for Robin Gibb, the rock star who had become an international one with the Bee Gees's soundtrack for *Saturday Night Fever*. Despite his glamorous image, he was a high-strung loner, eccentric even by rock royalty standards. One afternoon, Gibb saw some drawings in a house in Mayflower and their mythological subject matter, heavily inclined toward the erotic, piqued his interest. When he discovered the artist was his driver's relative, he asked to view more sketches and Ken arranged an introduction. Dwina recalls when they first met. Gibb was so shy he could only peep at her from behind a curtain. When he emerged, he commissioned some drawings and further requested she join him in house-hunting. During the search, they discovered they had many commonalities: they were both vegans and teetotalers and shared the same December 22 birthday and an interest in mythology, history, and old churches. She visited him regularly at his new home, and he did the same at her modest house, where she would not let him use the bathroom because it only had an old Victorian outdoor toilet.

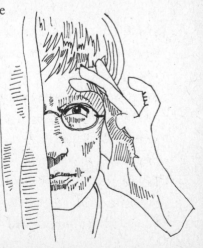

Just as the Grecian Penelope never finished weaving her shroud as she waited for Odysseus to return, the Irish Dwina never completed her pictures, as she felt if she did, her connection with Gibb would be severed.

A further bond was that they were both coming off aborted relationships: Dwina with David who, after his incarceration, had departed for Thailand, and Gibb from his divorce from Molly Hullis, former secretary for the Beatles' manager Brian Epstein. The former Mrs. Bee Gee, tired of Gibb's addiction to amphetamines and women, had forbidden him contact with son Spencer and daughter Melissa, who lived in Australia. Gibb said of the amputation from his children, "It was akin to bereavement. I felt as though I was on the verge of madness."

What rescued him was Dwina, whom he claimed he loved at first sight and added it may have been because he might have known her in a former life. They became a couple; although Dwina had become lesbian at this point, she agreed that for him she would be bisexual. Robin John, nicknamed RJ, their only child, arrived a year later. Marriage appeared on their horizon when Gibb wanted to move to the United States, and though it would be easy for the multimillionaire entertainer to obtain a green card, this would not prove the case with Dwina, who under occupation could only put Druid priestess (her new religion). They eschewed a celebrity nuptial, perhaps as many felt their union was more than a nod to his song "I Started a Joke." In 1985, they wed in a London registry office, and when they realized they had neglected to buy wedding rings, they improvised with former presents: Robin's an Anglo-Saxon king's ring and Dwina's one in the shape of a star with a diamond in its center.

Their new home was in Miami's Millionaire's Row, a ten-bedroom palatial estate overlooking Biscayne Bay. Its former owner was President John F. Kennedy, who had used it as a love nest for his trysts with Marilyn Monroe and a bevy of other beauties. It was this that led to Gibb's oft-repeated quip, "Our bedroom is where Kennedy made love to all his girlfriends." After his assassination, it had fallen into disrepair, and Dwina, along with a select group of lesbian lovers, was in charge of refurbishing the mansion. A unique touch was the erection of a stone circle in the garden so the chatelaine could celebrate the solstices at home. The estate provides ample space for Mrs. Gibb's tarot-card readings as well as her extensive collection of spinning wheels and pictures of unicorns and dragons.

However, the residence in which they felt most comfortable was their hundred-acre former medieval monastery in Oxfordshire (mentioned in the *Domesday Book*), where, as a patroness of the Order of Bards and Druids, Dwina fashioned a stone circle on an old tennis court. One of the reasons they were drawn to this one-of-a-kind estate was it was rife with history—the bishops decided Joan of Arc's fate in its chapel, and Henry VIII and Anne Boleyn stayed there prior to their marital troubles. Its interior is reminiscent of a dimly lit Hogwarts, where tapestries and tarot-card tiles adorn the walls, snarling stone griffins guard the doorway, suits of armor line the stairway, and Buddhas beckon from innumerable nooks and crannies. Their oversized Irish wolfhounds roam the ancient halls like some unreal creatures from *Harry Potter*. However, even the heavy spiritualism of the baronial manor could not ward off tragedy. It was in its hallowed halls they mourned the passing of Gibb's younger brother Andy, who died of a heart attack brought on by a long relationship with booze and cocaine.

To the neighbors, Gibb was never the usual bloke next door, especially in his relationship with the missus. They pushed the envelope in the term "open relationship," where they openly acknowledged they were into threesomes, cruising, and extramarital affairs (heterosexual and lesbian). Dwina said of her husband's wandering eye (one firmly hidden behind his trademark blue-tinted glasses), "Other women don't bother me at all. I don't mind being the head wife, a concubine, or whatever. As long as nobody tries to take my position." Nevertheless, when Gibb aired their sexual proclivities

on the *Howard Stern Show*, Dwina was irate, not because she cared what the world thought but because she worried the statements would have a negative effect on RJ. As a *mea culpa*, Robin bought Dwina a blue Jaguar with the license plate DRUID.

However, even Celtic priestesses have their breaking points, and Dwina reached hers in 2009. There were not many taboos in the Gibb household, and Dwina even approved of her husband's eight-year-long affair with their housekeeper Claire Yang. Unfortunately, Gibb shattered a sacrosanct commandment: thou shalt not impregnate the hired help. When Gibb broke it, Dwina hit the proverbial roof and ordered Claire's immediate expulsion. She and Robin John refused to have any relationship with the baby, Snow Robin, though her father doted on her and routinely visited her in the million-pound-plus estate he lavished on her mother. Perhaps Dwina's anger was she felt the housekeeper wanted to become the third Mrs. Gibb, something the Bee Gee had never considered. When a reporter asked about his mistress, half his age, Gibb responded of his wife, "It's about the relationship we have with each other now, and all I can say about that is that it is rock solid and that's the most important thing to me. I've never felt anything different."

Dwina's devotion proved mutual when she was at her husband's side through every stage of his two-and-a-half-year battle against cancer of the liver and colon. Dwina tried spider medicine (a potion from an Indian tribe) in a desperate bid to save his life, but Robin passed away in 2012. The grieving widow stated, "I am devastated to have lost my best friend, my husband, my brother. Robin was everything to me. I shall miss him for the rest of my life." Her final ministration was to plan a funeral of which he would have approved. As Gibb had once stated he did not like hearses, Dwina arranged for his body (wearing his blue-tinted glasses) to be transported to St. Mary's Church in a glass carriage pulled by four dark horses, while their beloved Irish wolfhounds, Ollie and Missy, wearing black bow ties, trailed behind. Before his body was interred, she read to the assembled mourners her poem-eulogy, "My Songbird Has Flown." Dwina took solace in the belief Robin was reunited with his twin Maurice, whom he had always missed, and the fact Claire Yang and Snow Robin, at her request, did not attend. The mourners departed St. Mary's Church in Oxfordshire to the accompaniment of the Bee Gees' song "I Started a Joke."

It is anyone's wildest guest what went on behind the doors of their twelfth-century home, as Dwina had in the latter part of their marriage embraced celibacy when she became a devotee of Brahma Kumaris (Daughters of Brahma). However, Gibb, who wore his unique glasses as much for armor as for sight, always expressed his endless adoration of Dwina, as she did for him. Their devoted thirty-two-year marriage proves ample answer to the question he penned in his classic song "How Deep is Your Love."

THE MEN YOU KNEW—
THE WOMEN YOU DIDN'T

The *Lady Vanishes* is a 1938 Alfred Hitchcock film whose title can be viewed as the essence of this book: through the vagaries of fate, the women in the previous chapters, despite playing pivotal roles in the lives of their alpha males, were whitewashed from the front pages of Time. For the most part, this was either because history did not approve of women stepping onto the stage at the time or because their men desired to stand in solitary splendor in the spotlight.

Often (though not always) their husbands' reasons for keeping the fame to themselves was either narcissism or insecurity. When Toto tugged at the curtain, the act revealed that the great and powerful Oz was just a man—something he had taken great pains to hide. In the same vein, the wizards of the world may have kept their leading ladies hidden in order to obscure their own shortcomings. As the man behind the emerald curtain lamented when the truth was out, "I'm really a very good man, but I'm a very bad wizard."

In exhuming the lives of these behind-the-scenes players, I was endlessly amazed how their extraordinary stories had been reduced to mere footnotes. By unearthing their lost legacies, I was able to discover the human faces—warts and all—of these men who changed the course of history in various ways and shaped the world. But rather than being just arm-candy or walking sticks, their ladyloves were often responsible for giving their partners the emotional life preservers needed in their varied quests. Rick, the bartender in *Casablanca*, understood a wife's importance when, despite his great love for Ilsa, insisted she follow her Resistance-fighter husband Laszlo; without her by his side, he would have faltered in his battle against the tyranny of the Reich. She boarded the plane and left her heart in Casablanca. So did all of the women here assembled.

"Marriage interferes," warns the writer Henry St. George in Henry James's *The Lesson of the Master*. But this does not hold true for legions of women who subjugated their own desires to keep their partners' dreams afloat. Sophia Tolstoy—literature's most put-upon wife—copied *War and Peace* several times to ready it for its publisher and aptly described her whole life "as a sacrifice." Vladimir Nabokov was never far from the side of his wife, Vera. She was her husband's most ardent admirer and fiercest critic; she cut up his food, carried a gun for his protection, and saved *Lolita* from the flames when he despaired of its worth, stating, "We'll not be throwing this away," as she salvaged the charred manuscript. James Joyce paid silent tribute to his wife, Nora Barnacle, when he set *Ulysses* on June 16, the momentous day when Nora first made a "man" out of him. As her maiden name suggests, she stuck with him to the tempestuous end.

Even author George Eliot (a woman) understood how the fairer sex had to go through life tied down by apron strings. In *Middlemarch*, she wrote of her character Dorothea Brooke, who filed her husband's notes in a bid to play a role in his work, "Many who knew her thought it a pity that so substantive and rare a creature should have been absorbed into the life of another." But what options did a nineteenth-century woman have? The best she could aspire to was to attach herself to a male host and bask in his reflected glory.

Today, it is somewhat easier for women to emerge from the shadows and be recognized in their own right. But many still remain behind great men, and their contributions continue to go unnoticed. Ignoring women and their influence on the monumental events leaves out crucial parts of history that can help us understand our past, our present, and our future. It makes it solely *his*-story. We can learn something from each and every one of these women and the trials and tribulations they have endured, as well as the genius contributions they have made to bring about some of the most amazing developments man- and womankind have ever seen. In *Behind Every Great Man*, I have tried to pay tribute to their silenced sacrifices, to the forgotten women who were co-creators of history with their men. After all, as the old adage states, "They also serve who only stand and wait." In these pages, I hope for the resurrection of the ladies who vanished so they can emerge from the shadows and take their rightful place beside—rather than behind—their men in whose footsteps they followed.

If you know of any great woman not included or would like to get in touch, please email me at onceagaintozelda@hotmail.com or leave a comment on my website, marlenewagmangeller.com. I would love to hear from you.

ACKNOWLEDGMENTS

The most difficult part of writing *Behind Every Great Man* was the acknowledgments page; the rest of the book required me to search outward, and this page required me to search inward. It is in this section where the author enters the confessional. Who were my great men—and women—to privately thank in this public forum? It takes a village to make a book and my heartfelt appreciation to those who populate mine. I love words but have trouble locating the letters on the keyboard with which to adequately show gratitude. This difficulty was expressed in the 1967 movie *To Sir, with Love* where Lulu sang, "But how do you thank someone who has taken you from crayons to perfume? It isn't easy but I'll try..."

My first nod of appreciation is for Roger Williams, literary agent extraordinaire and owner of New England Publishing Associates. If it were not for him—and wife, Gina—my manuscript would have ended in the great slush pile of broken dreams; its title would have remained a girl-power slogan. From first to last, he encouraged me, honed my idea, and placed it in the very capable hands of my publisher, Sourcebooks.

I am also extremely fortunate to work with senior editor Stephanie Bowen, whose intelligence and sweetness spring forth from every email. If one could envision the ideal editor, it would be Stephanie who comes to mind. Her love of books and enthusiasm for her authors show that her position as senior editor is a labor of love. Endless thanks to her for making my fourth book materialize; writing saves me from the destiny of Sisyphus and transforms the black-and-white to Technicolor.

Family is simultaneously the greatest impediment and the greatest asset in writing, and I am grateful for my husband, Joel Geller, who listened—albeit he was force-fed—to my monopolizing conversations centered on each current chapter. Joel never *kvetched* that the only meal I have ever served arrived via Styrofoam box; he understands the time constraints of a full-time teaching job coupled with the demands of writing. It could also be because when we were first married, he asked me to make tea and I set our kitchen ablaze. (Hint: don't stand too near a gas oven while wearing a polyester blazer.) It is safe to assume my name will never appear on the spine of a cookbook. I also appreciate the exhortations of my daughter, Jordanna, who, when my spirits flagged, repeated, "Keep on keeping on." More than a passing nod to my mother, Gilda Wagman, for fostering in me the belief that dreams do not just have to be for sleeping.

In the course of my research I was able to communicate with people who knew the women profiled and provided valuable insights. Valerie Leveroni Corral, who runs the (Santa Cruz Women's) Men's Alliance for Medical Marijuana, reminisced she was "Laura Huxley's devoted friend and humble servant." She was with Laura at the end and read to her the same passages Laura had read to Aldous from *The Tibetan Book of the Dead* and *This Timeless Moment.* She also clothed Laura in the shroud that had once covered her beloved Ginny. Denis Berry was Rosemary Leary's friend and housemate in Aptos, California (near Santa Cruz). Denis described her friend as "bright, funny, and warm" and recalled, "She was just kind of establishing a group of friends. After all those years on the run and couldn't tell people who she was. This was the first time she had to be social again and reintegrate her life, so she wasn't constantly looking over her shoulder." Mirandi Babitz, a therapist in Torrance, California, once had the unique experience of sharing a home with Pamela and Jim Morrison. She recalled the period as "very stoned times" and recalled of Pamela, "She really was beautiful. She had a prevailing innocence, in and of the fact that she lived hard and didn't stop at anything. She still managed to stay young and pretty. Men just fell in love with her, I guess because she always seemed to need protection." I want to thank the three of you for sharing your memories of a unique period in history and the women behind the shadows of the men who helped define the hippie era.

Lastly, I want to acknowledge all the women profiled in my book. My investigation into their lives proved that although they were submerged in the shadow of history, they were the pillars that kept their Samsons from destruction. I am thrilled *Behind Every Great Man* has made them more than a footnote to their alpha males.

Lulu asked in her song, "What can I give you in return?" To those mentioned, I offer this volume. It is my sincere hope you and my readers will enjoy the stories of these intrepid—oftentimes better—halves who prove the veracity of the old adage, "Behind every great man is a great woman."

Marlene Wagman-Geller
San Diego, California

BIBLIOGRAPHY

CHAPTER ONE The Enchanted Princess: Mrs. Karl Marx

Baird, Jonathan. "Book Review: 'Love and Capital: Karl and Jenny Marx and the Birth of a Revolution' by Mary Gabriel 1/19/12." *Jonathan P. Baird*, November 25, 2012, jpbaird.com/2012/11/25/book-review-love-and-capital-karl-and-jenny-marx -and-the-birth-of-a-revolution-by-mary-gabriel-11912/.

Gabriel, Mary. "Marx's Not-So-Marxist Marriage." *Daily Beast*, September 21, 2011, www .thedailybeast.com/articles/2011/09/21/love-and-capital-karl-marx-s-marriage-was -decidedly-not-marxian.html.

Lear, Linda. "Review of 'Love and Capital: Karl and Jenny Marx and the Birth of a Revolution.'" *Washington Independent Review of Books*, September 23, 2011, www.washington independentreviewofbooks.com/bookreview/love-and-capital-karl-and-jenny-marx -and-the-birth-of-a-revolution.

Orr, Lyndon. "The Story of Karl Marx." *Famous Affinities of History*, October 2003, www .authorama.com/famous-affinities-of-history-iii-7.html.

Schepers, Emile. "Love and revolution: Marx family biography has lessons." *People's World*, February 20, 2013, /love-and-revolution-marx-family-biography-has-lessons/.

Showalter, Elaine. "'Love and Capital: Karl and Jenny Marx and the Birth of a Revolution,' by Mary Gabriel." *Washington Post*, October 14, 2011, www.washingtonpost .com/entertainment/books/love-and-capital-karl-and-jenny-marx-and-the-birth -of-a-revolution-by-mary-gabriel/2011/08/29/gIQAwSsUkL_story.html.

Siegel, Jennifer. "At Home With Karl Marx." *Wall Street Journal*, September 23, 2011, online .wsj.com/news/articles/SB10001424053111904353504576566673280799508.

Wallechinsky, David and Irving Wallace. "Famous Marriages Karl Marx and Jenny von Westphalen Part 1." *Trivia-Library.com*, www.trivia-library.com/b/famous-marriages -karl-marx-and-jenny-von-westphalen-part-1.htm (accessed September 21, 2013).

Wardlaw, Shelby. "Review of 'Love and Capital: Karl and Jenny Marx and the Birth of a Revolution.'" *Bookreporter.com*, November 3, 2011, www.bookreporter.com /reviews/love-and-capital-karl-and-jenny-marx-and-the-birth-of-a-revolution.

Washburn, Michael. "Leaving his Marx: A man of weak character, strong ideas." *Boston.com*, October 2, 2011, www.boston.com/ae/books/articles/2011/10/02/love_and_capital _karl_and_jenny_marx_and_the_birth_of_a_revolution_by_mary_gabriel/.

CHAPTER TWO Senta: Mrs. Richard Wagner

Bruno, Debra. "Family saga stresses details over dysfunction." *Boston.com*, February 26, 2008, www.boston.com/ae/books/articles/2008/02/26/family_saga_stresses_details_over _dysfunction/.

Hensher, Philip. "Cosima Wagner: The Lady of Bayreuth: review." *Telegraph*, May 1, 2010, www.telegraph.co.uk/culture/books/bookreviews/7651774/Cosima-Wagner -the-Lady-of-Bayreuth-review.html.

Hilmes, Oliver. *Cosima Wagner: The Lady of Bayreuth*. New Haven, CT: Yale University Press, 2010.

Levy, Paul. "Cosima Wagner: Lady of Bayreuth by Oliver Hilmes." *Guardian*, May 2, 2010, www .theguardian.com/books/2010/may/02/cosima-wagner-bayreuth-hilmes-review.

Mourby, Adrian. "The Bayreuth Festival preview: Let the madness begin!" *Independent*, July 20, 2013, www.independent.co.uk/arts-entertainment/classical/features/the-bayreuth -festival-preview-let-the-madness-begin-8723000.html.

Rothschild, Richard. "Dark Side—Anti-Semitism, Affairs Paint An Ugly Portrait Of Richard Wagner." *Chicago Tribune*, March 3, 1996, articles.chicagotribune .com/1996-03-03/news/9603050316_1_richard-wagner-operas-jews.

Seymour, Miranda. "Cosima Wagner: The Lady of Bayreuth by Oliver Hilmes." *Guardian*, May 8, 2010, www.theguardian.com/books/2010/may/08/cosima-wagner-oliver -himes-review.

CHAPTER THREE The Importance of Being Constance: Mrs. Oscar Wilde

Evans, David. "Constance: The Tragic and Scandalous Life of Mrs. Oscar Wilde, by Franny Moyle." *Independent*, February 19, 2012, www.independent.co.uk/arts -entertainment/books/reviews/constance-the-tragic-and-scandalous-life-of-mrs -oscar-wilde-by-franny-moyle-7166351.html#.

Fox, Essie. "The Importance of Being Constant." *Virtual Victorian*, July 4, 2011, virtual victorian.blogspot.com/2011/07/importance-of-being-constant.html.

Mendelsohn, Daniel. "Proud Mary?" *NYMag.com*, nymag.com/nymetro/arts/books/reviews /4184/ (accessed June 6, 2013).

Moyle, Franny. *Constance: The Tragic and Scandalous Life of Mrs. Oscar Wilde*. London: John Murray, 2011 .

———. "Shameful agony of Oscar Wilde's wife." *Express*, June 12, 2011, www.express .co.uk/expressyourself/252152/Shameful-agony-of-Oscar-Wilde-s-wife.

Seymour, Miranda. "Constance: The Tragic and Scandalous Life of Mrs. Oscar Wilde by Franny Moyle—review." *Guardian*, June 24, 2011, www.theguardian.com /books/2011/jun/24/constance-mrs-wilde-franny-moyle-review.

CHAPTER FOUR Ba: Mrs. Mohandas Gandhi

Ara, Dr. Roshan. "Mother India." *Greater Kashmir*, January 31, 2013, www.greaterkashmir .com/news/2013/Jan/31/mother-india-21.asp.

"Biography of Kasturba Gandhi, Indian Freedom Fighter." *Indiavideo*, www.indiavideo .org/text/kasturba-gandhi-1209.php (accessed May 29, 2013).

Desai, Nachiketa. "'She, not Gandhi was the first Satyagrahi.'" *Weekend Leader*, February 26, 2013, www.theweekendleader.com/Culture/1527/his-better-half.html.

Gandhi, Arun and Sunanda. *The Forgotten Woman*. Huntsville, AR: Ozark Mountain Publishers, 1998.

"Gandhi's Life—Part 8, India: And Then Gandhi Came." *Progress Report*, February 20, 2004, www.progress.org/biographies/biography-of-gandhi-8-india-then-gandhi-came/.

"Gandhi's Life—Part 12, Purifying India." *Progress Report*, November 24, 2003, www .progress.org/biographies/biography-of-gandhi-12-purifying-india/.

Guha, Ramachandra. "Kasturba." *Hindu*, October 9, 2005, www.hindu.com/mag/2005/10/09 /stories/2005100900290300.htm.

"Kasturba Gandhi." *Iloveindia.com*, www.iloveindia.com/indian-heroes/kasturba-gandhi.html (accessed May 29, 2013).

"Kasturba Gandhi." *Wikipedia*, en.wikipedia.org/wiki/Kasturba_Gandhi (accessed May 29, 2013).

"Kasturba Gandhi (1869–1944)." *Streeshakti*, www.streeshakti.com/bookK.aspx?author=18 (accessed May 29, 2013).

"Kasturba Gandhi death...wife of Mahatma Gandhi." *Timothy Hughes Rare and Early Newspapers*, www.rarenewspapers.com/view/580498 (accessed May 29, 2013).

Kittanpahuwa, K. D. M. "Person beyond reform." *Sunday Observer*, September 14, 2008, www .sundayobserver.lk/2008/09/14/plus02.asp.

"Mahatma Gandhi." *Wikipedia*, en.wikipedia.org/wiki/Mahatma_gandhi (accessed May 29, 2013).

Manzoor, Sarfraz. "Father to a nation, stranger to his son." *Guardian*, August 10, 2007, www .theguardian.com/film/2007/aug/10/india.

Menon, Vikram. "The Other Mrs. Gandhi." *Outlook*, August 28, 2000, www.outlookindia .com/article.aspx?209922.

Mungur, Lorna. "Kasturba Gandhi." *South African History Online*, www.sahistory.org.za /people/kasturba-gandhi (accessed May 29, 2013).

Roberts, Glenys. "Sexual torment of a saint: A new book reveals Gandhi tortured himself with the young women who worshipped him, and often shared his bed." *Mail Online*, April 9, 2010, www.dailymail.co.uk/news/article-1264952/A-new -book-reveals-Gandhi-tortured-young-women-worshipped-shared-bed.html.

Rosenberg, Jennifer. "Gandhi—A Biography of Mahatma Gandhi." *About.com 20th Century History*, history1900s.about.com/od/people/a/gandhi.htm (accessed May 29, 2013).

Rushdie, Salman. "Mohandas Gandhi." *Time*, April 13, 1998, content.time.com/time /magazine/article/0,9171,988159,00.html.

Tanna, Ketan Narottam. "Ba's death left Gandhi shattered." *Ketan Tanna*, ketan.net/hin13 .html (accessed May 29, 2013).

"Thrill of the chaste: The truth about Gandhi's sex life." *Independent*, April 7, 2010, www .independent.co.uk/arts-entertainment/books/features/thrill-of-the-chaste -the-truth-about-gandhis-sex-life-1937411.html.

CHAPTER FIVE Doxerl and Johonzel: Mrs. Albert Einstein

Arthurs, Deborah. "Was Einstein the world's worst husband? Wife ordered to keep room tidy, serve three meals a day—but expect NO affection...and she must stop talking when he demands it." *Mail Online*, April 23, 2012, www.dailymail.co.uk/femail /article-2133922/Was-Einstein-worlds-worst-husband-Wife-ordered-room-tidy -serve-meals-day--expect-NO-affection--stop-talking-demands-it.html.

"August 4, 1948, The Death Of Mileva Maric." *On This Deity*, www.onthisdeity.com /4th-august-1948-the-death-of-mileva-maric/ (accessed September 15, 2013).

Calle, Carlos I. "Getting to Know Einstein's Wives." *Einstein For Dummies*, www .dummies.com/how-to/content/getting-to-know-einsteins-wives.navId-323259 .html?print=true (accessed September 15, 2013).

Friedman, Josh. "Film Explores The Chance Mileva Maric Was Einstein's Better Half." *SunSentinel*, October 28, 2003, articles.sun-sentinel.com/2003-10-28 /lifestyle/0310270252_1_einstein-s-ideas-einstein-s-death-mileva-maric.

Golden, Frederic. "Einstein's Lost Child." *Time*, September 26, 1999, content.time.com /time/magazine/article/0,9171,31490,00.html.

Jayaraman, T. "The private Einstein." *Hindu.com*, www.hindu.com/thehindu/thscrip/print.pl?file =2005052000490100.0.htm&date=fl2210/&prd=fline& (accessed September 15, 2013).

Jha, Alok. "Letters reveal relative truth of Einstein's family life." *Guardian*, July 11, 2006, www .theguardian.com/science/2006/jul/11/internationalnews.

Kinnes, Tormod. "Albert Einstein Anecdotes." *Gold Scales*, oaks.nvg.org/sa5ra17.html (accessed September 15, 2013).

Knapton, Sarah. "Family frustrations of Albert Einstein revealed in bitter letter to estranged wife." *Telegraph*, December 11, 2008, www.telegraph.co.uk/news/uknews/3710188/Family-frustrations-of-Albert-Einstein-revealed-in-bitter-letter-to-estranged-wife.html.

"Mileva Einstein-Maric." *Biography Channel*, www.biography.com/people/mileva-einstein-maric-282676 (accessed January 19, 2014).

"Mileva Maric." *Wikipedia*, en.wikipedia.org/wiki/Mileva_Maric (accessed September 14, 2013).

Overbye, Dennis. *Einstein in Love: A Scientific Romance*. New York: Penguin Group, 2000.

Popovic, Milan. *In Albert's Shadow: The Life and Letters of Mileva Maric, Einstein's First Wife*. Baltimore, MD: John Hopkins University Press, 2003.

Rowley, Storer H. "Einstein's Letters Show Unflattering Side Of Genius." *Chicago Tribune*, November 17, 1996, articles.chicagotribune.com/1996-11-17/news/9611170217_1_mileva-maric-letters-show-jerusalem.

Smith, Dinitia. "Dark Side of Einstein Emerges in His Letters." *New York Times*, November 6, 1996, www.nytimes.com/1996/11/06/arts/dark-side-of-einstein-emerges-in-his-letters.html?pagewanted=all&src=pm.

Verrengia, Joseph B. "Existence Was Relative to Einstein." *Los Angeles Times*, April 17, 2005, articles.latimes.com/2005/apr/17/news/adna-einstein17.

Zackheim, Michele. "A Genius Obscured by a Great Man." *Los Angeles Times*, November 14, 1999, articles.latimes.com/1999/nov/14/opinion/op-33310.

CHAPTER SIX A Rose is a Rose is a Rose is a Rose: Mrs. Gertrude Stein

"Alice Toklas, 89, Is Dead In Paris." *New York Times*, March 8, 1967, www.nytimes.com/books/98/05/03/specials/stein-toklasobit.html.

Benfer, Amy. "Gertrude and Alice." *Salon*, November 18, 1999, www.salon.com/1999/11/18/alice/.

"Gertrude Stein & Alice B. Toklas." *People*, February 12, 1996, www.people.com/people/article/0,,20102772,00.html.

Greenberg, Arnie. "We Still Love You, Alice B. Toklas." *Bonjour Paris*, www.bonjourparis.com/story/we-still-love-you-alice-b-toklas/ (accessed September 15, 2013).

Peril, Lynn. "Alice B. Toklas." *HiLoBrow*, April 30, 2011, hilobrow.com/2011/04/30/alice-b-toklas/.

Rosenthal, Tom. "Odd couple's great escape." *Mail Online*, October 25, 2007, www.dailymail.co.uk/home/books/article-489659/Odd-couples-great-escape.html.

Simon, Linda. "Alice Babette Toklas." *Jewish Women's Archive*, jwa.org/encyclopedia/article/toklas-alice-babette (accessed September 15, 2013).

CHAPTER SEVEN The Stepping Stone: Mrs. Bill Wilson

Black, Claudia. "Lois Wilson Story—Hallmark Hall of Fame Presentation." *Psychology Today*, April 12, 2010, www.psychologytoday.com/blog/the-many-faces-addiction/201004/lois-wilson-story-hallmark-hall-fame-presentation.

Borchert, William G. *The Lois Wilson Story: When Love Is Not Enough*. Center City, MN: Hazelden, 2005.

Cheever, Susan. "BILL W.: The Healer." *Time*, June 14, 1999, content.time.com/time/magazine/article/0,9171,991266,00.html.

———. "Susan Cheever on the Real Bill W." *Fix*, www.thefix.com/content/in-search-of-the-real-bill-w8998 (accessed October 1, 2013).

Homans, John. "Saint Booze." *NYMag.com*, nymag.com/nymetro/arts/books/reviews/n_9880/ (accessed September 2, 2013).

Hurley, Anne. "Bill Wilson is still a mystery." *Seattle Times,* March 14, 2004, seattletimes
.com/html/books/2001876685_bill14.html.

"Lois Burnham Wilson Dies; Founded Al-Anon for Alcoholics' Families." *Los Angeles Times,* October 9, 1988, articles.latimes.com/1988-10-09/news/mn-5528_1_
alcoholics-anonymous.

"Lois' Story." *Stepping Stones,* www.steppingstones.org/loisstory.html (accessed September 2, 2013).

Mcnamara, Mary. "Winona Ryder stars in CBS' 'Lois Wilson Story.'" *Los Angeles Times,* April 23, 2010, www.azcentral.com/offbeat/articles/2010/04/23/20100423winona-ryder
-tv-cbs-love-is-not-enough.html.

Pace, Eric. "Lois Burnham Wilson, a Founder Of Al-Anon Groups, Is Dead at 97." *New York Times,* October 6, 1988, www.nytimes.com/1988/10/06/obituaries
/lois-burnham-wilson-a-founder-of-al-anon-groups-is-dead-at-97.html.

Stasi, Linda. "'Love' drunk." *New York Post,* April 23, 2010, nypost.com/2010/04/23/love-drunk/.

Witzeman, Jeff. "AA: The Magic Of Bill Wilson." *Huffington Post,* November 16, 2009, www.huffingtonpost.com/jeff-witzeman/aa-the-magic-of-bill-wils_b_359534.html.

CHAPTER EIGHT Life's Leading Lady: Mrs. Alfred Hitchcock

"Alma Reville." *Biography Channel,* www.biography.com/people/alma-reville-21014017 (accessed January 12, 2014).

Anderson, John. "Alfred Hitchcock's Secret Weapon Becomes a Star." *New York Times,* November 16, 2012, www.nytimes.com/2012/11/18/movies/hitchcock-and-the
-girl-remember-alma-reville.html?_r=0.

Blair, Elizabeth. "A Look At 'The Girl' Who Caught Hitchcock's Eye." *NPR.org,* October 18, 2012, www.npr.org/2012/10/20/163182381/a-look-at-the-girl-who-caught-hitchcocks-eye.

DeFore, John. "Helen Mirren generating Oscar buzz for her performance in 'Hitchcock.'" *Washington Post,* November 23, 2012, www.washingtonpost.com/entertainment
/movies/helen-mirren-generating-oscar-buzz-for-her-performance-in-hitchcock
/2012/11/21/62a83258-3290-11e2-bfd5-e202b6d7b501_story.html.

Diu, Nisha Lilia. "Mrs Alfred Hitchcock: 'The Unsung Partner.'" *Telegraph,* February 8, 2013, www.telegraph.co.uk/culture/film/film-news/9832084/Mrs-Alfred-Hitchcock-The
-Unsung-Partner.html.

Fuller, Graham. "Helen Mirren Pays Tribute to Alma Reville, Alfred Hitchcock's Wife and Indispensable Collaborator." *BlouinArtinfocom,* February 7, 2012, www.blouinart
info.com/news/story/811786/helen-mirren-pays-tribute-to-alma-reville-alfred
-hitchcocks.

Guerrero, Amadís Ma. "The Master of Suspense's dark side: Hitchcock and his leading ladies." *Philippine Daily Inquirer,* August 26, 2012, lifestyle.inquirer.net/63578
/the-master-of-suspenses-dark-side-hitchcock-and-his-leading-ladies.

LaSalle, Mick. "'Hitchcock' review: 'Psycho' drama." *SFgate.com,* November 22, 2012, www.sfgate.com/movies/article/Hitchcock-review-Psycho-drama-4060092
.php#photo-3775922.

Lowman, Rob. "The other A. Hitchcock was director's wife, Alma." *Kentucky.com,* December 13, 2012, www.kentucky.com/2012/12/13/2442245/the-other-a-hitchcock-was-directors.html.

Mandell, Andrea. "In 'Hitchcock,' the marriage gives shape to the man." *USA Today,* November 23, 2012, www.usatoday.com/story/life/people/2012/11/22/hitchcock-movie-cover
-story/1716309/.

Mazmanian, Adam. "Movie Review: 'Hitchcock.'" *Washington Times,* November 22, 2012, www
.washingtontimes.com/news/2012/nov/22/movie-review-hitchcock/.

McLaren, Leah. "Alfred Hitchcock's indecent obsession with 'decent girls.'" *Globe and Mail,* July 20,

2012, www.theglobeandmail.com/arts/film/alfred-hitchcocks-indecent-obsession -with-decent-girls/article4430015/.

Norman, Neil. "The woman behind Alfred Hitchcock." *Daily Express*, December 24, 2012, www.express.co.uk/news/showbiz/366832/The-woman-behind-Alfred-Hitchcock.

O'Connell, Pat Hitchcock and Laurent Bouzereau. *Alma Hitchcock: The Woman Behind the Man*. New York: Berkeley Publishing Group, 2003.

Rampton, James. "Obsession: The dark side of Alfred Hitchcock." *Independent*, December 26, 2012, www.independent.co.uk/arts-entertainment/films/features/obsession-the-dark -side-of-alfred-hitchcock-8431033.html.

Stasi, Linda. "Truth behind Alfred Hitchcock's obsession with 'The Girl.'" *New York Post*, October 19, 2012, nypost.com/2012/10/19/truth-behind-alfred-hitchcocks-obsession-with -the-girl/.

Tanenhaus, Sam. "Alfred Hitchcock: The Psycho Genius of Hollywood." *Newsweek*, November 18, 2012, www.newsweek.com/alfred-hitchcock-psycho-genius-hollywood-63817.

Zakarin, Jordan. "How 'Hitchcock' Rights a Hollywood Wrong." *Hollywood Reporter*, December 3, 2012, www.hollywoodreporter.com/news/hitchcock-alma-reville-psycho-unexpected -396605.

CHAPTER NINE I Didn't Forget You: Mrs. Simon Wiesenthal

"About Simon Wiesenthal." *Simon Wiesenthal Center*, www.wiesenthal.com/site/pp .asp?c=lsKWLbPJLnF&b=4441293#.Us8mCLSQOdw (accessed August 22, 2013).

Bernstein, Adam. "SIMON WIESENTHAL: 1908–2005." *Washington Post*, September 21, 2005, www.sfgate.com/news/article/SIMON-WIESENTHAL-1908-2005-The-Holocaust -s-2607552.php#photo-2094875.

Blumenthal, Ralph. "Simon Wiesenthal Is Dead at 96; Tirelessly Pursued Nazi Fugitives." *New York Times*, September 21, 2005, www.nytimes.com/2005/09/21 /international/europe/21wiesenthal.html?pagewanted=all&_r=0.

"Cyla Wiesenthal." *Telegraph*, November 13, 2003, www.telegraph.co.uk/news/obituaries /1446534/Cyla-Wiesenthal.html.

"Cyla Wiesenthal, 95; Holocaust Survivor, Wife of Nazi Hunter." *Los Angeles Times*, November 12, 2003, articles.latimes.com/2003/nov/12/local/me-cyla12.

Frick, Lisa. "Simon Wiesenthal." *Encyclopedia of World Biography*, www.notablebiographies .com/newsmakers2/2006-Ra-Z/Wiesenthal-Simon.html (accessed August 22, 2013).

Friedmann, Jan. "A Critical Look at Simon Wiesenthal: Examining the Legacy of the Nazi Hunter." *Spiegel Online International*, September 16, 2010, www.spiegel.de /international/germany/a-critical-look-at-simon-wiesenthal-examining-the-legacy-of -the-nazi-hunter-a-716216.html.

"Nazi hunter was a 'deputy for the dead.'" *Veterans Today*, September 21, 2005, www .veteranstoday.com/2005/09/21/nazi-hunter-was-a-deputy-for-the-dead/.

Pick, Hella. *Simon Wiesenthal: A Life in Search of Justice*. London: Phoenix, 1997.

Seligmann, Rafael. "The Architect of Justice. Simon Wiesenthal remembered." *Atlantic Times*, www .atlantic-times.com/archive_detail.php?recordID=318 (accessed August 22, 2013).

Van der Vat, Dan. "Cyla Wiesenthal." *Guardian*, November 13, 2003, www.theguardian .com/news/2003/nov/14/guardianobituaries.

CHAPTER TEN The White Horse Girl and The Blue Wind Boy: Mrs. Frank Lloyd Wright

Churchwell, Sarah. "'Slow Pay Frank' and his many wives." *Guardian*, March 6, 2009, www .theguardian.com/books/2009/mar/07/women-tc-boyle-review.

Cryer, Dan. "'The Women,' by T. C. Boyle." *SFGate.com*, February 15, 2009, www.sfgate .com/books/article/The-Women-by-T-C-Boyle-3172164.php.

Field, Marcus. "Architect of desire: Frank Lloyd Wright's private life was even more unforgettable than his buildings." *Independent*, March 8, 2009, www.independent.co.uk/arts -entertainment/architecture/architect-of-desire-frank-lloyd-wrights-private-life -was-even-more-unforgettable-than-his-buildings-1637537.html.

Friedland, Roger and Harold Zellman. *The Fellowship: The Untold Story of Frank Lloyd Wright & the Taliesin Fellowship*. New York: Regan, an imprint of Harper Collins, 2006.

Kephart, Lore. "Couples Wright And His Wife, Olgivanna, Reshaped Ideas On Architecture." *Philly.com*, November 1, 1999, articles.philly.com/1999-11-01 /news/25493932_1_taliesin-west-taliesin-east-taliesin-fellowship.

Lansing, David. "Olgivanna Lloyd Wright: Devil or Angel?" *Davidlansing.com*, October 17, 2012, davidlansing.com/olgivanna-lloyd-wright-devil-or-angel/.

Obst, David. "Sex, Lies, and Frank Lloyd Wright." *Santa Barbara Independent*, September 6, 2006, www.independent.com/news/2006/sep/06/sex-lies-and-frank-lloyd-wrigh/.

"Olgivanna Lloyd Wright." *Wikipedia*, en.wikipedia.org/wiki/Olgivanna_Lloyd_Wright (accessed September 24, 2013).

Saxon, Wolfgang. "Olgivanna Lloyd Wright, Wife Of The Architect, Is Dead At 85." *New York Times Arts*, March 2, 1985.

Sheff, David. "In the Arizona Desert, Frank Lloyd Wright's Widow Keeps the Architect's Flame Burning and Her Students Building." *People*, January 1, 1983, www .people.com/people/article/0,,20084174,00.html.

Thornton, Richard. "One house of scandel [sic], one house of horror and one house of irony." *Examiner.com*, November 2, 2010, www.examiner.com/article/one -house-of-scandel-one-house-of-horror-and-one-house-of-irony.

CHAPTER ELEVEN Where Light and Shadow Meet: Mrs. Oskar Schindler

Connolly, Kate. "Emilie Schindler." *Guardian*, October 8, 2001, www.theguardian.com /news/2001/oct/09/guardianobituaries.kateconnolly.

———. "Schindler's widow left to die in bitterness and poverty." *Guardian*, July 28, 2001, www .theguardian.com/world/2001/jul/29/kateconnolly.theobserver.

"Emilie Schindler." *Telegraph*, October 8, 2001, www.telegraph.co.uk/news/obituaries/1358768 /Emilie-Schindler.html.

"Emilie Schindler." *Virtual Jewish Library*, www.jewishvirtuallibrary.org/jsource/biography /emilieschindler.html (accessed May 8, 2013).

"Emilie Schindler, 93, Dies; Saved Jews in War." *New York Times*, October 8, 2001, www .nytimes.com/2001/10/08/world/emilie-schindler-93-dies-saved-jews-in-war.html.

Gold, Alison Leslie. *Fiet's Vase and Other Stories of Survival, Europe 1939–1945*. New York: Jeremy P. Tarcher/Penguin, 2003.

Podesta, Don. "A Widow's Memories of a Flawed Saint." *Washington Post*, December 15, 1993, www.washingtonpost.com/wp-srv/style/longterm/movies/review97/emilie.htm.

"Schindler After The Second World War." *Southern Institute for Education and Research*, www .southerninstitute.info/holocaust_education/slguid5.html (accessed May 8, 2013).

Schindler, Emilie with Erika Rosenberg. *Where Light and Shadows Meet*. New York: W. W. Norton & Company, 1996.

Traynor, Ian. "Mrs. Schindler's list of grievances aired on TV." *Guardian*, May 30, 1999, www .theguardian.com/world/1999/may/31/iantraynor2.

CHAPTER TWELVE Tristan und Isolde: Mrs. Salvador Dalí

Brown, Mick. "My weekend with Salvador Dali." *Telegraph*, May 21, 2010, www.telegraph.co.uk/culture/art/art-features/7750501/My-weekend-with-Salvador-Dali.html.

"For the love of Gala." *Age*, June 13, 2009, www.theage.com.au/news/entertainment/arts/for-the-love-of-gala/2009/06/12/1244664839594.html.

"Gala Dali." *Voice of Russia*, July 7, 2005, voiceofrussia.com/2005/07/07/104205/.

"Gala Dali." *Wikipedia*, en.wikipedia.org/wiki/Gala_Dali (accessed June 10, 2013).

"Gala—She melted the man who melted the clocks." *Blackbook Unique Creatures*, www.theuniquecreatures.com/gala/ (accessed June 10, 2013).

Markham, James M. "Gala Dali, Impelled Her Artist Husband To Fame And Wealth." *New York Times*, June 11, 1982, www.nytimes.com/1982/06/11/obituaries/gala-dali-impelled-her-artist-husband-to-fame-and-wealth.html.

Meisler, Stanley. "The Surreal World of Salvador Dalí." *Smithsonian Magazine*, April 2005, www.smithsonianmag.com/arts-culture/the-surreal-world-of-salvador-dali-78993324/.

Richardson, John. "Dali's Demon Bride." *Vanity Fair*, December, 1998.

CHAPTER THIRTEEN Herr Wolff: Mrs. Adolf Hitler

Connolly, Kate. "Nazi loyalist and Adolf Hitler's devoted aide: the true story of Eva Braun." *Guardian*, February 13, 2010, www.theguardian.com/world/2010/feb/14/eva-braun-adolf-hitler.

Gallagher, Dorothy. "Adolf and Eva." *New York Times*, November 16, 2011, www.nytimes.com/2011/11/20/books/review/eva-braun-life-with-hitler-by-heike-b-gortemaker-translated-by-damion-searls-book-review.html.

Guest, Katy. "The Eva Braun story: Behind every evil man…" *Independent*, March 12, 2006, www.independent.co.uk/news/world/europe/the-eva-braun-story-behind-every-evil-man-469532.html.

Jones, Nigel. "Eva Braun: Life with Hitler by Heike Görtemaker: review." *Telegraph*, October 13, 2011, www.telegraph.co.uk/culture/books/historybookreviews/8840871/Eva-Braun-Life-with-Hitler-by-Heike-Gortemaker-review.html.

McCrum, Robert and Taylor Downing. "The Hitler home movies: how Eva Braun documented the dictator's private life." *Guardian*, January 26, 2013, www.theguardian.com/world/2013/jan/27/hitler-home-movies-eva-braun.

"No dumb blonde: New book reveals the other side of Hitler's mistress Eva Braun." *Mail Online*, February 10, 2010, www.dailymail.co.uk/news/article-1249724/No-dumb-blonde-new-book-reveals-Hitlers-mistress-Eva-Braun.html.

Roberts, Andrew. "New Biography Explores the Life and Myth of Eva Braun." *Daily Beast*, November 10, 2011, www.thedailybeast.com/articles/2011/11/10/new-biography-explores-the-life-and-myth-of-eva-braun.html.

Shakespeare, Nicholas. "Eva Braun: Life with Hitler: review." *Telegraph*, November 7, 2011, www.telegraph.co.uk/culture/books/bookreviews/8874350/Eva-Braun-Life-with-Hitler-review.html.

Sinha, Tuhin A. "Did Hitler love Eva Braun?" *Times of India*, April 17, 2011, articles.timesofindia.indiatimes.com/2011-04-17/people/28375073_1_adolf-hitler-eva-braun-personal-photographer-heinz-linge.

Wistrich, Robert S. "Eva Braun." *Jewish Virtual Library*, www.jewishvirtuallibrary.org/jsource/Holocaust/braun.html (accessed May 8, 2013).

CHAPTER FOURTEEN Fade Away: Mrs. Douglas MacArthur

Huff, Colonel Sid. *My Fifteen Years with General MacArthur*. Philadelphia, PA: Curtis Publishing Company, 1954.

"Jean MacArthur; Widow of Gen. Douglas MacArthur." *Los Angeles Times*, January 23, 2000, articles.latimes.com/2000/jan/23/local/me-56859.

Nemy, Enid. "Jean MacArthur, General's Widow, Dies at 101." *New York Times*, January 24, 2000, www.nytimes.com/2000/01/24/nyregion/jean-macarthur-general-s-widow-dies-at-101.html.

Reed, J. D. "The General's Lady." *People*, February 7, 2000, www.people.com/people/article/0,,20130434,00.html.

CHAPTER FIFTEEN Madame Butterfly: Mrs. Julius Rosenberg

Berger, Joseph. "Decades Later, Rosenberg Case Again Ignites Passions." *New York Times*, November 15, 2004, www.nytimes.com/2004/11/15/nyregion/15rosenberg.html.

Carton, Sydney. "Sobell Confesses: Julius Guilty, Ethel Was Framed." *TalkLeft*, September 17, 2008, dukeforums.talkleft.com/index.php?topic=1890.0#top.

Conklin, William R. "Atom Spy Couple Sentenced to Die; Aide Gets 30 Years." *New York Times*, April 6, 1951, www.nytimes.com/learning/general/onthisday/big/0405.html.

"Execution of Ethel Rosenberg." *Jewish Women's Archive*, jwa.org/thisweek/jun/19/1953/ethel-rosenberg (accessed May 13, 2013).

Hevesi, Dennis. "Ruth Greenglass, Key Witness in Trial of Rosenbergs, Dies at 83." *New York Times*, July 9, 2008, www.nytimes.com/2008/07/09/us/09greenglass.html?_r=1&.

"Julius and Ethel Rosenberg." *Atomicarchive.com*, www.atomicarchive.com/Bios/Rosenberg.shtml (accessed May 13, 2013).

"Julius and Ethel Rosenberg." *Wikipedia*, en.wikipedia.org/wiki/Julius_and_Ethel_Rosenberg (accessed May 13, 2013).

Linder, Douglas. "The Rosenberg Trial: Stories Of Love & Longing." *Famous Trials*, law2.umkc.edu/faculty/projects/ftrials/rosenb/ROS_STOR.HTM.

———. "Trial Of The Rosenbergs: An Account." *Western Michigan University*, brn227.brown.wmich.edu:7000/3228/ (accessed May 13, 2013).

Onion, Rebecca. "The Jell-O Box That Helped Convict the Rosenbergs." *Slate*, February 20, 2013, www.slate.com/blogs/the_vault/2013/02/20/ethel_and_julius_rosenberg_how_a_jell_o_box_helped_convict_them.html.

Price, Steven. "Ethel Rosenberg." *University of Missouri–K. C. School of Law*, law2.umkc.edu/faculty/projects/ftrials/rosenb/ros_bero.htm (accessed May 13, 2013).

Roberts, Sam. "The Informer." *New York Times*, October 28, 2001, www.nytimes.com/2001/10/28/books/the-informer.html.

———. "Yes, They Were Guilty. But of What Exactly?" *Free Republic*, June 15, 2003, www.freerepublic.com/focus/fr/929408/posts.

———. "The Rosenbergs Revisited." *New York Times*, October 8, 2010, www.nytimes.com/2010/10/10/books/review/Roberts-t.html?pagewanted=all.

"The Rosenbergs' Prison Cell." *Western Michigan University*, brn227.brown.wmich.edu:7000/1691/ (accessed May 13, 2013).

CHAPTER SIXTEEN The Man with the Golden Pen: Mrs. Ian Fleming

Hudson, Christopher. "Why it was Ian Fleming's wife who invented James Bond." *Mail Online*, February 1, 2008, www.dailymail.co.uk/femail/article-511863/Why-Ian-Flemings-wife-invented-James-Bond.html.

McGinness, Mark. "Licensed to Endure." *Australian*, May 12, 2008, www.theaustralian.com.au/news/features/licensed-to-endure/story-e6frg6z6-1111116308759.

Satterfield, Archie. "The House Where Bond Was Born." *Sun Sentinel*, July 9, 1989, articles.sun-sentinel.com/1989-07-09/features/8902200057_1_james-bond-ian-fleming-jamaican.

"The Man With The Golden Pen." *Express*, July 12, 2007, www.express.co.uk /expressyourself/13177/The-man-with-the-GOLDEN-PEN.

Thornton, Michael. "The Dark Secrets of the Volcano." *Telegraph*, August 18, 2012, www .telegraph.co.uk/culture/theatre/9483001/The-dark-secrets-of-the-Volcano.html.

CHAPTER SEVENTEEN Beloved Infidel: Mrs. F. Scott Fitzgerald

Allen, Brooke. "The Other Sides of Paradise." *New York Times*, July 23, 1995, www.nytimes .com/1995/07/23/books/the-other-sides-of-paradise.html.

Donaldson, Scott. "Fresh Voices, Familiar Story." *Chicago Tribune*, September 17, 1995, articles .chicagotribune.com/1995-09-17/entertainment/9509170068_1_sheilah-graham-zelda -fitzgerald-eleanor-lanahan.

Folkart, Burt A. "Sheilah Graham, Columnist, 'Beloved Infidel' Author, Dies." *Los Angeles Times*, November 19, 1988, articles.latimes.com/1988-11-19/local/me-660_1 _sheilah-graham.

Graham, Sheila and Gerold Frank. *Beloved Infidel*. New York: Bantam Books, 1959.

Krebs, Albin. "Sheilah Graham Is Dead at 84; Wrote Hollywood Gossip Column." *New York Times*, November 19, 1988, www.nytimes.com/1988/11/19/obituaries /sheilah-graham-is-dead-at-84-wrote-hollywood-gossip-column.html.

Kretzmer, Sybil Sever. "Fitzgerald Through Other Eyes: Fitzgerald's daughter and lover: Two tales of tragedy and triumph." *Los Angeles Times*, September 24, 1995, articles.latimes. com/1995-09-24/books/bk-49315_1_fitzgerald-through-other-eyes-frances-scott -fitzgerald-eleanor-lanahan.

Lauerman, Connie. "Sheilah Graham's 50 Years 'In The Gossip.'" *Chicago Tribune*, April 9, 1985, articles.chicagotribune.com/1985-04-09/features/8501200401_1_gossip-hedda -hopper-shirley-temple.

"Sheilah Graham." *Jewish Women's Archive*, jwa.org/weremember/graham-sheilah (accessed January 6, 2014).

CHAPTER EIGHTEEN Any Other Man: Mrs. Billy Graham

Baker, Mike. "Billy Graham's wife, Ruth, dies at 87." *Seattle Times*, June 14, 2007, seattletimes.com/html/nationworld/2003748172_webgraham14.html.

Cornwell, Patricia. *Ruth, A Portrait*. Colorado Springs, CO: WaterBrook Press, 1997.

Gibbs, Nancy and Michael Duffy. "Ruth Graham, Soulmate to Billy, Dies." *Time*, June 14, 2007, content.time.com/time/nation/article/0,8599,1633197,00.html.

"Reverend Billy Graham & Ruth Bell." *People*, February 12, 1996, www.people.com /people/article/0,,20102781,00.html.

Severo, Richard. "Wife of Rev. Billy Graham Dies at 87." *New York Times*, June 15, 2007, www .nytimes.com/2007/06/15/obituaries/15graham.html?_r=0.

Stepp, Laura Sessions. "Ruth Bell Graham, The Soul Mate Of the Preacher." *Washington Post*, June 16, 2007, www.washingtonpost.com/wp-dyn/content/article/2007/06/15 /AR2007061502363.html.

Stewart, Jocelyn Y. "Ruth Graham, 87; had active role as wife of famed evangelist." *Los Angeles Times*, June 15, 2007, articles.latimes.com/2007/jun/15/local/me-graham15.

CHAPTER NINETEEN Here's to You: Mrs. Jackie Robinson

Fitzpatrick, Frank. "Rachel Robinson: Still spreading the legacy." *Philly.com*, April 11, 2007, articles.philly.com/2007-04-11/sports/24993675_1_jackie-robinson-rachel -robinson-psychiatric-nurse.

Green, Mary. "Rachel Robinson: My Life with Jackie Robinson." *People*, April 19, 2013, www
.people.com/people/article/0,,20692184,00.html.

"Jackie Robinson & Rachel Isum."*People*, February 12, 1996, www.people.com/people
/article/0,,20102789,00.html.

Libman, Gary. "Rachel Robinson's Homecoming: She Recalls a Legend and Her Days
in L.A." *Los Angeles Times*, September 2, 1987, articles.latimes.com/1987-09
-02/news/vw-3579_1_house-today.

Long, Michael G. "Celebrate Rachel Robinson, Too!" *Huffington Post*, April 11, 2013, www
.huffingtonpost.com/michael-g-long/celebrate-rachel-robinson_b_3060876.html.

Robinson, Rachel with Lee Daniels. *Jackie Robinson: An Intimate Portrait*. New York: Harry N.
Abrams, 1996.

Wilkins, Roger. "Rachel Robinson: The Survivor." *New York Times Magazine*,
partners.nytimes.com/library/magazine/millennium/m5/album-robinson.html
(accessed January 2, 2014).

CHAPTER TWENTY The Lady and the Tramp: Mrs. Charlie Chaplin

Arditti, Michael. "A drunken widow in a gilded cage." *Independent*, July 8, 1995,
www.independent.co.uk/arts-entertainment/books/a-drunken-widow-in-a-gilded
-cage-1590369.html.

Bowman, David. "Oona O'Neill Chaplin Remains a Mysterious Presence." *SFGate*, December
13, 1998, www.sfgate.com/books/article/Oona-O-Neill-Chaplin-Remains-a
-Mysterious-Presence-2973341.php.

"Charlie Chaplin & Oona O'Neill." *People*, February 12, 1996, www.people.com/people
/article/0,,20102787,00.html.

"Lady Oona O'Neill Chaplin, 66." *Seattle Times*, September 28, 1991, community
.seattletimes.nwsource.com/archive/?date=19910928&slug=1307936.

Scovell, Jane. *Oona: Living in the Shadows*. New York: Warner Books, 1998.

Stanley, Alessandra. "Oona O'Neill Chaplin Dies at 66; She Lived in the Shadow of
Fame." *New York Times*, September 28, 1991, www.nytimes.com/1991/09/28
/obituaries/oona-o-neill-chaplin-dies-at-66-she-lived-in-the-shadow-of-fame.html.

Thomas, David. "When Chaplin played father." *Telegraph*, December 26, 2002, www
.telegraph.co.uk/culture/film/3587749/When-Chaplin-played-father.html.

CHAPTER TWENTY-ONE Not With Mice: Mrs. Pablo Picasso

Gilot, Françoise. *Life With Picasso*. London: Virago Press, 1964.

Hawley, Janet. "'Pablo was the greatest love of my life… I left before I was destroyed.'" *Sydney
Morning Herald*, July 7, 2011, newsstore.fairfax.com.au/apps/viewDocument.ac;
jsessionid=28E487188BF6E01A1648B30E382C034E?sy=afr&pb=allffx&dt
=selectRange&dr=1month&so=relevance&sf=text&sf=headline&rc=10
&rm=200&sp=brs&cls=7993&clsPage=1&docID=SMH1107234H7R11L5RFK.

Hudson, Mark. "Pablo Picasso's love affair with women." *Telegraph*, February 13, 2009, www
.telegraph.co.uk/culture/art/4610752/Pablo-Picassos-love-affair-with-women.html.

Huffington, Arianna Stassinopoulos. "Picasso: Creator and Destroyer." *Atlantic Monthly*, June
1988, www.theatlantic.com/past/unbound/flashbks/picasso/destroy.htm (accessed
December 15, 2013).

Kalter, Suzy. "At 57, Francoise Gilot Recalls Life with Picasso but Enjoys It with Scientist Jonas
Salk." *People*, July 30, 1979, www.people.com/people/article/0,,20074227,00.html.

Lacher, Irene. "A Place of Her Own: Culture: Francoise Gilot, Picasso's former lover and
Jonas Salk's wife, wants to be known not as the companion of great men, but as

their equal." *Los Angeles Times*, March 6, 1991, articles.latimes.com/1991-03
-06/news/vw-83_1_francoise-gilot.

Moye, David. "French Connection." *Pacific Magazine*, March 28, 2012, www.pacific
sandiego.com/2012/03/28/french-connection/.

Whitley, John. "Life with Pablo was a bullfight." *Telegraph*, September 19, 1998, www
.telegraph.co.uk/culture/4715712/Life-with-Pablo-was-a-bullfight.html.

CHAPTER TWENTY-TWO Camp Betty: Mrs. Gerald Ford

"Betty Ford." *Economist*, July 21, 2011, www.economist.com/node/18985759.

"Betty Ford." *Telegraph*, July 10, 2011, www.telegraph.co.uk/news/obituaries/politics
-obituaries/8627228/Betty-Ford.html.

"Betty Ford dies at 93." *Mirror News*, July 9, 2011, www.mirror.co.uk/news/uk-news/betty
-ford-dies-at-93-182983#.Uun4pnddW24.

"Betty Ford is dead at 93, founded addiction center." *Baltimore Sun*, July 8, 2011, articles
.baltimoresun.com/2011-07-08/news/bs-betty-ford-cnn-20110708_1_betty
-ford-center-elaine-didier-38th-president.

Douglas, Hilary. "Presidents' tributes to battling Betty Ford." *Express*, July 10, 2011, www
.express.co.uk/news/world/257774/Presidents-tributes-to-battling-Betty-Ford.

Hickey, Claire. "Betty Ford; an unconventional First Lady." *Washington Times*, July 20, 2011,
communities.washingtontimes.com/neighborhood/feed-mind-nourish-soul/2011
/jul/20/betty-ford-unconventional-first-lady/.

Jackson, Harold. "Betty Ford obituary." *Guardian*, July 10, 2011, www.theguardian.com
/world/2011/jul/10/betty-ford-obituary.

Kantrowitz, Barbara. "Betty Ford: A Singular First Lady." *Newsweek*, December 28, 2006, www
.newsweek.com/betty-ford-singular-first-lady-105867.

Mohajer, Shaya Tayefe and Mike Householder. "Betty Ford Dies: Former First Lady Dead
At Age 93." *Huffington Post*, July 8, 2008, www.huffingtonpost.com/2011/07/08
/betty-ford-dies-former-dead_n_893664.html.

Nemy, Enid. "Betty Ford, Former First Lady, Dies at 93." *New York Times*, July 8, 2011, www
.nytimes.com/2011/07/09/us/politics/betty-ford-dies.html?_r=0.

Smith, Richard Norton. "Remembering the legendary Betty Ford." *Chicago Tribune News*,
July 18, 2011, articles.chicagotribune.com/2011-07-18/news/ct-oped-0718
-eulogy-20110718_1_elizabeth-bloomer-betty-ford-president-ford.

Watson, Robert. "Hidden History: Betty Ford's honesty was refreshing." *Sun Sentinel*,
July 17, 2011, articles.sun-sentinel.com/2011-07-17/news/fl-rwcol-oped0717
-20110717_1_first-lady-betty-ford-black-children.

CHAPTER TWENTY-THREE The Polish Rider: Mrs. Aldous Huxley

Bernstein, Adam. "Laura Archera Huxley, 96; Self-help Author." *Washington Post*, December
15, 2007, www.washingtonpost.com/wp-dyn/content/article/2007/12/14/AR2007
121401997.html.

Fox, Margalit. "Laura Huxley, Her Husband's Biographer, Dies at 96." *New York Times*, December
19, 2007.

Hawtree, Christopher. "Laura Huxley." *Guardian*, December 16, 2007, www.theguardian.com
/news/2007/dec/17/guardianobituaries.booksobituaries.

Huxley, Laura. *This Timeless Moment: A Personal View of Aldous Huxley*. New York: Harper &
Row, 1962.

Thomson, Ian. "Laura Huxley: Widow of Aldous Huxley." *Independent*, December 17, 2007, www.
independent.co.uk/news/obituaries/laura-huxley-widow-of-aldous-huxley-765500.html.

Woo, Elaine. "Laura Huxley worked to save husband's legacy." *Seattle Times*, December 16, 2007, seattletimes.com/html/obituaries/2004076050_huxleyobit16.html.
———. "Writer, lay therapist was devoted to husband's legacy." *Los Angeles Times*, December 15, 2007, articles.latimes.com/2007/dec/15/local/me-huxley15.

CHAPTER TWENTY-FOUR And God Walked In: Mrs. C.S. Lewis

Allego, Donna M. "Joy Davidman Biography." *Modern American Poetry*, www.english.illinois.edu/maps/poets/a_f/davidman/bio.htm (accessed June 3, 2013).
Dorsett, Lyle W. "Helen Joy Davidman (Mrs. C. S. Lewis) 1915–1960: A Portrait." *C. S. Lewis Institute*, www.cslewisinstitute.org/node/31 (accessed June 3, 2013).
Finkle, David. "For C. S. Lewis, Does Love Conquer All?" *New York Times*, November 4, 1990, www.nytimes.com/1990/11/04/theater/theater-for-c-s-lewis-does-love-conquer-all.html.
Haven, Cynthia. "Lost in the shadow of C. S. Lewis' fame." *Sfgate.com*, January 1, 2006, www.sfgate.com/books/article/ESSAY-Lost-in-the-shadow-of-C-S-Lewis-fame-2524646.php.
———. "C. S. Lewis, 'carny classics,' Joy Davidman…it all comes together." *Book Haven*, October 22, 2010, bookhaven.stanford.edu/2010/10/c-s-lewis-carny-classics-joy-davidman-it-all-comes-together/.
Person, James E. Jr. "'Out of My Bone: The Letters of Joy Davidman.'" *Washington Times*, August 16, 2009, www.washingtontimes.com/news/2009/aug/16/books-out-my-bone-letters-joy-davidman/.
Smith, Gayle Rosenwald. "C. S. Lewis And Joy Gresham, Shared A Love Of Life And Literature." *Philly.com*, March 20, 2000, articles.philly.com/2000-03-20/news/25607267_1_clive-staples-lewis-joy-gresham-jewish-family.
Ylvisaker, Robert. "C. S. Lewis eventually finds joy." *MetroLutheran*, April 30, 2010, metrolutheran.org/2010/04/c-s-lewis-eventually-finds-joy/.

CHAPTER TWENTY-FIVE A Brief History of Love: Mrs. Stephen Hawking

Adams, Tim. "Brief history of a first wife." *Guardian*, April 3, 2004, www.theguardian.com/theobserver/2004/apr/04/features.review17.
Brooks, Richard. "Physicist Stephen Hawking's first wife tells how their marriage plunged into a 'black hole.'" *Australian*, July 28, 2013, www.theaustralian.com.au/news/world/physicist-stephen-hawkings-first-wife-tells-how-their-marriage-plunged-into-a-black-hole/story-fnb64oi6-1226687071098#.
Connor, Steve. "Jane—Hawking's life support: A new documentary on the cosmologist reveals his gratitude to his first wife." *Independent*, August 25, 2013, www.independent.co.uk/news/people/news/jane--hawkings-life-support-a-new-documentary-on-the-cosmologist-reveals-his-gratitude-to-his-first-wife-8783677.html.
———. "Personal, revealing memoir exposes Hawking's marriage traumas." *New Zealand Herald*, September 14, 2013, www.nzherald.co.nz/world/news/article.cfm?c_id=2&objectid=11124575.
Dewitt, David. "The Brilliance of His Universe." *New York Times*, September 12, 2013, www.nytimes.com/2013/09/13/movies/hawking-a-documentary-on-stephen-hawking.html.
Hawking, Jane. *Traveling to Infinity: My Life with Stephen*. Surrey, UK: Alma Books Ltd., 1999.
"Jane back in Stephen Hawking's universe." *Neurotalk*, June 13, 2007, neurotalk.psychcentral.com/showthread.php?t=21733.
John, Simi. "Stephen Hawking's Former Wife Refused Offer to Turn Off His Life Support in 1985." *International Business Times*, July 29, 2013, www.ibtimes.co.uk/stephen-hawking-wife-jane-wilde-doctors-lifesupport-495251.

Matyszczyk, Chris. "Hawking: I think about women most." *CNET*, January 6, 2012, www .cnet.com/news/hawking-i-think-about-women-most/.

Munez, Sofia. "Professor Stephen Hawking's [sic] pays tribute to first wife who saved him from depression after he was diagnosed with motor neurone disease." *USA-UK Online*, August 25, 2013, www.usaukonline.com/latest-news/29524 -professor-stephen-hawking-s-pays-tribute-to-first-wife-who-saved-him -from-depression-after-he-was-diagnosed-with-motor-neurone-disease.html.

Ng, Magdalen. "My life with a genius." *Star Online*, February 27, 2011, www.thestar.com.my /story.aspx/?file=%2f2011%2f2%2f27%2flifebookshelf%2f8118777&sec= lifebookshelf.

Packham, Chris. "Hawking Exhibits a Painstakingly Three-Dimensional View of the Genius Physicist's Life." *Village Voice*, September 11, 2013, www.villagevoice .com/2013-09-11/film/hawking/full/.

Sinha, Bikash. "A Dream Run." *Telegraph India*, January 3, 2014, www.telegraphindia .com/1140103/jsp/opinion/story_17741164.jsp#.U0GCS1f4Lxs.

Smith, Joan. "Books: Stephen Hawking: the man who mistook his wife for a nurse." *Independent*, August 15, 1999, www.independent.co.uk/arts-entertainment/books-stephen-hawking -the-man-who-mistook-his-wife-for-a-nurse-1112891.html.

CHAPTER TWENTY-SIX The Book of Ruth: Mrs. Bernie Madoff

"Bernard Madoff." *Wikipedia*, en.wikipedia.org/wiki/Bernard_Madoff (accessed May 5, 2013).

"Bernie Madoff's wife Ruth cuts him off and moves closer to surviving son." *Mail Online*, March 11, 2012, www.dailymail.co.uk/news/article-2113417/Bernie-Madoffs -wife-Ruth-cuts-moves-closer-surviving-son.html.

Browning, Lynnley. "The Loneliest Woman in New York." *New York Times*, June 12, 2009, www. nytimes.com/2009/06/14/fashion/14ruth.html?pagewanted=all.

Cahalan, Susannah. "Bernie Madoff's wife seeking redemption through char- ity work in Florida." *New York Post*, July 18, 2010, nypost.com/2010/07/18 /bernie-madoffs-wife-seeking-redemption-through-charity-work-in-florida/.

Henriques, Diana B. "Madoffs Aim to Write Their Own Future." *New York Times*, October 30, 2011, www.nytimes.com/2011/10/31/business/madoff-family-aims-to-write-its-own -future.html?_r=0&pagewanted=print.

Honan, Corinna. "Why IS Ruth Madoff, the wife of history's biggest fraudster, still devoted to a monster?" *Mail Online*, January 27, 2012, www.dailymail.co.uk/news /article-2092941/Ruth-Madoff-Why-IS-wife-historys-biggest-fraudster-devoted -monster.html.

Kolhatkar, Sheelah. "Poor Ruth. Why does Bernie's better half inspire such vitriol?" *New York Magazine*, July 2, 2009, nymag.com/news/features/57772/.

"Madoff's alleged affair was Ruth's 'final straw.'" *CBSNews*, October 31, 2011, www .cbsnews.com/news/madoffs-alleged-affair-was-ruths-final-straw/.

Mcneil, Liz and Alex Tresniowski. "The Trials of Ruth Madoff." *People*, February 21, 2011, www .people.com/people/article/0,,20467587,00.html.

Seal, Mark. "Ruth's World." *Vanity Fair*, September 2009, www.vanityfair.com/politics /features/2009/09/ruth-madoff200909-2.print.

Segal, David and Alison Leigh Cowan. "Madoffs Shared Much: Question Is How Much." *New York Times*, January 14, 2009, www.nytimes.com/2009/01/15 /business/15ruth.html?pagewanted=all.

Williams, Mary Elizabeth. "Should we feel sorry for Ruth Madoff?" *Salon*, October 31, 2011, www.salon.com/2011/10/31/should_we_feel_sorry_for_ruth_madoff/.

CHAPTER TWENTY-SEVEN Maza Shelaza: Mrs. Jim Henson

Barnes, Mike. "Muppets Co-Creator Jane Henson Dies at 78." *Hollywood Reporter*, April 2, 2013, www.hollywoodreporter.com/news/muppets-jane-henson-dies-432527.

Borovitz, Abby. "Jim Henson: The man behind the muppet." *MSNBC*, October 14, 2013, www.msnbc.com/the-cycle/jim-henson-the-man-behind-the-muppet.

Harrigan, Stephanie. "It's Not Easy Being Blue." *Muppet Central*, www.muppetcentral.com/articles/tributes/henson/hensonarticle6.shtml (accessed November 11, 2013).

"Jane Henson." *Telegraph*, April 4, 2013, www.telegraph.co.uk/news/obituaries/9972657/Jane-Henson.html.

Jones, Brian Jay. *Jim Henson: The Biography*. New York: Ballantine Books, 2013.

Mai-Duc, Christine. "Jane Nebel Henson dies at 78; partner with Jim Henson in Muppets." *Los Angeles Times*, April 3, 2013, articles.latimes.com/2013/apr/03/local/la-me-jane-nebel-henson-20130404.

———. "Jane Nebel Henson, wife and collaborator of Muppets creator, dies at 78." *Washington Post*, April 5, 2013, www.washingtonpost.com/local/obituaries/jane-nebel-henson-wife-and-collaborator-of-muppets-creator-dies-at-78/2013/04/05/de9986b0-9e0f-11e2-a941-a19bce7af755_story.html.

Schindehette, Susan. "Legacy of a Gentle Giant." *People*, June 18, 1990, www.people.com/people/archive/article/0,,20117981,00.html.

Theis, Michael. "Cancer Takes Jane Henson, Wife of Jim Henson." *Hyattsville Patch*, May 7, 2013, hyattsville.patch.com/groups/editors-picks/p/cancer-takes-jane-henson-wife-of-jim-henson.

Vitello, Paul. "Jane Henson, a Partner in Creating the Muppets, Dies at 78." *New York Times*, April 3, 2013, www.nytimes.com/2013/04/04/arts/television/jane-henson-early-collaborator-on-the-muppets-dies-at-78.html.

CHAPTER TWENTY-EIGHT What's In a Name?: Mrs. Malcolm X

"Betty Shabazz." *Answers.com*, www.answers.com/topic/betty-shabazz (accessed May 3, 2013).

"Betty Shabazz." *Wikipedia*, en.wikipedia.org/wiki/Betty_Shabazz (accessed May 5, 2013).

Swarns, Rachel L. "At Funeral For Shabazz, Grief, Prayer And Respect." *New York Times*, June 28, 1997, www.nytimes.com/1997/06/28/nyregion/at-funeral-for-shabazz-grief-prayer-and-respect.html.

CHAPTER TWENTY-NINE The Stolen Hours: Mrs. Samuel Beckett

"Barbara Bray." *Telegraph*, April 18, 2010, www.telegraph.co.uk/news/obituaries/culture-obituaries/tv-radio-obituaries/7604308/Barbara-Bray.html.

"Barbara Bray." *Wikipedia*, en.wikipedia.org/wiki/Barbara_Bray (accessed November 30, 2013).

Dirda, Michael. "The Letters of Samuel Beckett." *Washington Post*, October 12, 2011, www.washingtonpost.com/entertainment/books/the-letters-of-samuel-beckett-reviewed-by-michael-dirda/2011/10/07/gIQAKwq2fL_story.html.

Gussow, Mel. "Samuel Beckett Is Dead at 83; His 'Godot' Changed Theater." *New York Times*, December 27, 1989, www.nytimes.com/books/97/08/03/reviews/20046.html.

———. "Barbara Bray: In Her Own Words." *Modernism/modernity* 18.4 (November 2011): 887–897, muse.jhu.edu/login?auth=0&type=summary&url=/journals/modernism-modernity/v018/18.4.k-dzierski.pdf.

Martin, Tim. "Samuel Beckett." *Telegraph*, August 28, 2009, www.telegraph.co.uk/culture/books/6105016/Samuel-Beckett.html.

Morrison, Blake. "The Poet Of Less." *Independent*, October 6, 1996, www.independent.co.uk/arts-entertainment/the-poet-of-less-1357073.html.

Murdoch, Jim. "Better halves." *The Truth About Lies*, December 9, 2010, jim-murdoch
.blogspot.com/2010/12/better-halves.html.

"Obituaries: Barbara Bray." *Journal of Beckett Studies* 20.1 (2011): 96–101, www
.euppublishing.com/doi/pdfplus/10.3366/jobs.2011.0007.

"Samuel Beckett, Author Of 'Godot,' Is Dead At 83." *Philly.com*, December 26, 1989,
articles.philly.com/1989-12-26/news/26158372_1_godot-samuel-beckett-nazi.

Smith, Sid. "Samuel Beckett Dies." *Chicago Tribune*, December 27, 1989, articles
.chicagotribune.com/1989-12-27/news/8903210066_1_nobel-prize-winning
-playwright-godot-montparnasse-cemetery.

Todd, Andrew. "Barbara Bray obituary." *Guardian*, March 4, 2010, www.theguardian.com
/tv-and-radio/2010/mar/04/barbara-bray-obituary.

CHAPTER THIRTY One Hundred Times More: Mrs. Nelson Mandela

Bayliss, Deborah. "Winnie Mandela: Her Life and Legacy." *Chicago Weekly
Citizen*, December 18, 2013, thechicagocitizen.com/news/2013/dec/18
/winnie-mandela-her-life-and-legacy/.

Boynton, Graham. "Nelson Mandela and Winnie—portrait of a marriage." *Telegraph*, December
6, 2013, www.telegraph.co.uk/news/worldnews/nelson-mandela/10502171/Nelson
-Mandela-and-Winnie-portrait-of-a-marriage.html.

Carlin, John. "Whatever Went Wrong With Winnie?" *Independent*, March 29, 1995, www
.independent.co.uk/life-style/whatever-went-wrong-with-winnie-1613232.html.

du Preez Bezdrob, Anné Mariè. *Winnie Mandela: A Life*. Cape Town: Zebra Press, 2003.

Hewitt, Bill. "Against a Background of Black Anger and Bloodshed, Winnie Mandela Is
Accused of Kidnapping and Assault." *People*, October 8, 1990, www.people
.com/people/archive/article/0,,20118949,00.html.

Lydall, Ross. "Nelson Mandela walked out of prison hand-in-hand with Winnie—but two
years later they separated." *London Evening Standard*, December 6, 2013, www
.standard.co.uk/news/world/nelson-mandela-walked-out-of-prison-handinhand
-with-winnie--but-two-years-later-they-separated-8659535.html.

Lyman, Rick. "In Mandela Legacy, a Place for Winnie?" *New York Times*, August 2, 2013, www
.nytimes.com/2013/08/03/world/africa/in-mandela-legacy-a-place-for-winnie
.html?_r=0.

"Mandela illness revives ex-wife Winnie's fading star." *Inquirer*, July 1, 2013, newsinfo
.inquirer.net/436487/mandela-illness-revives-ex-wife-winnies-fading-star.

"Nelson Mandela death: The women who loved him." *BBC News Africa*, December 6, 2013, www.
bbc.co.uk/news/world-africa-22114543.

Sheets, Connor Adams. "Winnie Madikizela-Mandela: Nelson's Former Wife & Controversial
'Mother Of The Nation.'" *International Business Times*, December 5, 2013, www.ibtimes
.com/winnie-madikizela-mandela-nelsons-former-wife-controversial-mother
-nation-1498034.

Silverman, Stephen M. "Nelson Mandela Dies." *People*, December 5, 2013, www.people
.com/people/package/article/0,,20763535_20461287,00.html.

Smith, David. "Nelson and Winnie Mandela's marriage ended, but the bond was never
broken." *Guardian*, December 6, 2013, www.theguardian.com/world/2013
/dec/06/nelson-winnie-mandela-marriage.

"Winnie Mandela Describes Nelson Mandela's Last Moments." *Huffington Post*,
December 12, 2013, www.huffingtonpost.com/2013/12/12/winnie-mandela
-describes-nelson-mandelas-last-moments_n_4435200.html.

CHAPTER THIRTY-ONE Mrs. Blue Eyes: Mrs. Frank Sinatra

Busciglio, Rick. "What is Barbara Marx Sinatra's background? How many times was she married?" *Examiner.com*, July 5, 2011, www.examiner.com/article/what-is-barbara-marx-sinatra-s-background-how-many-times-was-she-married.

Daniel, Douglass K. "Barbara Sinatra tells it her way in her new memoir." *Christian Science Monitor*, May 31, 2011, www.csmonitor.com/Books/Latest-News-Wires/2011/0531/Barbara-Sinatra-tells-it-her-way-in-her-new-memoir.

Di Nunzio, Miriam. "Living, loving Frank Sinatra." *Lake County News Sun*, June 11, 2011, newssun.suntimes.com/entertainment/5904567-421/living-loving-frank-sinatra.html.

Elsworth, Catherine. "My life with Frank Sinatra." *Telegraph*, June 5, 2011, www.telegraph.co.uk/news/features/8556824/My-life-with-Frank-Sinatra.html.

"Frank Sinatra's Widow on Man Behind the Legend: 'Big Tipper...Romantic Husband.'" *ABC News*, May 31, 2011, abcnews.go.com/Entertainment/lady-blue-eyes-life-frank-sinatra-excerpt/story?id=13563176.

Goldman, Andrew. "Barbara Sinatra's Way." *New York Times*, June 3, 2011, www.nytimes.com/2011/06/05/magazine/barbara-sinatras-way.html?_r=0.

Loudon, Christopher. "Excess Blather: The Barbara Sinatra Story." *Jazztimes*, June 6, 2011, jazztimes.com/articles/27790-excess-blather-the-barbara-sinatra-story.

"'Obsessive Frank Sinatra took 12 showers a day and always smelled of lavender,' reveals his widow." *Mail Online*, June 3, 2011, www.dailymail.co.uk/tvshowbiz/article-1392767/Obsessive-Frank-Sinatra-took-12-showers-day-smelled-lavender-reveals-widow.html.

"Sinatra, my Jekyll and Hyde husband: His fourth wife lays bare his terrifying mood swings and sadistic manipulation." *Mail Online*, June 6, 2011, www.dailymail.co.uk/news/article-1394161/Frank-Sinatra-Jekyll-Hyde-husband-4th-wife-Barbara-sadistic-manipulation.html.

Uhland, Vicky. "Book review: 'Lady Blue Eyes: My Life With Frank,' by Barbara Sinatra." *Denver Post*, June 12, 2011, www.denverpost.com/ci_18242433.

Wilson, Craig. "Lady Blue Eyes: My Life with Frank." *USA Today*, May 31, 2011, books.usatoday.com/book/barbara-sinatra-lady-blue-eyes-my-life-with-frank/r172400.

CHAPTER THIRTY-TWO After the Fall: Mrs. Arthur Miller

"Inge Morath." *Telegraph*, February 1, 2002, www.telegraph.co.uk/news/obituaries/1383341/Inge-Morath.html.

"Inge Morath." *Wikipedia*, en.wikipedia.org/wiki/Inge_Morath (accessed October 19, 2013).

Martin, Douglas. "Inge Morath, Photographer With a Poetic Touch, Dies at 78." *New York Times Arts*, January 31, 2002.

Miller, Arthur. "'A wide-eyed view of a crazy country.'" *Guardian*, November 19, 2006, www.theguardian.com/artanddesign/2006/nov/20/photography.usa.

Rustin, Susanna. "Inge Morath: In living colour." *Guardian*, December 4, 2009, www.theguardian.com/artanddesign/2009/dec/05/inge-morath-colour-photographs.

Seymore, Jim. "Arthur Miller and Inge Morath Find Themselves In the Country—and Write a Book About It." *People*, April 4, 1977, www.people.com/people/archive/article/0,,20067600,00.html.

CHAPTER THIRTY-THREE For Remembrance: Mrs. Timothy Leary

Greeenfield, Robert. *Timothy Leary: A Biography*. Orlando, FL: Harcourt Inc., 2006.

Hoffmann, Martina and others. "Rosemary Woodruff Leary—Psychedelic Pioneer." *Maps* XII.2 (Summer, 2002), www.maps.org/news-letters/v12n2/12253hof.html.

Martin, Douglas. "Rosemary Woodruff, 66, Wife And Fellow Fugitive of Leary." *New*

York Times, February 16, 2002, www.nytimes.com/2002/02/16/us/rosemary-woodruff-66-wife-and-fellow-fugitive-of-leary.html.

Mclellan, Dennis. "Rosemary W. Leary, 66; Ex-Wife of 1960s Psychedelic Guru." Los Angeles Times, February 9, 2002, articles.latimes.com/2002/feb/09/local/me-leary9.

Phillips, David. "The Magician's Daughter with Rosemary Woodruff Leary." Mavericks of the Mind, Interview, November 11, 2011, www.mavericksofthemind.com/rosemary.htm.

"Rosemary Woodruff Leary." Los Angeles Times, February 11, 2002, articles.chicagotribune.com/2002-02-11/news/0202110041_1_rosemary-woodruff-leary-timothy-leary-denis-berry.

Schou, Nick. "How the Brotherhood of Eternal Love Is Connected to the Weather Underground Via the Black Panthers." OC Weekly, September 17, 2009, www.ocweekly.com/2009-09-17/news/brotherood-of-eternal-love-weather-underground-black-panthers/full/.

Sward, Susan. "Rosemary Woodruff—LSD guru's ex-wife." SFGate, February 9, 2002, www.sfgate.com/news/article/Rosemary-Woodruff-LSD-guru-s-ex-wife-2876113.php.

"Timothy Leary's Wife Drops Out." Village Voice, February 5, 2002, www.villagevoice.com/2002-02-05/news/timothy-leary-s-wife-drops-out/.

CHAPTER THIRTY-FOUR The Merry Prankster: Mrs. Jerry Garcia

Barry, John W. "Mountain Girl: Her tale begins in Hyde Park." Poughkeepsie Journal, August 8, 2009, www.poughkeepsiejournal.com/article/20090809/LIFE/908090304/Mountain-Girl-Her-tale-begins-Hyde-Park.

Carlin, Plter. "War of the Wives." People, January 27, 1997, www.people.com/people/article/0,,20143324,00.html.

"Carolyn Garcia." RobertDespain.com, www.robertdespain.com/node/307 (accessed September 24, 2013).

"Carolyn Garcia." Wikipedia, en.wikipedia.org/wiki/carolyn_garcia (accessed September 24, 2013).

Cornwell, Tim. "'Dead' wives go head to head over Garcia's will." Guardian, January 12, 1997, www.independent.co.uk/news/world/dead-wives-go-head-to-head-over-garcias-will-1282795.html.

Downes, Lawrence. "In Mexico, on the Lam With Ken Kesey." New York Times, March 23, 2008, www.nytimes.com/2008/03/23/travel/23Kesey.html?pagewanted=all&_r=0.

Golden, Tim. "Why a Star Is Spinning In the Grave." New York Times, January 3, 1997, www.nytimes.com/1997/01/03/us/why-a-star-is-spinning-in-the-grave.html.

Haigwood, William. "Journeying the Sixties: A Counterculture Tarot: Page of Cups." Counter Culture Creations, www.counterculturecreations.com/card46.html (accessed September 24, 2013).

Helmore, Edward. "How Ken Kesey's LSD-fueled bus trip created the psychedelic 60s." Guardian, August 6, 2011, www.theguardian.com/film/2011/aug/06/lsd-ken-kesey-pranksters-film.

Hubler, Shawn. "Rock's Family Feud." Los Angeles Times, October 22, 2001, articles.latimes.com/2001/oct/22/news/cl-60093.

"Jerry Garcia: American Beauty." Fader, www.thefader.com/2011/08/01/jerry-garcia-american-beauty/?single_paged=1 (accessed September 24, 2013).

La Ganga, Maria L. "Airing Jerry's Dirty Tie-Dyed Laundry." Los Angeles Times, January 19, 1997, articles.latimes.com/1997-01-19/news/mn-20215_1_jerry-garcia.

Robins, Cynthia. "She Never Got Off The Bus." SFGate, May 25, 1997, www.sfgate.com/magazine/article/SHE-NEVER-GOT-OFF-THE-BUS-3117809.php.

CHAPTER THIRTY-FIVE Set the Night on Fire: Mrs. Jim Morrison

Butler, Patricia. *Angels Dance and Angels Die*, New York: Simon & Schuster, 1998.

Saroyan, Wayne A. "The Twisted Tale Of How Late Rocker Jim Morrison's Poetry Found." *Chicago Tribune*, March 22, 1989, articles.chicagotribune.com/1989-03-22 /features/8903280648_1_frank-lisciandro-jim-morrison-doors.

Simms, Judith. "Pamela Morrison: A Final Curtain On Her Affair With Life." *The Official John Densmore Forum*, January 16, 2014, forum.johndensmore.com/index .php?showtopic=3281.

Soler, Andrew. "Personal Life." *Hyperink*, www.hyperink.com/Personal-Life-b1114a12 (accessed January 16, 2014).

CHAPTER THIRTY-SIX Little Frog: Mrs. Lech Walesa

Apple, R. W. Jr. "Mrs. Walesa Parries The Press In Oslo." *New York Times*, December 10, 1983, www.nytimes.com/1983/12/10/world/mrs-walesa-parries-the-press-in-oslo.html.

Baczynska, Gabriela. "Lech Walesa's wife shakes Poland with frank biography." *Reuters*, November 22, 2011, www.reuters.com/article/2011/11/22/us-poland-walesa-book -idUSTRE7AL19H20111122.

Driscoll, Molly. "Former Polish first lady Danuta Walesa felt isolated, left to raise children alone." *Christian Science Monitor*, November 28, 2011, www.csmonitor.com /Books/chapter-and-verse/2011/1128/Former-Polish-first-lady-Danuta-Walesa -felt-isolated-left-to-raise-children-alone.

"Lech Walesa—Acceptance Speech." *Nobelprize.org*, Nobel Media AB 2013, January 10, 2014, www.nobelprize.org/nobel_prizes/peace/laureates/1983/walesa-acceptance.html.

MacShane, Denis. "Hero who toppled a tyranny." *Guardian*, August 13, 2000, www.theguardian .com/world/2000/aug/13/Poland.

Moreno, Kasia. "Behind Every Great Man Is the Mother of His Children. One of Them Finally Comes Out." *Forbes*, May 13, 2012, www.forbes.com/sites/forbes insights/2012/05/13/behind-every-great-man-is-the-mother-of-his-children-one -of-them-finally-comes-out/.

"My torment living with Lech Walesa: Wife of Polish Solidarity legend reveals her loneliness and jealousy as he rose to power from the shipyard." *Mail Online*, November 19, 2011, www .dailymail.co.uk/news/article-2063344/My-torment-living-legend-Lech-Walesa -Wife-Polish-Solidarity-hero-reveals-loneliness-jealousy-rose-power-shipyard.html.

Pawlicki, Maciej. "Walesa Taught Poles How They Could Win." *Philly.com*, July 5, 1989, articles .philly.com/1989-07-05/news/26133708_1_solidarity-danuta-walesa-lech-walesa.

"Politics took my husband away from me, says Danuta Walesa." *Polski Radio*, November 23, 2011, www.thenews.pl/1/9/Artykul/59032,Politics-took-my-husband-away-from-me -says-Danuta-Walesa.

CHAPTER THIRTY-SEVEN Heart: Mrs. Larry Flynt

Abdulali, Sohaila. "The Life & Death Of Althea Flynt The Porn King's Wife Stick By Him To The End." *Philly.com*, July 15, 1987, articles.philly.com/1987-07-15 /entertainment/26198388_1_hustler-magazine-publisher-larry-flynt-public-eye.

"Althea Flynt." *Wikipedia*, en.wikipedia.org/wiki/Althea_Flynt (accessed August 16, 2013).

Ansen, David. "Naked Ambition." *Daily Beast*, December 22, 1996, www.thedailybeast .com/newsweek/1996/12/22/naked-ambition.html.

Ebert, Roger. "The People Vs. Larry Flynt." *RogerEbert.com*, December 27, 1996, www .rogerebert.com/reviews/the-people-vs-larry-flynt-1996.

Fry, Donn. "Tolerance According To Larry Flynt." *Seattle Times*, December 13, 1996, community.seattletimes.nwsource.com/archive/?date=19961213&slug=2364946.

Gordon, Alex. "The People vs. Larry Flynt." *Chronicle*, January 22, 1997, www.duke chronicle.com/articles/1997/01/23/people-vs-larry-flynt.

Gorney, Cynthia. "The Brief, Brittle Life Of Althea Flynt 'She Was Extremely Stylized… A Devastatingly Smart Woman.'" *Timesunion.com*, July 12, 1987, alb.merlinone .net/mweb/wmsql.wm.request?oneimage&imageid=5425653.

Green, Michelle. "Her Death Ends the Improbable Love Match of Porn Merchants Althea and Larry Flynt." *People*, July 20, 1987, www.people.com/people/archive /article/0,,20096764,00.html.

Janos, Leo. "Porn Publisher Larry Flynt Beats Drugs but Remains Unashamedly Hooked on Sleaze." *People*, August 1, 1983, www.people.com/people/article/0,,20085591,00.html.

Kempley, Rita. "'Larry Flynt': An Unlikely Hero Porn in the U.S.A." *Washington Post*, December 27, 1996, www.washingtonpost.com/wp-srv/style/longterm/review96/peoplevslarry flyntkemp.htm.

Maslin, Janet. "The People vs. Larry Flynt (1996)." *New York Times*, October 12, 1996, www .nytimes.com/movie/review?res=9400E6D8103EF931A25753C1A960958260.

Mcgurk, Margaret A. "'Flynt' hustles with style, power, ideas." *Cincinnati Enquirer*, enquirer .com/columns/mcgurk/010797_mm.html (accessed August 16, 2013).

Rainer, Peter. "Porn Again." *Houston Press*, January 9, 1997, www.houstonpress .com/1997-01-09/film/porn-again/.

Shulgasser, Barbara. "Larry Flynt: The pornographer you have to love." *SFgate.com*, December 27, 1996, www.sfgate.com/news/article/Larry-Flynt-The-pornographer-you-have -to-love-3108064.php.

CHAPTER THIRTY-EIGHT The Dragon's Roar: Mrs. Stieg Larsson

Caeser, Ed. "Furious Eva's Legal Battle." *Sunday Telegraph*, July 10, 2011, www.dailytelegraph .com.au/the-girl-who-loved-stieg-larsson/story-fn6b3v4f-1226091352850.

Carr, David. "Remembering Stieg Larsson." *New York Times*, July 8, 2011, www.nytimes .com/2011/07/10/books/review/book-review-there-are-things-i-want-you-to -know-about-stieg-larsson-and-me-by-eva-gabrielsson.html?pagewanted=all.

Cochrane, Kira. "Stieg Larsson's partner: 'It's odd to have to prove our life together existed.'" *Guardian*, October 4, 2011, www.theguardian.com/books/2011/oct/04/stieg -larsson-partner-eva-gabrielsson.

Cooke, Rachel. "Stieg Larsson—by the woman who shared his life." *Guardian*, February 20, 2010, www.theguardian.com/books/2010/feb/21/stieg-larsson-eva-gabrielsson.

Fuller, David Jón. "Real-life Stieg Larsson tale like a Norse saga." *Winnipeg Free Press*, June 25, 2011, www.winnipegfreepress.com/arts-and-life/entertainment/books/real-life -stieg-larsson-tale-like-a-norse-saga-124532494.html.

Gabrielsson, Eva. "Stieg Larsson's Long Good-Bye." *Vanity Fair*, www.vanityfair.com /culture/features/2011/07/stieg-larsson-201107 (accessed July 27, 2013).

Hickman, Angela. "The girl who was left behind: Eva Gabrielsson on her life with Stieg Larsson." *National Post*, July 7, 2011, arts.nationalpost.com/2011/07/07 /the-girl-who-was-left-behind-eva-gabrielsson-on-her-life-with-stieg-larsson/.

James, Susan Donaldson. "Stieg Larsson's Girlfriend Rages in Memoir." *ABCNews*, February 21, 2011, abcnews.go.com/Health/stieg-larsson-girlfriend-eva-gabrielsson-rages -memoir/story?id=12950542.

McDonnell, Evelyn. "Book review: 'There Are Things I Want to Know You to Know' About Stieg Larsson and Me' by Eva Gabrielsson." *Los Angeles Times*, June 22, 2011, articles .latimes.com/2011/jun/22/entertainment/la-et-book-20110622.

Mcgrath, Charles. "The Afterlife of Stieg Larsson." *New York Times*, May 20, 2010, www
.nytimes.com/2010/05/23/magazine/23Larsson-t.html?pagewanted=all.
————. "Eva Gabrielsson: The Girl Who Cast a Viking Spell." *New York Times*, June 21, 2011,
www.nytimes.com/2011/06/22/books/eva-gabrielssons-memoir-of-her-life-with
-stieg-larsson.html?pagewanted=all&_r=0.
Pevere, Geoff. "Life after Larsson." *Toronto Star*, June 27, 2011, www.thestar.com
/entertainment/2011/06/27/life_after_larsson.html.
Sales, Nancy Jo. "Eva Gabrielsson: The Woman Behind the Girl." *Harper's Bazaar*, June 22,
2011, www.harpersbazaar.com/beauty/health-wellness-articles/eva-gabriellson-on
-steig-larsson.
Spörl, Gerhard. "Swedish author Stieg Larsson's controversial legacy." *Toronto Star*, August 10,
2012, www.thestar.com/news/insight/2012/08/10/swedish_author_stieg_larssons
_controversial_legacy.html.
Watson, Sasha. "The Girl Who Wanted Revenge." *Slate*, February 14, 2011, www.slate
.com/articles/double_x/doublex/2011/02/the_girl_who_wanted_revenge.html.

CHAPTER THIRTY-NINE The Sting: Mrs. Gordon Sumner (Mrs. Sting)

D'Souza, Christa. "Every little thing she does." *Telegraph*, November 17, 2001, www
.telegraph.co.uk/culture/4726627/Every-little-thing-she-does.-.-..html.
Gordon, Bryony. "Trudie Styler: 'Tantric sex? All day long? With Sting? If only...'" *Telegraph*,
December 29, 2011, www.telegraph.co.uk/news/celebritynews/8980773/Trudie
-Styler-Tantric-sex-All-day-long-With-Sting-If-only....html.
Higginbotham, Adam. "Truly Trudie." *Guardian*, August 3, 2002, www.theguardian.com
/theobserver/2002/aug/04/features.magazine37.
Hyde, Marina. "Trudie Styler is threatening to leave Britain, taking Sting with her." *Guardian*,
October 17, 2013, www.theguardian.com/lifeandstyle/lostinshowbiz/2013/oct/17
/trudie-styler-threatening-to-leave-britain.
La Ferla, Ruth. "More Than Mrs. Sting." *New York Times*, April 18, 2012, www.nytimes
.com/2012/04/19/fashion/trudie-styler-is-so-much-more-than-mrs-sting.html.
"PROFILE / Mockery, where is thy Sting?: Gordon Sumner, causing a buzz at the Grammys."
Independent, March 5, 1994, www.independent.co.uk/voices/profile--mockery
-where-is-thy-sting-gordon-sumner-causing-a-buzz-at-the-grammys-1427088.html.

CHAPTER FORTY How Deep Was Their Love?: Mrs. Robin Gibb

Coleman, Maureen. "Druid priestess from Tyrone who's been a rock for her Bee Gee husband Robin." *Belfast Telegraph*, April 27, 2012, www.belfasttelegraph.co.uk
/news/local-national/northern-ireland/druid-priestess-from-tyrone-whos-been
-a-rock-for-her-bee-gee-husband-robin-28742464.html.
Craig, Olga. "Robin Gibb: a Bee Gee's secret history." *Telegraph*, July 13, 2008, www
.telegraph.co.uk/culture/music/3556425/Robin-Gibb-a-Bee-Gees-secret-history
.html.
Fisher, Luchina. "Robin Gibb's Unconventional Family." *ABCNews*, April 19, 2012, abcnews
.go.com/Entertainment/robin-gibbs-unconventional-family/story?id=16163800.
Gallagher, Ian, Dennis Rice, and Sharon Churcher. "The PM's wife, the Druid priestess
and the no sex guru." *Mail Online*, January 6, 2007, www.dailymail.co.uk/news
/article-426903/The-PMs-wife-Druid-priestess-sex-guru.html.
"How deep is their love." *Belfast Telegraph*, January 5, 2007, www.belfasttelegraph.co.uk
/lifestyle/how-deep-is-their-love-28439835.html.
"'I want to go home': Bee Gee Robin Gibb's last words revealed as widow says she sleeps

with singer's teddy to ease her grief." *Mirror News*, June 10, 2012, www.mirror
.co.uk/news/uk-news/robin-gibb-bee-gee-stars-871138.

Kelly, Antoinette. "Robin Gibb's Irish wife tried desperate measures to save him." *Irish
Central*, May 21, 2012, www.irishcentral.com/ent/Robin-Gibbs-Irish-wife
-tried-desperate-measures-to-save-him--152260905.html.

Leigh, Wendy. "House of decadence where JFK took his mistresses." *Mail Online*, December
28, 2006, www.dailymail.co.uk/news/article-425104/House-decadence-JFK-took
-mistresses.html.

Moodie, Clemmie. "My life without Robin Gibb: Widow Dwina still makes him tea and lis-
tens to his music daily." *Mirror News*, November 10, 2012, www.mirror.co.uk
/news/uk-news/robin-gibb-widow-dwina-still-1427755.

Price, Richard and Ben Todd. "Picture: The baby who tested Bee Gee's marriage to the
limit." *Mail Online*, December 12, 2009, www.dailymail.co.uk/tvshowbiz
/article-1235213/Pictured-The-baby-tested-Bee-Gees-marriage-limit.html.

Rice, Dennis and Sharon Churcher. "Revealed: Blair host stood by jailed porn baron
lover." *Mail Online*, December 30, 2008, www.dailymail.co.uk/news/article
-425574/Revealed-Blair-host-stood-jailed-porn-baron-lover.html.

"Robin Gibb: A somewhat sleazy Bee Gee." *London Evening Standard*, December 29, 2006, www
.standard.co.uk/news/robin-gibb-a-somewhat-sleazy-bee-gee-7220634.html.

"Robin Gibb's Widow Dwina Reveals She Thought Husband Was Coming Home."
Huffington Post, October 6, 2012, www.huffingtonpost.co.uk/2012/06/10
/robin-gibb-funeral-widow-dwina-grief_n_1584261.html.

Wigg, David. "'My songbird has gone' Robin Gibb's wife Dwina speaks exclusively about
the pain of losing her husband." *Mail Online*, August 17, 2012, www.dailymail
.co.uk/femail/article-2189167/My-songbird-gone-Robin-Gibbs-wife-Dwina
-speaks-exclusively-pain-losing-husband.html.

ABOUT THE AUTHOR

Marlene Wagman-Geller received her BA from York University and her teaching credentials from the University of Toronto and San Diego State University. She made the great sacrifice of leaving her Winter Wonderland for Southern California and currently teaches high school English in National City, California. The author of several books, her works have been reviewed in the *New York Times*, *Chicago Tribune*, and *Washington Post*. An Associated Press article was picked up in dozens of newspapers such as the *Denver Post*, *Huffington Post*, and *San Diego Tribune*, among others. She lives in San Diego, California.